HALF HOURS WITH THE

Best Thinkers

HALF HOURS WITH THE
Best
Thinkers

Edited by
Frank J. Finamore

GRAMERCY BOOKS
New York

Introduction and compilation
copyright © 1999 by Random House Value Publishing, Inc.
All rights reserved under International and Pan-American
Copyright Conventions

This 1999 edition is published by Gramercy Books™,
an imprint of Random House Value Publishing, Inc.
201 East 50th Street, New York, New York 10022.

Gramercy Books™ and colophon are trademarks of
Random House Value Publishing, Inc.

Random House
New York • Toronto • London • Sydney • Auckland

Printed and bound in the United States of America

Compiled, edited, designed, and composited by Frank J. Finamore

A CIP catalog record for this book is available from the Library of Congress.

Half Hours with the Best Thinkers
ISBN 0–517–20432–0

8   7   6   5   4   3   2   1

Contents

Introduction

Man lives by his ideas. He understands the world through his beliefs and hypotheses. The ability to think rationally and abstractly makes us uniquely different from the rest of the animal kingdom. And unlike other animals, humans are the only beings on earth who have died merely for their beliefs. *Half Hours with the Best Thinkers* is a compendium of the greatest and most famous ideas—ethical, religious, political, economic, and scientific—of the last two thousand years. This collection ranges from the ancient philosophers Lao Tzu, Confucius, Plato, and Aristotle to the religious thinkers Saint Augustine and Saint Thomas Aquinas to the political theorists Machiavelli and Thomas Jefferson to the scientific thinkers Charles Darwin and Sigmund Freud. This book is an introduction to the development of human thought and a concise overview of the ideas that have literally shook the world.

The *Tao Te Ching*, composed over two thousand years ago, is one of China's most ancient books of wisdom. Legend attributes the work to Lao Tzu—which means "The Old Master"—who wrote it before he disappeared into the mountains—never to be seen again—on the back of a blue water buffalo. It is now believed to have been written by several hands and compiled around 500 B.C. The central concept of this work is the idea of *Tao*, which is translated in English as the Way. It is the unnamable source of everything, which flows through everything, and the only way life itself could be understood.

Confucius lived from 551 to 479 B.C., and was one of China's greatest and most influential philosophers. Unable to secure a position in government, he devoted himself as a teacher to pass on his ideas and gathered around himself many disciples; the *Analects* are the sayings of Confucius as collected by his followers. The work deals with his precepts on political, social, and personal matters, and outlines the proper behavior of the *chun-tzu*, or ideal man. His concept of *jen*, or perfect virtue of

humanity, is central to his philosophy as he believed a stable
social order could only be founded upon humaneness.

Plato—born Aristocles, the son of Ariston—was born in
Athens about the year 427 B.C. He was a disciple of Socrates,
and when the Athenian people put his master to death, Plato
continued to expound the wisdom of his teacher. Plato lived to
the age of eighty and died in Athens in 347. The *Apology* is
believed to be an accurate facsimile of the defense made by
Socrates when he was indicted for "corrupting the youth" of
Athens, as Plato was himself present at the trial. Socrates was
found guilty by a small majority of votes, and a sentence of
death was passed, as set forth in the last section of the *Apology*.
The Republic is undoubtedly the work of Plato that has had the
widest general influence. In this dialogue, Socrates endeavors
to discover what Justice means, which leads to the description
of the ideal state or commonwealth, from which this work
derives its title.

Aristotle was born at Stagira, a Greek colony on the
Macedonian frontier, in 384 B.C. He went to Athens and became
one of Plato's pupils at the age of twenty. In 342 he became
tutor to the future Alexander the Great, and some years later
opened his own school, whose disciples were called the
Peripatetics. He died in 322 B.C. His works laid the foundation
for every science known in his time and the *Nicomachean
Ethics* profoundly influenced ethical and political thought from
his own day to ours and laid the foundation upon which almost
the entire Western conception of ethics has been built. In particular, his classification of the virtues—courage, temperance,
honor, justice, mercy, wisdom, continence, friendship, moderation, and contemplation—and his doctrine that virtue lies in a
"mean," have dominated a vast amount of moral speculation.

Saint Augustine was born Aurelius Augustinus in 354 at
Tagaste in the Roman Province of Numidia, North Africa. He
became a consecrated bishop in 395 and he built up the dio-
cese of Hippo. His lasting fame is from his *Confessions*, his
autobiography, and *The City of God*. Begun in 413 and finished
in 426, it is a huge treatise in twenty-two books. Augustine
ascribes the origin of the work as his attempt to refute the widely
held belief that the fall of Rome by Alaric's invasion in 410 was
caused by the desertion of the old gods of Rome and to the wide

extension of Christianity throughout the empire. It is a great defense of Christ's kingdom, the "Catholic Church, which should include all nations and speak in all tongues."

Saint Thomas Aquinas was born around 1225, the son of Landolfo of Aquino, a minor public official in Sicily. He entered the Dominican Order in 1244. By his early thirties he was a well-known scholar and teacher. His *Summa Theologica,* which he began in 1269, is one of his most important works. It epitomizes Christian wisdom of the Middle Ages and remains among the most finely argued expositions of humanity's need for God. He died in a Cistercian monastery at Fossanova on March 7, 1274, and his works have since exercised a continuing and growing influence in philosophy, religion, and education.

Niccolò di Bernardo dei Machiavelli was born in Florence, Italy, on May 3, 1469, and died June 22, 1527. At an early age he took an active part in Florentine politics, and was employed on numerous diplomatic missions. He wrote several plays and historical studies, but his most notable achievement is *The Prince*—written about 1514, and not published until 1532— which many regard as the first work that treated politics as a science. In it he emphasizes how moral principles must yield to the dictates of expediency, and that a successful ruler must pay little or no respect to right and wrong. Hence the book has been mercilessly condemned.

René Descartes was born March 31, 1596, of a noble family at La Haye, in the province of Touraine, France. He was educated at the College of La Fleche by the Jesuits. Descartes died in Stockholm in 1649. *Discourse on Method,* written around 1637 and published four years later, is his most famous work. Primarily interested in mathematics, Descartes worked to extend mathematical methods into other areas of human thought. He is considered the father of modern philosophy and his work stands a landmark in the history of philosophy.

John Locke was born at Wrington, Somersetshire, England, on August 29, 1632. He was educated at Westminster and at Christ Church, Oxford. His *An Essay Concerning Human Understanding* was published in 1690. It was a popular and influential work that had twenty editions before 1700. The purpose of the book was to inquire "into the origin, certainty, and

extent of human knowledge, together with the grounds and
degrees of belief, opinion, and assent." Locke died on October
28, 1704.

Jean Jacques Rousseau was born in Geneva in 1712. He was
one of the major figures of the French Enlightenment. His most
famous concept is the "natural man." He believed that human
beings are essentially good in the state of nature but were corrupted by society. *The Social Contract* of 1762 is probably the
most influential treatise on politics written in modern times. In
it Rousseau states: "Man is born free, and yet is everywhere in
chains." Highly controversial, it directly inspired one of history's great events, the French Revolution. After its publication
Rousseau fled to England, where he displayed marked symptoms of insanity that would plague him until his death in 1778.

Adam Smith was born at Kirkcaldy, Scotland, on June 5,
1723. He attended Glasgow University and Balliol College,
Oxford, where he studied for seven years. In 1751 he became
professor of Logic at Glasgow University, and in the following
year professor of Moral Philosophy. In 1776, the *Wealth of
Nations* was published and at once achieved renown. Smith was
appointed, in 1778, Commissioner of Customs for Scotland,
and died on July 17, 1790. Today he is considered the greatest
of discoverers in the science of political economy.

Immanuel Kant, the most celebrated of German metaphysi-
cians, was born at Konigsberg on April 22, 1724, and died on
February 12, 1804. Taking his degree at University of
Konigsberg, he quickly entered on a professional career as a
teacher and writer. His lasting reputation is built upon *The
Critique of Pure Reason*, published in 1781. His aim in the
work was "to separate the necessary and universal in the realm
of knowledge from the merely experimental or empirical." In
The Critique of Practical Reason, published in 1788, Kant
takes up the position of vindicator of the truth of Christianity,
establishing positive affirmations of the immortality of the soul
and the existence of God.

Thomas Paine was born in England in 1737. He emigrated to
Philadelphia in 1774. He had a wide-ranging career that took
him into many occupations, including corset-maker, tobac-
conist and grocer, and schoolteacher. When he arrived in
America, he became, with the help of Benjamin Franklin, a

journalist and published *Common Sense,* a pamphlet that urged independence from Britain. He later enlisted in the Revolutionary Army. After the war he returned to England where he wrote *The Rights of Man,* a defense of the French Revolution. It was published in two parts in 1790 and 1792, and because of his controversial arguments against monarchy, led to his fleeing England. He spent his last years in New York and died in 1809.

Thomas Jefferson was born in Shadwell, Virginia, in 1743. He was a philosopher, architect, political theorist, diplomat, educator, and one of the Founding Fathers. His service to the American colonies and nation began with his election to the Virginia House of Burgesses in 1769 and the issuing of his 1774 revolutionary pamphlet *A Summary View of the Rights of British America.* A member of the Continental Congress in 1775 and 1776, Jefferson was requested to create a document declaring the colonies independent of England. His draft, with some minor changes, was adopted on July 4, 1776, as the *Declaration of Independence.* He was elected the third president of the United States in 1800. And somewhat fittingly, Jefferson died on July 4, 1826.

Georg Wilhelm Friedrich Hegel was born on August 27, 1770, at Stuttgart, the capital of Württemberg, where his father had a humble position in government service. Hegel was educated at Tubingen for the ministry. In 1805, he became Professor Extraordinarius at the University of Lena, and in 1807, his first great work, *Phenomenology of Mind,* was published. In 1816, Hegel secured a professorship at Heidelberg, but, after two years, he went to Berlin, where he remained until his death on November 14, 1831. His *Philosophy of History* was not published until a year after his death. He was a major influence on idealistic philosophers like Kierkegaard and Sartre, as well as Karl Marx.

Arthur Schopenhauer was born in Danzig, Germany, on February 22, 1788, and died September 21, 1860. His mother, Johanna Schopenhauer, was a noted author. After graduating from Jena in 1813, he spent the winter of that year at Weimar, where he met Goethe. In 1819, Schopenhauer published his important work, *The World as Will and Idea.* He believed that the sole essential reality in the universe is the will, and that all visible and tangible phenomena are merely subjective representations, or formal manifestations of that will, which is the only thing-in-itself that actually subsists.

Ralph Waldo Emerson, one of America's most influential writers and thinkers, was born on May 25, 1803, in Boston. A member of a family of preachers, he was educated at Harvard for the Unitarian ministry and became a pastor in Boston before he was twenty-six. Three years later he resigned his charge owing to theological disagreements. In 1833 he visited Europe and England. When he returned to America, he settled at Concord, where he lived until his death on April 27, 1882. In 1836, his first book, *Nature*, was published. The appeal of *Self-Reliance*, published in 1841, is its belief in individual integrity. He believed deeply in the universality of the soul and in the godlike attributes of man, and it is as the spokesman for American idealism and optimism that Emerson retains an undiminished influence.

John Stuart Mill was born in London on May 20, 1806. By the age of fourteen he had an extensive knowledge of Greek, Latin, and mathematics, and had begun to study logic and political economy. In 1823, he received an appointment at the India Office, and in the same year he became a member of a small Utilitarian society, and soon became the leader of the Utilitarian movement. Mill's great work, *Principles of Political Economy*, published in 1848, embodies the results of many years of study, disputation, and thought. Throughout, it manifests a belief in the possibility of great social improvement to be achieved upon individualistic lines. Mill died at Avignon on May 8, 1873. He was one of the great liberal thinkers of the nineteenth century and had a great influence on modern economics, politics, and philosophy.

Charles Robert Darwin was born on February 12, 1809. He failed to follow in the family tradition of medicine as a vocation because he could not stand the sight of blood. He instead became a naturalist and signed on in that capacity on the H.M.S. *Beagle* during its world voyage from 1831 to 1836, when he gathered data and formulated his concept of natural selection and evolution. In 1859, he published his great work, *The Origin of Species*, which caused violent controversy and has been called "the most fundamental of all intellectual revolutions in the history of mankind."

Henry David Thoreau today remains one of America's most influential writers. He was a nonconformist and rebel. Under the tutelage of his friend Ralph Waldo Emerson he began to write. In 1845, he built a cabin at Walden Pond, near Concord, Massachussetts, and stayed there in solitude for two years. There he sharpened his metaphysical response to nature. In *Civil Disobedience*, first published in 1849, Thoreau issues a call for anarchy in which he argues against government itself, for rejection of unjust laws, and for rebellion when necessary. He tells why he went to jail rather than pay a tax to a government that condones human slavery. In 1854, *Walden*, his paean to self-reliance and the contemplative life he found in nature, was published.

Heinrich Karl Marx was born on May 5, 1818, at Treves, in Rhenish Prussia. He died in London on March 14, 1883. He was a brilliant university graduate both at Berlin and Bonn and became one of the leaders of the modern socialist movement in Germany. Marx, from the beginning of his career as a journalist, was known as a socialist. He was expelled from Germany, France, and Belgium, but eventually found refuge in England, where he lived from 1849. In his most famous work, *Capital: A Critical Analysis of Capitalist Production*, published in 1867, he advances his advocacy of the claims of labor against those of capitalism. Although the failure of Communism at the end of the twentieth century has cast doubt upon many of his theories, Marx's analysis of the economic development of modern society has been justified in many respects by the events of history.

William James, brother of novelist Henry James, was one of America's great nineteenth-century thinkers. He was an influential psychologist and the founder of Pragmatism, the uniquely American school of philosophy. The publication of his *Principles of Psychology* in 1890 brought him renown in the field of psychology. The Varieties of Religious Experience, published in 1902, is probably his most famous book. This work summarizes and analyzes the evidence concerning belief in the supernatural and mystical experiences.

Born in 1844, the German philosopher Friedrich Wilhelm Nietzsche became one of the most influential and widely-known names in philosophy—though also one of the most misunderstood. After his death in 1900, his ideas of the Superman and "the will to power" were appropriated and misused by the Nazis for their propaganda. Nietzsche was as much a poet as a philosopher, and saw himself as an iconoclast and destroyer of old values in an effort to clear the way for the virtues of strength against meekness, health against decadence, and the spirit of freedom against slave morality of traditional religious thought." *Beyond Good and Evil,* published in 1886, is one of his major works and representative of his argument against conventional morality.

The Austrian psychiatrist Sigmund Freud—born in 1856—is one of the founders of modern psychology. But his ideas have had an enormous impact upon art and culture as well. His concepts—like the subconscious, repressed urges, inhibitions, and complexes—have entered the mainstream. Freud essentially reconceived the theory of the human mind with a thoroughly scientific methodology and uncovered the sexual motivation at the basis of human nature. Freud believed that "the dream is the royal road to the unconscious" and that it represented the hidden fulfillment of unconscious desires, which, when repressed, produce a chain of psychic consequences. *The Interpretation of Dreams,* published in 1900, was his groundbreaking book and one of the century's most influential.

FRANK JAMES FINAMORE

May 1999
New York

Lao Tzu

(c. 600 B.C.–?)

From

TAO TE CHING

CHAPTER 1

1. The Tao that can be trodden is not the enduring and unchanging Tao. The name that can be named is not the enduring and unchanging name.

2. (Conceived of as) having no name, it is the Originator of heaven and earth; (conceived of as) having a name, it is the Mother of all things.

3. Always without desire we must be found,
If its deep mystery we would sound;
But if desire always within us be,
Its outer fringe is all that we shall see.

4. Under these two aspects, it is really the same; but as development takes place, it receives the different names. Together we call them the Mystery. Where the Mystery is the deepest is the gate of all that is subtle and wonderful.

CHAPTER 2

1. All in the world know the beauty of the beautiful, and in doing this they have (the idea of) what ugliness is; they all know the skill of the skillful, and in doing this they have (the idea of) what the want of skill is.

2. So it is that existence and non-existence give birth the one to (the idea of) the other; that difficulty and ease produce the one (the idea of) the other; that length and shortness fashion out the one the figure of the other; that (the ideas of) height and lowness arise from the contrast of the one with the other; that the musical notes and tones become harmonious through the relation of one with another; and that being before and behind give the idea of one following another.

3. Therefore the sage manages affairs without doing anything, and conveys his instructions without the use of speech.

4. All things spring up, and there is not one which declines to show itself; they grow, and there is no claim made for their ownership; they go through their processes, and there is no expectation (of a reward for the results). The work is accomplished, and there is no resting in it (as an achievement).

The work is done, but how no one can see;

'Tis this that makes the power not cease to be.

CHAPTER 3

1. Not to value and employ men of superior ability is the way to keep the people from rivalry among themselves; not to prize articles which are difficult to procure is the way to keep them from becoming thieves; not to show them what is likely to excite their desires is the way to keep their minds from disorder.

2. Therefore the sage, in the exercise of his government, empties their minds, fills their bellies, weakens their wills, and strengthens their bones.

3. He constantly (tries to) keep them without knowledge and without desire, and where there are those who have knowledge, to keep them from presuming to act (on it). When there is this abstinence from action, good order is universal.

CHAPTER 4

1. The Tao is (like) the emptiness of a vessel; and in our employment of it we must be on our guard against all fullness. How deep and unfathomable it is, as if it were the Honored Ancestor of all things!

2. We should blunt our sharp points, and unravel the complications of things; we should attemper our brightness, and bring ourselves into agreement with the obscurity of others. How pure and still the Tao is, as if it would ever so continue!

3. I do not know whose son it is. It might appear to have been before God.

CHAPTER 5

1. Heaven and earth do not act from (the impulse of) any wish to be benevolent; they deal with all things as the dogs of grass are dealt with. The sages do not act from (any wish to be) benevolent; they deal with the people as the dogs of grass are dealt with.

2. May not the space between heaven and earth be compared to a bellows?
'Tis emptied, yet it loses not its power;
'Tis moved again, and sends forth air the more.
Much speech to swift exhaustion lead we see;
Your inner being guard, and keep it free.

<h3 align="center">CHAPTER 6</h3>

The valley spirit dies not, aye the same;
The female mystery thus do we name.
Its gate, from which at first they issued forth,
Is called the root from which grew heaven and earth.
Long and unbroken does its power remain,
Used gently, and without the touch of pain.

<h3 align="center">CHAPTER 7</h3>

1. Heaven is long-enduring and earth continues long. The reason why heaven and earth are able to endure and continue thus long is because they do not live of, or for, themselves. This is how they are able to continue and endure.

2. Therefore the sage puts his own person last, and yet it is found in the foremost place; he treats his person as if it were foreign to him, and yet that person is preserved. Is it not because he has no personal and private ends, that therefore such ends are realized?

<h3 align="center">CHAPTER 8</h3>

1. The highest excellence is like (that of) water. The excellence of water appears in its benefiting all things, and in its occupying, without striving (to the contrary), the low place which all men dislike. Hence (its way) is near to (that of) the Tao.

2. The excellence of a residence is in (the suitability of) the place; that of the mind is in abysmal stillness; that of associations is in their being with the virtuous; that of government is in its securing good order; that of (the conduct of) affairs is in its ability; and that of (the initiation of) any movement is in its timeliness.

3. And when (one with the highest excellence) does not wrangle (about his low position), no one finds fault with him.

CHAPTER 9

1. It is better to leave a vessel unfilled, than to attempt to carry it when it is full. If you keep feeling a point that has been sharpened, the point cannot long preserve its sharpness.

2. When gold and jade fill the hall, their possessor cannot keep them safe. When wealth and honors lead to arrogancy, this brings its evil on itself. When the work is done, and one's name is becoming distinguished, to withdraw into obscurity is the way of Heaven.

CHAPTER 10

1. When the intelligent and animal souls are held together in one embrace, they can be kept from separating. When one gives undivided attention to the (vital) breath, and brings it to the utmost degree of pliancy, he can become as a (tender) babe. When he has cleansed away the most mysterious sights (of his imagination), he can become without a flaw.

2. In loving the people and ruling the state, cannot he proceed without any (purpose of) action? In the opening and shutting of his gates of heaven, cannot he do so as a female bird? While his intelligence reaches in every direction, cannot he (appear to) be without knowledge?

3. (The Tao) produces (all things) and nourishes them; it produces them and does not claim them as its own; it does all, and yet does not boast of it; it presides over all, and yet does not control them. This is what is called "The mysterious Quality" (of the Tao).

CHAPTER 11

The thirty spokes unite in the one nave; but it is on the empty space (for the axle), that the use of the wheel depends. Clay is fashioned into vessels; but it is on their empty hollowness, that their use depends. The door and windows are cut out (from the walls) to form an apartment; but it is on the empty space (within), that its use depends. Therefore, what has a (positive) existence serves for profitable adaptation, and what has not that for (actual) usefulness.

CHAPTER 12

1. Color's five hues from th' eyes their sight will take;

Music's five notes the ears as deaf can make;
The flavors five deprive the mouth of taste;
The chariot course, and the wild hunting waste
Make mad the mind; and objects rare and strange,
Sought for, men's conduct will to evil change.

2. Therefore the sage seeks to satisfy (the craving of) the belly, and not the (insatiable longing of the) eyes. He puts from him the latter, and prefers to seek the former.

CHAPTER 13

1. Favor and disgrace would seem equally to be feared; honor and great calamity, to be regarded as personal conditions (of the same kind).

2. What is meant by speaking thus of favor and disgrace? Disgrace is being in a low position (after the enjoyment of favor). The getting that (favor) leads to the apprehension (of losing it), and the losing it leads to the fear of (still greater calamity)—this is what is meant by saying that favor and disgrace would seem equally to be feared.

And what is meant by saying that honor and great calamity are to be (similarly) regarded as personal conditions? What makes me liable to great calamity is my having the body (which I call myself); if I had not the body, what great calamity could come to me?

3. Therefore he who would administer the kingdom, honoring it as he honors his own person, may be employed to govern it, and he who would administer it with the love which he bears to his own person may be entrusted with it.

CHAPTER 14

1. We look at it, and we do not see it, and we name it "the Equable." We listen to it, and we do not hear it, and we name it "the Inaudible." We try to grasp it, and do not get hold of it, and we name it "the Subtle." With these three qualities, it cannot be made the subject of description; and hence we blend them together and obtain The One.

2. Its upper part is not bright, and its lower part is not obscure. Ceaseless in its action, it yet cannot be named, and then it again returns and becomes nothing. This is called the Form of the Formless, and the Semblance of the Invisible; this is called the Fleeting and Indeterminable.

3. We meet it and do not see its Front; we follow it, and do not see its Back. When we can lay hold of the Tao of old to direct the things of the present day, and are able to know it as it was of old in the beginning, this is called (unwinding) the clue of Tao.

CHAPTER 15

1. The skillful masters (of the Tao) in old times, with a subtle and exquisite penetration, comprehended its mysteries, and were deep (also) so as to elude men's knowledge. As they were thus beyond men's knowledge, I will make an effort to describe of what sort they appeared to be.

2. Shrinking looked they like those who wade through a stream in winter; irresolute like those who are afraid of all around them; grave like a guest (in awe of his host); evanescent like ice that is melting away; unpretentious like wood that has not been fashioned into anything; vacant like a valley, and dull like muddy water.

3. Who can (make) the muddy water (clear)? Let it be still, and it will gradually become clear. Who can secure the condition of rest? Let movement go on, and the condition of rest will gradually arise.

4. They who preserve this method of the Tao do not wish to be full (of themselves). It is through their not being full of themselves that they can afford to seem worn and not appear new and complete.

CHAPTER 16

1. The (state of) vacancy should be brought to the utmost degree, and that of stillness guarded with unwearying vigor. All things alike go through their processes of activity, and (then) we see them return (to their original state). When things (in the vegetable world) have displayed their luxuriant growth, we see each of them return to its root. This returning to their root is what we call the state of stillness; and that stillness may be called a reporting that they have fulfilled their appointed end.

2. The report of that fulfillment is the regular, unchanging rule. To know that unchanging rule is to be intelligent; not to know it leads to wild movements and evil issues. The knowl-

edge of that unchanging rule produces a (grand) capacity and forbearance, and that capacity and forbearance lead to a community (of feeling with all things). From this community of feeling comes a kingliness of character; and he who is king-like goes on to be heaven-like. In that likeness to heaven he possesses the Tao. Possessed of the Tao, he endures long; and to the end of his bodily life, is exempt from all danger of decay.

CHAPTER 17

1. In the highest antiquity, (the people) did not know that there were (their rulers). In the next age they loved them and praised them. In the next they feared them; in the next they despised them. Thus it was that when faith (in the Tao) was deficient (in the rulers) a want of faith in them ensued (in the people).

2. How irresolute did those (earliest rulers) appear, showing (by their reticence) the importance which they set upon their words! Their work was done and their undertakings were successful, while the people all said, "We are as we are, of ourselves!"

CHAPTER 18

1. When the Great Tao (Way or Method) ceased to be observed, benevolence and righteousness came into vogue. (Then) appeared wisdom and shrewdness, and there ensued great hypocrisy.

2. When harmony no longer prevailed throughout the six kinships, filial sons found their manifestation; when the states and clans fell into disorder, loyal ministers appeared.

CHAPTER 19

1. If we could renounce our sageness and discard our wisdom, it would be better for the people a hundredfold. If we could renounce our benevolence and discard our righteousness, the people would again become filial and kindly. If we could renounce our artful contrivances and discard our (scheming for) gain, there would be no thieves nor robbers.

2. Those three methods (of government)
Thought olden ways in elegance did fail

And made these names their want of worth to veil;
But simple views, and courses plain and true
Would selfish ends and many lusts eschew.

CHAPTER 20

1. When we renounce learning we have no troubles.
The (ready) "yes" and (flattering) "yea"—
Small is the difference they display.
But mark their issues, good and ill—
What space the gulf between shall fill?
What all men fear is indeed to be feared; but how wide and
without end is the range of questions (asking to be discussed)!

2. The multitude of men look satisfied and pleased; as if
enjoying a full banquet, as if mounted on a tower in spring. I
alone seem listless and still, my desires having as yet given no
indication of their presence. I am like an infant which has not
yet smiled. I look dejected and forlorn, as if I had no home to
go to. The multitude of men all have enough and to spare. I
alone seem to have lost everything. My mind is that of a stupid
man; I am in a state of chaos.

Ordinary men look bright and intelligent, while I alone seem
to be benighted. They look full of discrimination, while I alone
am dull and confused. I seem to be carried about as on the sea,
drifting as if I had nowhere to rest. All men have their spheres
of action, while I alone seem dull and incapable, like a rude
borderer. (Thus) I alone am different from other men, but I
value the nursing-mother (the Tao).

CHAPTER 21

The grandest forms of active force
From Tao come, their only source.
Who can of Tao the nature tell?
Our sight it flies, our touch as well.
Eluding sight, eluding touch,
The forms of things all in it crouch;
Eluding touch, eluding sight,
There are their semblances, all right.
Profound it is, dark and obscure;
Things' essences all there endure.

Those essences the truth enfold
Of what, when seen, shall then be told.
Now it is so; 'twas so of old.
Its name—what passes not away;
So, in their beautiful array,
Things form and never know decay.

How know I that it is so with all the beauties of existing things?
By this (nature of the Tao).

CHAPTER 22

1. The partial becomes complete; the crooked, straight; the empty, full; the worn out, new. He whose (desires) are few gets them; he whose (desires) are many goes astray.

2. Therefore the sage holds in his embrace the one thing (of humility), and manifests it to all the world. He is free from self-display, and therefore he shines; from self-assertion, and therefore he is distinguished; from self-boasting, and therefore his merit is acknowledged; from self-complacency, and therefore he acquires superiority. It is because he is thus free from striving that therefore no one in the world is able to strive with him.

3. That saying of the ancients that "the partial becomes complete" was not vainly spoken—all real completion is comprehended under it.

CHAPTER 23

1. Abstaining from speech marks him who is obeying the spontaneity of his nature. A violent wind does not last for a whole morning; a sudden rain does not last for the whole day. To whom is it that these (two) things are owing? To Heaven and Earth. If Heaven and Earth cannot make such (spasmodic) actings last long, how much less can man!

2. Therefore when one is making the Tao his business, those who are also pursuing it, agree with him in it, and those who are making the manifestation of its course their object agree with him in that; while even those who are failing in both these things agree with him where they fail.

3. Hence, those with whom he agrees as to the Tao have the happiness of attaining to it; those with whom he agrees as to its manifestation have the happiness of attaining to it; and those with

whom he agrees in their failure have also the happiness of attaining (to the Tao). (But) when there is not faith sufficient (on his part), a want of faith (in him) ensues (on the part of the others).

CHAPTER 24

He who stands on his tiptoes does not stand firm; he who stretches his legs does not walk (easily). (So), he who displays himself does not shine; he who asserts his own views is not distinguished; he who vaunts himself does not find his merit acknowledged; he who is self-conceited has no superiority allowed to him. Such conditions, viewed from the standpoint of the Tao, are like remnants of food, or a tumor on the body, which all dislike. Hence those who pursue (the course) of the Tao do not adopt and allow them.

CHAPTER 25

1. There was something undefined and complete, coming into existence before Heaven and Earth. How still it was and formless, standing alone, and undergoing no change, reaching everywhere and in no danger (of being exhausted)! It may be regarded as the Mother of all things.

2. I do not know its name, and I give it the designation of the Tao (the Way or Course). Making an effort (further) to give it a name I call it The Great.

3. Great it passes on (in constant flow). Passing on, it becomes remote. Having become remote, it returns. Therefore the Tao is great; Heaven is great; Earth is great; and the (sage) king is also great. In the universe there are four that are great, and the (sage) king is one of them.

4. Man takes his law from the Earth; the Earth takes its law from Heaven; Heaven takes its law from the Tao. The law of the Tao is its being what it is.

Confucius

(c. 551–c. 479 B.C.)

From

ANALECTS

BOOK I
Concerning Fundamental Principles

1. The Master said: "Is it not indeed a pleasure to acquire knowledge and constantly to exercise oneself therein? And is it not delightful to have men of kindred spirit come to one from afar? But is not he a true philosopher who, though he be unrecognized of men, cherishes no resentment?"

2. The philosopher Yu said: "He who lives a filial life, respecting the elders, who yet is wishful to give offense to those above him, is rare; and there has never been any one unwishful to offend those above him, who has yet been fond of creating disorder. The true philosopher devotes himself to the fundamentals, for when those have been established right courses naturally evolve; and are not filial devotion and respect for elders the very foundations of an unselfish life?"

3. The Master said: "Artful speech and an ingratiating demeanor rarely accompany virtue."

4. The philosopher Tseng said: "I daily examine myself on three points—In planning for others have I failed in conscientiousness? In intercourse with friends have I been insincere? And have I failed to practice what I have been taught?"

5. The Master said: "To conduct the government of a State of a thousand chariots there must be religious attention to business and good faith, economy in expenditure and love of the people, and their employment on public works at the proper seasons."

6. The Master said: "When a youth is at home let him be filial, when abroad respectful to his elders; let him be circumspect and truthful and, while exhibiting a comprehensive love

for all men, let him ally himself with the good. Having so acted, if he have energy to spare, let him employ it in polite studies."

7. Tzu Hsia said: "He who transfers his mind from feminine allurement to excelling in moral excellence; who in serving his parents is ready to do so to the utmost of his ability; who in the service of his prince is prepared to lay down his life; and who in intercourse with his friends is sincere in what he says—though others may speak of him as uneducated—I should certainly call him educated."

8. The Master said: "A scholar who is not grave will not inspire respect and his learning will therefore lack stability. His chief principles should be conscientiousness and sincerity. Let him have no friends unequal to himself. And when in the wrong let him not hesitate to amend."

9. The philosopher Tseng said: "Solicitude on the decease of parents, and the pursuit of this for long after, would cause an abundant restoration of the people's morals."

10. Tzu Ch'in inquired of Tzu Kung saying: "When the Master arrives at any State he always hears about its administration. Does he ask for this information, or, is it tendered to him?" "The Master," said Tzu Kung, "is benign, frank, courteous, temperate, deferential and thus obtains it. The Master's way of asking—how different it is from that of others!"

11. The Master said: "While a man's father lives, mark his tendencies; when his father is dead, mark his conduct. If for three years he does not change from his father's ways, he may be called filial."

12. The philosopher Yu said: "In the usages of decorum it is naturalness that is of value. In the regulations of the ancient kings this was the admirable feature, both small and great deriving therefrom. But there is a naturalness that is not permissible; for to know to be natural, and yet to be so beyond the restraints of decorum is also not permissible."

13. The philosopher Yu said: "When you make a promise consistent with what is right, you can keep your word. When you show respect consistent with good taste, you keep shame and disgrace at a distance. When he in whom you confide is one who does not fail his friends, you may trust him fully."

14. The Master said: "The scholar who in his food does not seek the gratification of his appetite, nor in his dwelling is

solicitous of comfort, who is diligent in his work, and guarded
in his speech, who associates with the high-principled, and
thereby directs himself aright—such a one may really be said
to love learning."

15. "What do you think," asked Tzu Kung, "of the man who
is poor yet not servile, or who is rich yet not proud?' "He will
do," replied the Master, "but he is not equal to the man who is
poor and yet happy, or rich and yet loves courtesy." Tzu Kung
remarked: "The Ode says this is

> Like cutting, then filing;
> Like chiseling, then grinding.

That is the meaning of your remark, is it not?" "Tz'u!" said the
Master. "Now indeed I can begin to talk with him about the
Odes, for when I tell him the premise he knows the conclu-
sion."

15. The Master said: "I will not grieve that men do not know
me; I will grieve that I do not know men."

BOOK II
Concerning Government

1. The Master said: "He who governs by his moral excellence may be compared to the pole-star, which abides in its
place, while all the stars bow towards it."

2. The Master said: "Though the Odes number three hundred, one phrase can cover them all, namely, 'With purpose
undiverted.'"

3. The Master said: "If you govern the people by laws, and
keep them in order by penalties, they will avoid the penalties,
yet lose their sense of shame. But if you govern them by your
moral excellence, and keep them in order by your dutiful conduct, they will retain their sense of shame, and also live up to
this standard."

4. The Master said: "At fifteen I set my mind upon wisdom.
At thirty I stood firm. At forty I was free from doubts. At fifty I
understood the laws of Heaven. At sixty my ear was docile. At
seventy I could follow the desires of my heart without transgressing the right."

5. When Meng I Tzu asked what filial duty meant, the Master

answered: "It is not being disobedient." Afterwards when Fan
Ch'ih was driving him the Master told him, saying: "Meng Sun
asked me what filial piety meant, and I replied 'Not being disobedient.'" Fan Ch'ih thereupon asked, "What did you mean?"
The Master answered: "While parents live serve them rightful-
ly; when they are dead bury them with filial rites, and sacrifice
to them with proper ordinances."

6. When Meng Wu Po asked what filial duty meant the
Master answered: "Parents should only have anxiety when their
children are ill."

7. When Tzu Yu asked the meaning of filial piety the Master
said: "The filial piety of the present day merely means to feed
one's parents; but even one's dogs and horses receive their
food—without reverence wherein lies the difference?"

8. When Tzu Hsia asked the meaning of filial piety the
Master said: "The behavior is the difficult matter. When anything is to be done, then the young should undertake the burden of it, when there is wine and food then they should serve
them to their seniors. But is this alone to be considered filial
piety?"

9. The Master said: "I could talk to Hui for a whole day and,
as if he were stupid, he never raised an objection; but when he
withdrew and I examined into his conduct when not with me, I
nevertheless found him fully competent to demonstrate what I
had taught him. Hui! he was not stupid."

10. The Master said: "Observe what he does; look into his
motives; find out in what he is at peace. Can a man hide himself? Can a man hide himself?"

11. The Master said: "He who keeps on reviewing his old
and acquiring new knowledge may become a teacher of others."

12. The Master said: "The higher type of man is not a
machine."

13. On Tzu Kung asking about the nobler type of man the
Master said: "He first practices what he preaches and afterwards preaches according to his practice."

14. The Master said: "The nobler type of man is broad-minded and not prejudiced. The inferior man is prejudiced and not
broad-minded."

15. The Master said: "Learning without thinking is useless.
Thinking without learning is dangerous."

16. The Master said: "To devote oneself to irregular speculations is decidedly harmful."

17. The Master said: "Yu! Shall I teach you the meaning of knowledge? When you know a thing to recognize that you know it; and when you do not, to know that you do not know—that is knowledge."

18. Tzu Chang was studying with a view to preferment. The Master said to him: "Hear much, be reserved in what causes you doubt, and speak guardedly of the rest; you will then suffer little criticism. See much, be reserved in what seems imprudent, and act guardedly as to the rest; you will then have few regrets. With little for criticism in your speech, and little to regret in your conduct—herein you will find preferment."

19. Duke Ai inquired saying: "What should I do to insure the contentment of the people?" "If you promote the upright and dismiss the ill-doer," replied Confucius, "the people will be contented; but if you promote the ill-doer and dismiss the upright, the people will be discontented."

20. When Chi K'ang Tzu asked how to inspire the people with respect and loyalty, so that they might be mutually emulous (for the welfare of the state), the Master said: "Lead them with dignity and they will also be dutiful; be filial and kind and they will be loyal; promote those who excel and teach the incompetent, and they will encourage each other."

21. Someone addressed Confucius with the remark: "Why, Sir, are you not in the public service?" The Master answered: "Does not the *Book of History* say concerning filial duty—'But one's duty as a son and friendliness to one's brethren are shown forth in the public service?' These then are also public service. Why should your idea alone be considered as constituting public service?"

22. The Master said: "A man who is without good faith—I do not know how he is to manage! How can a wagon without its yoke-bar for the ox, or a carriage without its collar-bar for the horses, be made to move?"

23. Tzu Chang asked whether the condition of things ten ages hence could be foreknown. The Master answered: "The Yin dynasty perpetuated the civilization of the Hsia; its modifications and accretions can be known. The Chou perpetuated the civilization of the Yin, and its modifications and accretions

can be known. Whatever others may succeed the Chou, their character, even a hundred ages hence, can be known."

24. The Master said: "To sacrifice to a spirit of an ancestor not one's own is sycophancy. To see the right and not do it is cowardice."

BOOK III

The Eight Dancers: Concerning Manners and Morals

1. Confucius said of the head of the House of Chi, who had eight rows of dancers performing in his Temple: "If he can bear to do this, what can he not bear to do?"

2. The members of the three great Houses of Lu used the Yung Ode at the removal of the sacrifices. The Master said:

> "'Assisted by princes and noblemen,
> Solemnly stands the Son of Heaven'—
> What application can this have in the hall
> merely of the three Families?"

3. The Master said: "A man who is not virtuous, what has he to do with worship? A man who is not virtuous, what has he to do with the music of the temple?"

4. Lin Fang asked what was the chief principle in observances of ritual. The Master answered: "A great question indeed! In ceremonies in general, it is better to be simple than lavish: and in the rites of mourning heartfelt distress is better than observance of detail."

5. The Master said: "The tribes of the east and north have their princes, and are not, like all our great land, without leaders."

6. When the chief of the Chi family was going to sacrifice on Mount T'ai the Master addressing Jan Yu said: "Can you not save him from this sin?" "I cannot," he replied. "Alas!" said the Master, "is that not saying that the Spirit of Mount T'ai is not equal to that of Lin Fang?"

7. The Master said: "A gentleman never contends in anything he does—except perhaps in archery. Even then, he bows to his rival and yields him the way as they ascend the pavilion; in like manner he descends and offers him the penalty cup—in his contentions he is still a gentleman."

8. Tzu Hsia asked: "What is the meaning of the passage—

> 'As she artfully smiles
> What dimples appear!
> Her bewitching eyes
> Show their colors so clear.
> Ground spotless and candid
> For tracery splendid!'?"

"The painting comes after the groundwork," answered the Master. "Then manners are secondary?" said Tzu Hsia. "'Tis Shang who unfolds my meaning," replied the Master. "Now indeed, I can begin to discuss the poets with him."

9. The Master said: "I can describe the civilization of the Hsia dynasty, but the descendant State of Ch'i does not yield adequate documentation. I can describe the civilization of the Yin dynasty, but the descendant State of Sung does not yield adequate documentation. And all because of the deficiency of their records and wise men. Were those sufficient, then I could confirm my views."

10. The Master said: "At the Quinquennial Sacrifice in the Lu Ancestral Temple, after the libation has been sprinkled, I have no further wish to look on."

11. When some one asked the meaning of the Quinquennial Sacrifice, the Master replied: "I do not know. He who knew its meaning, would he not find himself in regard to the whole Empire as if he were looking upon this?"—pointing to his palm.

12. He sacrificed to his forefathers as if they were present; he sacrificed to the gods as if the gods were present. The Master said: "For me not to be present at a sacrifice is as if I did not sacrifice."

13. Wang-sun Chia inquired: "What is the meaning of the saying, 'It is better to pay court to the god of the Hearth than to the god of the Hall?'" "Not so," answered Confucius, "He who sins against Heaven has nowhere left for prayer."

14. The Master said: "Chou had the advantage of surveying the two preceding dynasties. How full was its culture! I follow Chou dynasty ideas."

15. When the Master first entered the Grand Temple he asked about everything, whereupon someone remarked: "Who says the son of the man of Tsou knows the correct forms? On

entering the Grand Temple he asks about everything." The Master hearing of it remarked: "This too is correct form."

16. The Master said: "In archery piercing the target is not the essential, for men are not of equal strength. Such was the rule of yore."

17. Tzu Kung wished to dispense with the live sheep presented in the Ducal Temple at the announcement of the new moon. The Master said: "T'zu! You care for the sheep. I care for the ritual."

18. The Master said: "If one were to serve one's prince with perfect homage, people today would deem it sycophancy."

19. When Duke Ting asked how a prince should employ his ministers and how ministers should serve their prince, Confucius replied saying "A prince should employ his ministers with courtesy. A minister should serve his prince with loyalty."

20. The Master said: "The Kuan Chu Ode is passionate without being sensual, is plaintive without being morbid."

21. When Duke Ai asked Tsai Wo concerning the altars to the tutelary deities of the land, Tsai Wo responded: "The sovereign of Hsia adopted the pine, the men of Yin the cypress, but the men of Chou the chestnut, intimating that the people should stand in dread." On the Master hearing of this he said: "When a deed is done it is useless to discuss it, when a thing has taken its course it is useless to remonstrate, what is past and gone it is useless to blame."

22. The Master said: "The caliber of Kuan Chung's mind was but limited!" Someone observed: "Do you mean that Kuan Chung was economical?" "Kuan," he replied, "maintained his San Kuei palace, and the members of his staff performed no double duties—how can he be considered economical?" "But surely Kuan Chung understood etiquette?" "The prince of a state," said Confucius, "has a screen to mask his gate—Kuan too had his gate-screen. Princes of state, when two of them have a friendly meeting, use a stand for their inverted pledge-cups— Kuan too used such a cup-stand. If Kuan understood etiquette, who does not understand it?"

23. The Master discoursing to the state Band Master of Lu on the subject of music said: "The art of music may be readily understood. The attack should be prompt and united, and as

the piece proceeds it should do so harmoniously, with clearness of tone, and continuity of time, and so on to its conclusion."

24. The Officer in charge of the frontier town of I requested an interview, saying: "Whenever a man of virtue has come here I have never failed to obtain an interview"—whereupon the followers of the Sage introduced him. On coming out he observed: "Why do you grieve, gentlemen, over this loss of office? The Empire for long has been without light and leading; but Heaven is now going to use your Master as an arousing tocsin."

25. The Master spoke of the Shao music as perfectly beautiful in form and perfectly good in its influence. He spoke of the Wu music as perfectly beautiful in form but not perfectly good in its influence.

26. The Master said: "High station filled without magnanimity, religious observances performed without reverence, and 'mourning' conducted without grief—from what standpoint shall I view such ways?"

BOOK IV
Concerning Virtue

1. The Master said: "It is the moral character of a neighborhood that constitutes its excellence, and how can he be considered wise who does not elect to dwell in moral surroundings?"

2. The Master said: "A man without virtue cannot long abide in adversity, nor can he long abide in happiness; but the virtuous man is at rest in virtue, and the wise man covets it."

3. The Master said: "Only the virtuous are competent to love or to hate men."

4. The Master said: "He who has really set his mind on virtue will do no evil."

5. The Master said: "Wealth and rank are what men desire, but unless they be obtained in the right way they may not be possessed. Poverty and obscurity are what men detest; but unless prosperity be brought about in the right way, they are not to be abandoned. If a man of honor forsakes virtue how is he to fulfill the obligations of his name? A man of honor never disregards virtue, even for the space of a single meal. In moments of haste he cleaves to it; in seasons of peril he cleaves to it."

6. The Master said: "I have never seen one who loved virtue, nor one who hated what was not virtuous. He who loved virtue would esteem nothing above it; and he who hated what is not virtuous would himself be so virtuous that he would allow nothing evil to adhere to him. Is there anyone able for a single day to devote his strength to virtue? I have never seen such a one whose ability would be sufficient. If perchance there be such I have never seen him."

7. The Master said: "A man's faults all conform to his type of mind. Observe his faults and you may know his virtues."

8. The Master said: "He who heard the truth in the morning might die content in the evening."

9. The Master said: "The student who aims at wisdom, and yet who is ashamed of shabby clothes and poor food, is not yet worthy to be discoursed with."

10. The Master said: "The wise man in his attitude towards the world has neither predilections nor prejudices. He is on the side of what is right."

11. The Master said: "The man of honor thinks of his character, the inferior man of his position. The man of honor desires justice, the inferior man favor."

12. The Master said: "He who works for his own interests will arouse much animosity."

13. The Master said: "Is a prince able to rule his country with courtesy and deference—then what difficulty will he have? And if he cannot rule his country with courtesy and deference, what use are the forms of courtesy to him?"

14. The Master said: "One should not be concerned at lack of position, but should be concerned about what will fit him to occupy it. One should not be concerned at being unknown, but should seek to be worthy of being known."

15. The Master said: "Shen! My teaching contains one all-pervading principle." "Yes," replied Tseng Tzu. When the Master had left the room the disciples asked, "What did he mean?" Tseng Tzu replied, "Our Master's teaching is simply this: Conscientiousness within and consideration for others."

16. The Master said: "The wise man is informed in what is right. The inferior man is informed in what will pay."

17. The Master said: "When you see a man of worth, think how to rise to his level. When you see an unworthy man, then look within and examine yourself."

18. The Master said: "In his duty to his parents a son may gently remonstrate with them. If he see that they are not inclined to yield, he should be increasingly respectful but not desist, and though they deal hardly with him he must not complain."

19. The Master said: "While a father or mother are alive, a son should not travel far. If he travel he must have a stated destination."

20. The Master said: "If for three years a son does not change from his father's ways, he may be called filial."

21. The Master said: "The age of one's parents should ever be kept in mind, as an occasion at once for joy and for fear."

22. The Master said: "The men of old were reserved in speech out of shame lest they should come short in deed."

23. The Master said: "The self-restrained seldom err."

24. The Master said: "The wise man desires to be slow to speak but quick to act."

25. The Master said: "Virtue never dwells alone; it always has neighbors."

26. Tzu Yu said: "In serving one's prince importunity results in disgrace; as importunity between friends results in estrangement."

Plato

(427–347 B.C.)

From

THE APOLOGY, OR DEFENSE OF SOCRATES

The Official Indictment, and the Real Charges

What my accusers have said, Athenians, has been most specious, but none of it is true. The falsehood which most astonished me was that you must beware of being beguiled by my consummate eloquence; for I am not eloquent at all, unless speaking pure truth be eloquence. You will hear me speak with adornments and without premeditation in my everyday language, which many of you have heard. I am seventy years old, yet this is my first appearance in the courts, and I have no experience of forensic arts. All I ask is that you will take heed whether what I say be just.

It is just that I should begin by defending myself against my accusers from of old, in priority to Anytus and these other latter-day accusers. For, skillful as these are, I fear those more—those who from your youth have been untruthfully warning you against one Socrates, a wise man, who speculates about everything in heaven and under the earth, and tries to make the worse cause the better. Their charge is the craftier, because you think that a man who does as they say has no thought for the gods. I cannot name these gentlemen precisely, beyond indicating that one is a writer of comedies; I cannot meet and refute them individually. However, I must try to enter a brief defense. I think I know where my difficulty will lie; but the issue will be as the gods choose.

Now, what is the basis of this charge, on which Meletus also relies? "Socrates is an evildoer, a busybody, who pries into things in heaven and under the earth, and teaches these same things to others." You all saw the Socrates in the comedy of Aristophanes engaged in these pursuits. I have nothing to say

against such inquiries; but do not let Meletus charge me with
them, for I have no part nor lot in them. Many of you have heard
me talk, but never one on these subjects. Witness you yourselves. From this you should be able to gauge the other things
that are said against me.

Equally untrue is the charge that I make a paid business of
teaching my neighbors. It is a fine thing to be able to impart
knowledge, like Gorgias, and Prodicus, and Hippias, who can
go from city to city and draw to converse with them young men
who pay for the privilege instead of enjoying their companions'
society for nothing. I am told there is one Evenus, a Parian,
practicing now, whose fee is five minas. It must be delightful to
possess such valuable knowledge and to impart it—if they do
possess it. I should like to do it myself, but I do not possess the
knowledge.

"Whence, then, comes the trouble, Socrates?" you will say;
"if you have been doing nothing unusual, how have these
rumors and slanders arisen?" I will tell you what I take to be
the explanation. It is due to a certain wisdom with which I seem
to be endowed—not superhuman at all like that of these gentlemen. I speak not arrogantly, but on the evidence of the
Oracle of Delphi, who told Chaerephon, a man known to you,
that there was no wiser man than Socrates. Now, I am not conscious of possessing wisdom; but the God cannot lie. What did
he mean?

Well, I tried to find out, by going to a man reputed wise,
thinking to prove that there were wiser men. But I found him
not wise at all, though he fancied himself so. I sought to show
him this, but he was only very much annoyed. I concluded that,
after all, I was wiser than he in one particular, because I was
under no delusion that I possessed knowledge, as he was. I
tried all the men reputed wise, one after the other, and made
myself very unpopular, for the result was always the same. It
was the same with the poets as with the politicians, and with
the craftsmen as with the poets. The last did know something
about their own particular art, and therefore imagined that they
knew all about everything.

I went on, taking every opportunity of finding out whether
people reputed wise, and thinking themselves so, were wise in
reality, and pointing out that they were not. And because of my

exposing the ignorance of others, I have got this groundless reputation of having knowledge myself, and have been made the object of many other calumnies. And young gentlemen of position who have heard me follow my example, and annoy people by exposing their ignorance; and this is all visited on me; and I am called an ill-conditioned person who corrupts youth. To prove which my calumniators have to fall back on charging me with prying into all things in heaven and under the earth, and the rest of it.

The Cross-Examining of Meletus

Such is my answer to the charges which have been poured into your ears for a long time. Now let me defend myself against these later accusations of Meletus and the rest—the virtuous patriot Meletus. I am an evildoer, a corrupter of youth, who pays no reverence to the gods who the city reveres, but to strange demons. Not I, but Meletus is the evil-doer, who rashly makes accusations so frivolous, pretending much concern for matters about which he has never troubled himself. Answer me, Meletus, You think it of the utmost importance that our youth should be made as excellent as possible.
MELETUS: Certainly.
SOCRATES: Tell us, then, who is it that makes them better; for of course, you know. You are silent. The laws, you say? The question was, "Who?"
MELETUS: The judges; all the judges.
SOCRATES: In other words, all the Athenian people—everyone but me? And I alone corrupt them? Truly, I am in an ill plight! But in the case of all other animals, horses, for instance, there are only a few people who are able to improve them. Your answer shows that you have never bestowed attention on the care of young people. Next, tell me is it better for a man to dwell among good citizens or bad? The good, since the bad will injure him. I cannot, then, set about making bad citizens designedly. My friend, no man designedly brings injury upon himself. If I corrupt them, it must be undesignedly—reason good for admonishing and instructing me, which you have not done; but not for bringing me into court, which you have done! However, I corrupt them by teaching them not to believe in the

gods in whom the city believes, but in strange deities? Do I teach that there are some gods, or that there are no gods at all?
MELETUS: I say that you believe in no gods. You say the sun is a stone, and the moon earth.
SOCRATES: Most excellent Meletus, everyone knows that Anaxagoras says so; you can buy that information for a drachma! Do I really appear to you to revere no gods?
MELETUS: No, no gods at all.
SOCRATES: Now, that is incredible! You must have manufactured this riddle out of sheer wantonness, for in the indictment you charge me with reverencing gods! Can anyone believe that there are human affairs, or equine affairs, or instrumental affairs without believing that there are men, or horses, or instruments? You say expressly that I believe in demonic affairs, therefore in demons; but demons are a sort of gods or the offspring of gods. Therefore, you cannot possibly believe that I do not believe in gods. Really, I have sufficiently answered the indictment. If I am condemned, it will not be on the indictment of Meletus, but on popular calumnies; which have condemned good men before me, and assuredly I shall not be the last.

The Defense

It may be suggested that I ought to be ashamed of practices which have brought you in danger of death. Risk of death is not to be taken into account in any action which really matters at all. If it ought to be, the heroes before Troy were bad characters! Every man should stand to his post, come life, come death. Should I have stood to my post and faced death when on service at Potidaca, but have failed through fear of death when the deity imposed on me a certain course of action? Whether to die be evil or good, I know not, though many think they know it to be evil. But to disobey authority, human or divine, I know to be evil; and I will not do what I know to be evil to avoid what may in fact be a good. Insomuch that if you now offer to set me free on condition that I should cease from these pursuits on pain of death, I should reply: "Men of Athens, I love and honor you, but I will obey the god rather than you; and while I breathe and have the power I will not cease from the pursuit of philosophy, or from exhorting and warning you as I have done hitherto, against caring much for riches and nothing for the perfecting of your souls. This is the bidding of the god. If to speak thus be to corrupt youth, then I corrupt youth. But he who says I speak other things than this talks vanity; and this I will do, though the penalty were many deaths.

Do not murmur, but listen, for you will profit. If you put me to death, you will harm yourselves more than me, for it is worse to do wrong than to suffer it. You will not easily find another to serve as the gadfly which rouses a noble horse—as I have done, being commissioned thereto by the god. For that I have made no profit for myself from this course, my poverty proves. If it seems absurd that I should meddle thus with each man privately, but take no part in public affairs, that is because of the divine or demonic influence of which I have spoken, named also in mockery by Meletus in the indictment. This is a voice which checks but never urges me on. Indeed, had I meddled with politics, I should have been dead long ago.

That I will prove by facts. When you chose to condemn the ten generals, my phyle supplied the Prytanes, and I alone stood out against you. And in the time of the thirty, I was ordered with four others to bring Leon from Salamis to be executed, and I alone would not; and it may be that my own life was saved only because that government was broken up. Judge, then, if my life would not have been shorter, had I taken part in public life.

But I have never posed as an instructor or taken money for giving instruction. Anyone who chooses can question me and hear what I have to say. People take pleasure in my society, because they like to hear those exposed who deem themselves wise but are not. This duty the god has laid on me by oracles and dreams and every mode of divine authority. If I am corrupting or have corrupted youth, why do none of them bear witness against me, or their fathers or brothers or other kinsmen? Many I see around me who should do so if this charge were true; yet all are ready to assist me.

This, and the like, is what I have to say in my defense. Perhaps some of you, thinking how, in a like case with mine but less exigent, he has sought the compassion of the court with tears and pleadings of his children and kinsfolk, will be indignant that I do none of these things, though I have three boys of my own. That is not out of disrespect to you, but because I think it would be unbeseeming to me. Such displays, as though death were something altogether terrifying, are to me astonishing and degrading to our city in the sight of strangers, for persons reputed to excel in anything, as in some respects I am held to excel the generality.

But apart from credit, I count that we ought to inform and convince our judges, not seek to sway them by entreaties; that they may judge rightly according to the laws, and not by favor. For you are sworn. And how should I persuade you to break your oath, who am charged by Meletus with impiety. For by so doing, I should be persuading you to disbelief in the gods, and making that very charge against myself. To you and to the god I leave it, that I may be judged as shall be best for you and for me.

After the Verdict

Your condemnation does not grieve me for various reasons, one of which is that I fully expected it. What surprises me is the small majority by which it was carried. Evidently Meletus, if left to himself, would have failed to win the few votes needed to save him from the fine. Well, the sentence he fixes is death, and I have to propose an alternative—presumably, the sentence I deserve. I have neglected all the ordinary pursuits and ambitions of men—which would have been no good either to me or to you—that I might benefit each man privately, by persuading him to give attention to himself first—how to attain his own best and wisest—and his mere affairs afterwards, and the city in like manner. The proper reward is that I should be maintained in the Prytaneum as a public benefactor.

You may think this merely a piece of insolence, but it is not so. I am not conscious of having wronged any man. Time does not permit me to prove my case, and I will not admit guilt by owning that I deserve punishment by a fine. What have I to fear? The penalty fixed by Meletus, as to which I do not know whether it is good or bad? Shall I, to escape this, choose something which is certainly bad? Imprisonment, to be the slave of the Eleven? A fine, to be a prisoner till I pay it—which comes to the same thing, as I cannot pay. Exile? If my fellow-citizens cannot put up with me, how can I expect strangers to do so?

The young men will come to listen to me. If I repulse them, they
will drive me out; and if I do not their elders will drive me out,
and I shall live wandering from city to city.

Why cannot I go and hold my tongue, you may ask. That is
the one thing which I cannot do. That would be to disobey the
god, and the life would not be worth living, though you do not
believe me. I might undertake to pay a mina. However, as Plato
and Crito and Apollodorus urge me to name thirty minae, for
which they will be security, I propose thirty minae.

. . . .

Your enemies will reproach you, Athenians, for having put to
death that wise man Socrates. Yet you would have had but a
short time to wait, for I am old. I speak to those of you who have
condemned me. I am condemned, not for lack of argument, but
because I have not chosen to plead after the methods that
would have been pleasant and flattering to you, but degrading
to me. There are things we may not do to escape death, for
baseness is worse than death, and swifter. Death has overtaken
me, who am old, but baseness my accusers, who are strong.
Truth condemns them, as you have condemned me, and each of
us abides sentence. And for you who have condemned me there
will be a penalty swift and sure, and so I take my leave of you.

But to you, my true judges, who voted for my acquittal, I
would speak while yet we may. I have to tell you that my warning demon has in no way withstood the course I have taken, and
the reason, assuredly, is that I have done what is best, gaining
blessing, death being no evil at all. For death is either only to
cease from sensations altogether as in a dreamless sleep, and
that is no loss; or else it is a passing to another place where all
the dead are—the heroes, the poets, the wise men of old. How
priceless were it to hold converse with them and question them!
And surely the judges there pass no death-sentences!

But be you hopeful with regard to death, for to the good man,
neither in life nor in death is there anything that can harm him.
And for me, I am confident that it is better to die than to live.
Therefore the demon did not check me, and I have no resentment
against those who have caused my death. And now we go, I to death
and you to life; but which of us to the better state, God knoweth
alone.

From

The Republic

How the Argument Arose

I had gone with Glaucon to attend the celebration of the festival of Bendis—the Thracian Artemis—a picturesque affair, and we were just leaving, when Polemarchus insisted on carrying us off by main force to the house of his father, Cephalus. There we found a small company assembled. The old gentleman received us with hearty geniality; he is aging, but would not see any hardship in that, if you take age good-humoredly. Of course, he owned that being wealthy makes a difference, but not all the difference. The best of wealth is that you need not do things which anger the gods and entail punishment in the hereafter; you need not lie, or be in debt to gods or men. And this consciousness of your own justice is a great consolation.

"But," said I, "what is justice? Is it always to speak the truth, and always to let a man have his property? There are circumstances——"

"I must go," said he. "Polemarchus shall do the arguing."

This set us discussing the nature of justice. Glaucon took up the cudgels, after a preliminary skirmish with Thrasymachus.

Assuming justice to be desirable—is it so for itself and by itself, or only for its results; or both? The world at large puts it in the second category as an inconvenient necessity. To suffer injustice is an evil, and to protect themselves from that the weak combine to prevent injustice from being done. But if anyone had the ring of Gyges, which made him invisible, so that he could go his own way without let or hindrance, he would get all the pleasures he could out of life without troubling about the justice of it. Again, imagine on the one hand your really consummate rogue who gets credit for all the virtues and is surrounded by all the material factors of happiness; and, on the other hand, a man of utter rectitude, on whom circumstances combine to fix the stigma of iniquity. He will be rejected, scourged, crucified; while the other is enjoying wealth, honor, everything, and can afford to make his peace with the gods into the bargain.

Then Adeimantus took the field in support of his brother. "The poets," he said, "hold forth about the rewards of virtue here and hereafter. But we see the unrighteous prospering mightily; and the religious mendicants come to rich folks and offer to sell them indulgences on easy terms. A keen-witted lad is bound to argue that it is only the appearance of justice that is needed for prosperity; while the gods can be reconciled cheaply. This dwelling on the temporal rewards of justice is fatal. What we expect of you is to show us the inherent value of justice—justice itself, not the appearance of it."

"Well argued," said I, "especially as you reject your own conclusion. I can but try, though the task be hard. But my weak sight may enable me to read large characters better than small. Justice is the virtue of the state as well as of the individual; finding it in the state, the greater, may help us to find it in the individual, the less."

The Socratic Utopia

Society arises because different people are the better skilled to supply different wants, and the wants of each are supplied by mutual arrangement and division of labor. Wants multiply; the community grows; it exchanges its own foreign products; merchants and markets are added to the producers; and when folk begin to hire servants you have a complete city or state living a life of simplicity. "A city of pigs," said Glaucon, "with no refinements." We will go on and develop every luxury of civilization. But then our city and its neighbors will be wanting each other's lands. We must have soldiers. Our best guardians will be a select band, those who are of the right temper and thoroughly trained; fierce to foes but gentle to friends, like that true philosopher, the dog, to whom knowledge is the test. The known are friends, the unknown foes—knowledge begets gentleness.

So our guardians must be trained to knowledge; we must educate them. Music and gymnastic, our national intellectual and physical training, must be taught. Literature comes first, and really we teach things that are not true before we teach things that are true—fables before facts. But over these we must exercise a rigid censorship, excluding what is essentially false.

We must have no stories which attribute harmful doings to the gods. God must be represented as He is—the author of good always, of evil never; also as having in him no variableness, neither shadow of turning. God has no need of disguises. The lie in the soul—essential falsehood—is to Him abhorrent, and He has no need of such deceptions as may be innocent or even laudable for men. God must be shown always as utterly true.

Similarly, we must not have stories which inspire dread of death; no Achilles saying in the underworld that it were better to be a slave in the flesh than Lord of the Shades. And again, no heroes—and gods still less—giving way to frantic lamentations and uncontrolled emotions, even uncontrolled laughter. Truth must be inculcated; medicinal untruths, so to speak, are the prerogative of our rulers alone, and must be permitted to no one else. Temperance, which means self-control and obedience to authority, is essential, and is not always characteristic of Homer's gods and heroes! We must exclude a long list of most unedifying passages on this score. As for pictures of the afflictions of the righteous and the prosperity of the unjust, we must wait, as we have not yet defined justice. We turn to the poetical forms in which the stories should be embodied.

The possible forms are the simply descriptive, the imitative, and the mixture of the two: narrative drama, and narrative mixed with dialogue. Our guardians ought to eschew imitation altogether, or at least to imitate only the good and noble. The act of imitating an evil character is demoralizing, just as no self-respecting person will imitate the lower animals, and so on. Imitation must be restricted within the narrowest practicable limits.

But who are to be our actual rulers? The best of the elders, whose firmness and consistency have stood the test of temptation. To them we transfer the title of guardians, calling the younger men auxiliaries. And we must try to induce everyone— guardians, soldiers, citizens—to believe in one quite magnificent lie: that they were like the men in the Cadmus myth, fashioned in the ground, their common mother.

"I don't wonder at your blushing," said Glaucon.

That they are brothers and sisters, but of different metals— gold, silver, brass, iron; not necessarily of the same metal as their parents in the flesh; and must take rank according to the metal whereof they are made. No doubt it will take a generation or two to get them to believe it.

And now our soldiers must pitch their camp for the defense of the city. Soldiering is their business, not money-making. They must live in common, supported efficiently by the state, having no private property. The gold and silver in their souls is of God. For them, though not for the other citizens, the earthly dross called gold is the accursed thing. Once let them possess it, and they will cease to be guardians, and become oppressors and tyrants.

Of Justice and Communism

But now we have to look for justice. Find the other three cardinal virtues first, and then justice will be distinguishable. Wisdom is in the guardians; if they be wise, the whole state will be wise. Courage we find in the soldiers; courage is the true estimate of danger, and that has been ingrained in them by their education. Temperance, called mastery of self, is really the mastery of the better over the baser qualities; as in our state the better class controls the inferior. Temperance would seem to lie in the harmonious inter-relation of the different classes. Obviously, the remaining virtue of the state is the constant performance of his own particular function in the state, and not his neighbor's, by each member of the state. Let us see how that works out in the individual.

Shall we not find that there are three several qualities in the individual, each of which must in like manner do its own business, the intellectual, the passionate or spirited, and the lustful? They must be separate, because one part of a thing cannot be doing contradictory things at the same time; your lusts bid you do what your intelligence forbids; and the emotional quality is distinct from both desire and reason, though in alliance with reason. Well, here you have wisdom and courage in the intellectual and spiritual parts, temperance in their mastery over desire; and justice is the virtue of the soul as a whole; of each part never failing to perform its own function and that alone. To ask, now, whether justice or injustice is the more profitable becomes ridiculous.

Now we shall find that virtue is one, but that vice has several forms; as there is but one form of perfect state—ours—whether it happens to be called a monarchy if there be but one guardian, or an aristocracy if there be more; and, as it has four principal imperfect forms, so there are four main vices.

Here Glaucon and Adeimantus refused to let me go on; I had shirked a serious difficulty. What about women and children? My saying that the soldiers were to live in common might mean anything. What kind of communism was I demanding? Well, there are two different questions: What is desirable? And, What is possible? First, then, our defenders are our watchdogs. Glaucon knows all about dogs; we don't differentiate in the case of males and females; the latter hunt with the pack. If women are similarly to have the same employments as men, they must have the same education in music and gymnastic. We must not mind ribald comments. But should they share masculine employments? Do they differ from men in such a way that they should not? Women bear children, and men beget them; but apart from that the differences are really only in degrees of capacity, not essential distinctions of quality; even as men differ among themselves. The natures being the same, the education must be the same, and the same careers must be open.

But a second and more alarming wave threatens us: Community of wives and children. "You must prove both the possibility and desirability of that." Men and women must be trained together and live together, but not in licentiousness. They must be mated with the utmost care for procreation, the best being paired at due seasons, nominally by lot, and for the occasion. The offspring of the selected will have a common nursery; the mothers will not know which were their own children. Parentage will be permissible only between twenty-five and fifty-five, and between twenty and forty. The children begotten in the same batch of espousals will be brothers and sisters.

The absence of "mine" and "thine" will ensure unity, because it abolishes the primary cause of discord: common maintenance by the state removes all temptation either to meanness or cringing. Our guardians will be uncommonly happy. As to practicability: communism is suitable for war. The youngsters will be taken to watch any fighting; cowards will be degraded; valor will be honored, and death on the field, with

other supreme services to the state, will rank the hero among
demigods. Against Greeks war must be conducted as against
our own kith and kin. But as to the possibility of all this—this
third threatening wave is the most terrific of all.

Of Philosophy in Rulers

It will be possible then, and only then, when kings are philosophers or philosophers kings. "You will be mobbed and pelted
for such a proposition." Still, it is the fact. The philosopher
desires all knowledge. You know that justice, beauty, good, and
so on, are single, though their presentation is multiplex and
variable. Curiosity about the multiplex particulars is not desire
of knowledge, which is of the one constant idea—of that which
is, as ignorance is of that which is not. What neither is nor is
not, that which fluctuates and changes, is the subject matter of
opinion, a state between knowledge and ignorance. Beauty is
beauty always and everywhere; the things that look beautiful
may be ugly from another point of view. Experience of beautiful things, curiosity about them, must be distinguished from
knowledge of beauty; the philosopher is not to be confounded
with the connoisseur, not knowledge with opinion. The philosopher is he who has in his mind the perfect pattern of justice,
beauty, truth; his is the knowledge of the eternal; he contem-
plates all time and all existence; no praises are too high for his
character. "No doubt; still, if that is so, why do professed
philosophers always show themselves either fools or knaves in
ordinary affairs?" A ship's crew which does not understand that
the art of navigation demands a knowledge of the stars, will
stigmatize a properly qualified pilot as a star-gazing idiot, and
will prevent him from navigating. The world assumes that the
philosopher's abstractions are folly, and rejects his guidance.
The philosopher is the best kind of man; the corrupted philosopher is the worst; and the corrupted influences brought to bear
are irresistible to all but the very strongest natures. The professional teachers of philosophy live not by leading popular
opinion, but by pandering to it; a bastard brood trick themselves out as philosophers, while the true philosopher withdraws himself from so gross a world. Small wonder that philosophy gets discredited! Not in the soil of any existing state can

philosophy grow naturally; planted in a suitable state, her divinity will be apparent.

I need no longer hesitate to say that we must make our guardians philosophers. The necessary combination of qualities is extremely rare. Our test must be thorough, for the soul must be trained up by the pursuit of all kinds of knowledge to the capacity for the pursuit of the highest—higher than justice and wisdom—the idea of the good. "But what is the good— pleasure, knowledge?" No. To see and distinguish material things, the faculty of sight requires the medium of light, whose source is the sun. The good is to the intellectual faculty what the sun is to that of vision: it is the source and cause of truth, which is the light whereby we perceive ideas; it is not truth nor the ideas, but above them; their cause, as the sun is the source of light and the cause of growth.

Again, as the material things with which the eye is concerned are in two categories—the copies, reflections or shadows of things, and actual things—correspondingly the things perceived by the intellect are in a secondary region—as the mathematical—where everything is derived from hypotheses which are assumed to be first principles; or in a supreme region, in which hypotheses are only the steps by which we ascend to the real ultimate first principles themselves. And it will follow further that the mind has four faculties appropriate to these four divisions, which we call respectively pure reason (the highest), understanding, conviction, and perception of shadows; the first pair being concerned with being, the field of the intellect; the second pair with becoming, the field of opinion.

Of Shadows and Realities

Let me speak a parable. Humanity—ourselves—are as people dwelling ever bound and fettered in a twilit cave, with our backs to the light. Behind us is a parapet, and beyond the parapet a fire; all that we see is the shadows thrown on the wall that faces us by figures passing along the parapet behind us; all we hear is the echo of their voices. Now, if some of us are turned round to face the light and look on the real figures, they will be dazzled at first, and much more if they are taken out into the light, and up to face the sun himself; but presently they will see

perfectly, and have all the joy thereof. Now send them back into
the cave, and they will be apparently much blinder than the
folk who have been there all the time, and their talk of what
they have seen will be taken for the babbling of fools, or worse.
Small wonder that those who have beheld the light have but little mind to return to the twilight cave which is the common
world. But remember—everyone in the cave possesses the faculty of sight if only his eyes be turned to the light. Loose the
fetters of carnal desires which hold him with his back to the
light, and every man may be converted and live. So we must
select those who are most capable of facing the light, and see
to it that they return to the cave, to give the cave-dwellers the
benefit of their knowledge. And if this be for them a hardship,
we must bear in mind as before, that the good of the whole is
what matters, not whether one or another may suffer hardship
for the sake of the whole.

How, then, shall we train them to the passage from darkness
to light? For this, our education in music and gymnastic is
wholly inadequate. We must proceed first to the science of
numbers, then of geometry, then of astronomy. And after astronomy, there is the sister science of abstract harmonics—not of
audible sounds. All of which are but the prelude to the ultimate
supreme science of dialectic, which carries the intelligence to
the contemplation of the idea of the good, the ultimate goal.
And here to attempt further explanation would be vanity. This
is the science of the pure reason, the coping-stone of knowledge.

We saw long ago that our rulers must possess every endowment of mind and body, all cultivated to the highest degree.
From the select we must again select, at twenty, those who are
most fit for the next ten years' course of education; and from
them, at thirty, we shall choose those who can, with confidence,
be taken to face the light; who have been tested and found
absolutely steadfast, not shaken by having got beyond the conventional view of things. We will give them five or six years of
philosophy; then fifteen years of responsible office in the state;
and at fifty they shall return to philosophy, subject to the call
upon them to take up the duties of rulership and of educating
their successors.

Of State Types and Individual Types

Before this digression we were on the point of discussing the four vitiated forms of the state, and the corresponding individual types. The four types of state as we know them in Hellas, are: the Spartan, where personal ambition and honor rule, which we call timocracy; the oligarchical, where wealth rules; the democratic; and the arbitrary rule of the individual, which we call tyranny. The comparison of this last—the supremely unjust—with our own—the supremely just—will show whether justice or injustice be the more desirable.

The perfect state degenerates to timocracy when the state's numerical law of generation [an unsolved riddle] has not been properly observed, and inferior offspring have entered in consequence into the ruling body. The introduction of private property will cause them to assume towards the commonalty the attitude, not of guardians, but of masters, and to be at odds among themselves; also, in their education gymnastic will acquire predominance over music. Ambition and party spirit become the characteristic features. When, in an ill-ordered state a great man withdraws from the corruption of politics into private life, we see the corresponding individual type in the son of such a one, egged on by his mother and flattering companions, to win back for himself at all costs the prestige which his father had resigned; personal ambition becomes his dominant characteristic.

Oligarchy is the next outcome of the introduction of private property; riches outweigh virtue, love of money the love of honor, and the rich procure for themselves the legal monopoly of political power. Here the state becomes divided against itself—there is one state of the rich and another of the poor—and the poor will be divided into the merely incompetent and the actively dangerous or predatory. And your corresponding individual is he whose father had won honors which had not saved him from ultimate ruin; so that the son rejects ambition and makes money his goal, till, for the sake of money, he will compass any baseness, though still only under a cloak of respectability.

In the oligarchy the avaricious encourage and foster extravagance in their neighbors. Men, ruined by moneylenders, turn on their moneyed rulers, overthrow them, and give everyone a share in the government. The result is that the state is not one, nor two, but diverse. Folk say what they like and do what they like, and anyone is a statesman who will wave the national flag. That is democracy. Such is the son of your miserly oligarch; deprived of unnecessary pleasures, he is tempted to wild dissipation. He has no education to help him to distinguish, and the vices of dissipation assume the aspect and titles of virtue. He fluctuates from one point of view to another—is one thing today and another tomorrow.

And last we come to tyranny and the tyrannical man. Democratic license develops into sheer anarchy. Jack is as good as his master. The predatory population becomes demagogues; they squeeze the decent citizens, and drive them to adopt oligarchical methods; then the friend of the people appears; the protector, champion, and hero, by a familiar process becomes a military autocrat, who himself battens, as must also his mercenary soldiery, on the citizens; and our unhappy Demos finds that it has jumped out of the reek into the fire. Now our democratical man was swayed by the devices and moods of the moment; his son will be swayed by the most irrational and most bestial of his appetites; be bully and tyrant, while slave of his own lusts. Your thorough blackguard of every species comes of this type, and the worst of all is he who achieves the tyranny of a state. See, then, how, even as the tyrannic state is the most utterly enslaved, so the tyrannic man is of all men the least free; and, beyond all others, the tyrant of a state. He is like a slave-owner, who is at the mercy of his slaves—the passions which he must pamper, or die, yet cannot satisfy. Surely such a one is the veriest slave—yea, the most wretched of men. It follows that he who is the most complete opposite of the tyrant is the happiest—the individual who corresponds to our state. Proclaim it, then, son of Ariston, that the most just of men is he who is master of himself, and is of all men the most miserable, whether gods and men recognize him or no.

Of the Happiness of the Just

Now for a second proof. Three kinds of pleasure correspond to the three elements of the soul—reason, spirit, desire. In each man one of the three is in the ascendant. One counts knowledge vain in comparison with the advantages of riches, another with

those of honor; to the philosopher only truth counts. But he is
the only one of them who makes his choice from experience of
all three kinds. And he, the only qualified judge, places the
satisfaction of the spirit second, and of desire lowest. And yet
a third proof: I fancy the only quite real pleasures are those of
the philosopher. There is an intermediate state between pleasure and pain. To pass into this from pleasure is painful, and
from pain is pleasurable. Now, the pleasures of the body are
really nothing more than reliefs from pains of one kind or
another. And, next, the pleasures of the soul, being of the eternal order, are necessarily more real than those of the body,
which are fleeting—in fact, mere shadows of pleasure.

Much as I love and admire Homer, I think our regulations as
to poetry were particularly sound; but we must inquire further
into the meaning of imitation. We saw before that all particular
things are the presentations of some universal idea. There is
one ultimate idea of bed, or chair, or table. What the joiner
makes is a copy of that. All ideas are the creation of the master artificer, the demiurge; of his creations all material things
are copies. We can all create things in a way by catching reflections of them in a mirror. But these are only copies of particular things from one point of view, partial copies of copies of the
idea. Such precisely are the creations of the painter, and in like
manner of the poet. What they know and depict is not the realities, but mere appearances. If the poets knew the realities they
would have left us something other than imitations of copies.
Moreover, what they imitate is not the highest but the lower; not
the truth of reason, but emotions of all sorts, which it should be
our business not to excite but to control and allay. So we continue to prohibit the poetry which is imitation, however
supreme, and allow only hymns to the gods, and praises of great
men. We must no more admit the allurements of poesy than the
attractions of ambition or of riches.

Greater far are the rewards of virtue than all we have yet
shown; for an immortal soul should heed nothing that is less
than eternal. "What, is the soul then immortal? Can you prove
that?" Yes, of a surety. In all things there is good and evil; a
thing perishes of its own corruption, not of the corruption of
ought external to it. If disease or injury of the body cannot corrupt the soul, *a fortiori* they cannot slay it; but injustice, the
corruption of the soul, is not induced by injury to the body. If,

then, the soul be not destroyed by sin, nothing else can destroy
it, and it is immortal. The number of existing souls must then
be constant; none perish, none are added, for additional immortal souls would have to come out of what is mortal, which is
absurd. Now, hitherto we have shown only that justice is in
itself best for the soul, but now we see that its rewards, too, are
unspeakably great. The gods, to whom the just are known, will
reward them hereafter, if not here; and even in this world they
have the better lot in the long run. But of this nothing is com-
parable to their rewards in the hereafter, revealed to us in the
mythos of Er, called the Armenian, whose body being slain in
battle, his soul was said to have returned to it from the underworld—renewing its life—a messenger to men of what he had
there beheld. For a thousand years the souls, being judged,
enjoyed or suffered a tenfold retribution for all they had done
of good or evil in this life, and some for a second term, or it
might be for terms without end. Then for the most part they
were given again, after the thousand years, a choice of another
lot on the earth, being guided therein by their experience in
their last life; and so, having drunk of the waters of forgetful-
ness, came back to earth once more, unconscious of their past.

Let us, then, believing that the soul is indeed immortal, hold
fast to knowledge and justice, that it may be well with us both
here and hereafter.

Aristotle
(384–322 B.C.)

From

NICOMACHEAN ETHICS

The End of Life and the Meaning of Virtue

Every art and science, every action, has for its end some good, whether this be a form of activity or an actual product. The ends of minor arts are only means to the ends of superior arts. If there is one supreme end, this is The Good, inquiry into which belongs to the supreme Social Science [for which the Greek term is Politics]. The name given to this supreme good, the attainment of which is the object of Politics, is Happiness, good living, or welfare.

But Happiness itself is variously defined; some identify it with Pleasure, others with Honor—the first a degrading, and the second an inadequate view. Platonists find it in an abstract Idea of Good, a Universal which precludes particulars. There is a great deal to be said against this doctrine, even as a question of logic or metaphysic; but apart from that, the theory is out of court, for the all sufficient reason that its practical value is *nil*—knowledge of the great Universal Good in the abstract is of no practical use whatever in everyday life, which is a fundamental point for us.

If, then, there is a supreme dominating Good to be aimed at, what are the essential characteristics it must display? The Good of all Goods, the Best, must be complete in itself, a consummation. Whatsoever is a means to some end beyond fails so far of completeness; when we say that our end must be "complete," it follows that it must always be an end, never a means. It is not merely one amongst others of which it is the best, but the one in which all the others are summed up. It is of itself quite sufficient for the individual, and that not merely in isolation, but as a member of society—which it is his nature to be.

Let us then define Happiness as Man's *Work*—the perfor-

mance of his function as man. Everything has some specific
function, the performance of which is its Good, and man, too,
must have a specific function. Now, this cannot be the kind of
life which he shares with the vegetable or with the brute creation, therefore it must be the active life of his distinctive—
i.q., his rational—part, exercised in accordance with the virtue
or virtues which perfect it, and in his life as a whole, not merely at moments.

Testing our conclusions by the judgments of common experience, we gather support from them. Goods external, and goods
of the body, are reckoned inferior to goods of the soul, which is
recognized as the seat of activities. The identification of happiness with virtue, however, necessitates the distinction between
active virtue and virtuousness. As conducing to active virtue,
the other kinds of goods are elements in happiness. We must
assume it to be not something granted to us, outside our own
control, but attainable by effort and education.

Virtues are of two kinds: of the intellect, acquired by study;
and moral, acquired by practice. The moral virtues are not
implanted by nature, but we have the capacity for them by
nature, and achieve them by practice, as by practice we
acquire excellence in the arts, or control over our passions.
Education, then, is of the utmost importance, since the state or
habit of virtue is the outcome of virtue in act.

The manner, the "how" of action, must be in accord with
Right Reason, whereof we shall speak elsewhere. Here we must
recognize that we are not laying down universal propositions,
but general rules which are modified by circumstances. Our
activities must lie in a mean between the two extremes of
excess and defect, and this applies both to the process of gen-
erating virtue, and to its manifestation. The virtues are concerned with pleasure and pain, because these act as inducements or opposing influences; Beauty, Advantage, and Pleasure
being the three standing inducements, and Pleasure entering
into both the others; so that in one aspect Virtue is the Best
action in respect to pleasure.

But it does not lie in the mere act; the act must be born of
knowledge and of choice done for its own sake, and persistent-
ly—the first, knowledge, being the least important; to make it
the most important is a speculative error.

Now, there are three modes of mind: feeling or passion, faculty, and habit. We do not praise or blame passion in itself, or the faculty; therefore virtue can lie in neither, but must be found in habit or condition. The virtuous habit or condition is what enables that whereof it is the virtue to perform its function, which, in the case of man, is the activity of the soul, preserving always a middle course between excess and deficiency, by choice.

In another sense, however, we must remember that there are qualities in themselves wrong, and that virtue may be presented as not something intermediate, but a consummation. But when we name each of these virtues—Courage, Temperance, Liberality, etc.; the social virtues, or good manners; the virtues concerned with the passions—we can name the corresponding excess or deficiency. Justice and the intellectual virtues demand a separate analysis.

Each virtue stands in opposition to each of the extremes, and each of these to the other extreme, though in some cases the virtue may be more antagonistic to one extreme than to the other, as courage to cowardice more than to rashness. In individual cases, it is difficult to avoid being deflected towards one or other of the extremes.

Before proceeding with this analysis, we must examine the question of choice. To be praiseworthy, an act must be voluntary. An act is not voluntary if it is the outcome of external compulsion. Where there is a margin of choice, an act must still, on the whole, be regarded as voluntary, though done "against our will." Of properly involuntary acts, we must distinguish between the unintentional and the unwilling, meaning by the latter, in effect, what the agent would not have done if he had known.

Choice is not the same thing as a voluntary act; nor is it desire, or emotion, or exactly "wish," since we may wish for, but cannot make choice of, the unattainable. Nor is it Deliberation—rather, it is the act of decision following deliberation. If man has the power to say yes, he has equally the power to say no, and is master of his own action. If we make a wrong choice through ignorance for which we are ourselves responsible, the ignorance itself is culpable, and cannot excuse the wrong choice, and so, when the choice is the outcome of a

judgment disordered by bad habits, men cannot escape by saying they were made so—they made themselves so. To say they
"could not help" doing wrong things is only an evasion.

The Moral Virtues Examined

Virtues, then, are habits, issuing in acts corresponding to those
by which the habit was established, directed by Right Reason,
every such act being voluntary, and the whole process a voluntary process.

We may now turn to the analysis of the several virtues.

Courage has to do with fear. Not all kinds; for there are some
things we ought to fear, such as dishonor and pauperism, the
fear of which is compatible with dauntless courage, while the
coward may not fear them. Fearlessness of what is in our control, and endurance of what is not, for the sake of true honor,
constitute the courageous habit. Its excess is rashness or fool-
hardiness, the deficiency cowardice. Akin to it, but still spurious, is the courage of which the motive is not Honor but honors
or reputation. Spurious also is the courage which arises from
the knowledge that the danger is infinitesimal; so is that which
is born of blind anger, or of elated self-confidence, or of mere
unconsciousness of danger. True Courage lies in resisting a
temptation to pleasure or to escaping pain, and, above all,
death, for Honor's sake. The exercise of a virtue may be very far
from pleasant, except, of course, in so far as the end for which
it was exercised is achieved.

Temperance is concerned with pleasures of the senses;
mainly of touch, in a much less degree of taste; but not of sight,
hearing, or smell, except indirectly. Of carnal pleasures, some
are common to all, some have an individual application.
Temperance lies in being content to do without them, and
desiring them only so far as they conduce to health and comfort. The characteristic of intemperance is that it has to do with
pleasures only, not with pains. Hence, it is more purely voluntary than cowardice, as being less influenced by perturbing outward circumstances as concerns the particular case, though not
the habit.

Liberality is concerned with money matters, and lies
between extravagance and meanness. Really it means the right

treatment of money, both in spending and receiving it—the former rather than the latter. A man is not really liberal who lav-
ishes money for baser purposes, or takes it whence he should
not, or fails to take due care of his property. The liberal man
tends to err in the direction of lavishness. Extravagance is curable, but is frequently accompanied by carelessness as to the
objects on which the money is spent and the sources from
which it is obtained. The habit of meanness is apt to be inerad-
icable, and is displayed both in the acquisition and in the
hoarding of money.

Munificence is a virtue concerned only with expenditure on
a large scale, and it implies liberality. It lies between vulgar
ostentation and niggardliness. It is possible only for the
wealthy, and is concerned mainly with public works, but also
with private occasions of ceremony. The error of vulgar ostentation is misdirection of expenditure, not excess. Niggardliness
abstains from a proper expenditure.

Magnanimity is the virtue of the aristocrat; its excess is self-
glorification, its deficiency self-depreciation. The magnani-
mous man will bate nothing of his claim to honor, power and
wealth, not as caring greatly for them, but as demanding what
he knows to be his due. This character involves the possession
of the virtues; the man must act in the grand manner and on the
grand scale. He knows his own superiority, does not conceal it,
and acts up to it. Self-glorification overrates its own capacities;
self-depreciation underrates them and shuns its responsibili-
ties, being the more reprehensible of the two.

There is a nameless virtue which stands to magnanimity in
the same relation as that of liberality to munificence; these
being concerned with honors, as those with money. The excess
is ambition, the deficiency is the lack of it; but here terminology fails us.

Good temper is a mean between ill-temper—whether of the
irascible, the sulky, or the cantankerous kind—and something
for which we have no name (poor-spiritedness). Friendliness
comes between the excessive desire to please and boorishness.
It is a social virtue which might be defined as goodwill *plus*
tact. Sincerity [there is no English term quite corresponding to
the Greek] is the quality opposed on the one side to boastful-
ness, and on the other to mock-modesty; it is displayed by the

man who acknowledges, but who never exaggerates his own merits. In the social display of wit and humor, there is a marked mean between the buffoon and the dullard or prig. Shame is a term implying a feeling rather than a habit; like fear, it has a physical effect, producing blushes, and seems, in fact, to be fear of disrepute. To the young, it is a safeguard against vice; the virtuous man need never feel it; to be unable to feel it implies the habit of vice. Continence is not properly in the category of moral virtues.

Justice

We come now to Justice. A specific habit differs from a specific faculty or science, as each of the latter covers opposites, *e.g.*, the science of health is also the science of sickness; whereas the habit of Justice does not cover but is opposed to the habit of Injustice. Justice itself is a term used in various senses; and the senses in which injustice is used vary correspondingly. Confusion is apt to arise from these varying senses not being distinguished. Injustice includes law-breaking, grasping and unfairness. Grasping is taking too much of what is good only; unfairness is concerned with both what is good and what is injurious. But in the legal sense, whatever law lays down is assumed to be just. Law, however, covers the whole field of virtuous action as it affects our neighbors, so that in this general sense justice is an inclusive term equivalent to righteousness. We, however, must confine ourselves to the specific sense of the terms.

Grasping is, in fact, included in unfairness, which is the real opposite of specific justice; it includes law-breaking only so far as the law is broken for the sake of gain. The justice with which we are concerned has two branches: Distributive, of honors and the like among citizens by the State, and of private property by contract and agreement; and Corrective, the remedying of unfair distribution. There are always two parties, and justice is the mean between the unfairness which favors A and the unfairness which favors B. Distributive justice takes into consideration the merits of the parties; corrective justice is concerned only with restoring a balance which has been disturbed. The distribution is a question not of equality, but of right proportion; and this applies to retribution, which is recognized as one of its aspects, *e.g.*, the retribution for an officer striking a private and for a private striking an officer. Proportional requital is the economic basis of society, arrived at by the existence of a comparatively unfluctuating currency which provides a criterion.

In the State, as such, justice is obtained from the law and its administrators; justice is the virtue of the magistrate. Since he has nothing to gain or lose himself, it has been supposed that justice is "another's good," not our own. In the family, justice does not come in, the whole household being, in a sense, parts of the *pater familias*; and as you cannot be unjust to yourself, you cannot be unjust to your household. In the State, what is just is fixed partly by the nature of things, partly by law or convention.

As to individual acts: injury may arise from a miscalculation, or from an incalculable accident; it becomes a wrong when it was intentional but not premeditated, an injustice when premeditated. An act *prima facie* unjust is not so if done with the free consent of the person injured. It is the agent of distribution, not the recipient, who is unjust (when they are different persons); and similarly, the agent, not the instrument. And even the agent of unjust distribution is not really unjust unless he was really actuated by motives of personal gain

The performance of a particular act is easy. To perform it rightly as the outcome of a right habit, is not; nor is it easy to be confident as to what is right in the particular case. The man who is just, having the habit does not find it easy to act unjustly.

What we must call equity may be opposed to justice, but only in the legal sense of that term. It is justice freed from the errors incidental to the particular cases for which the law cannot provide. Injustice, again, is found in self-injury or suicide; which the law penalizes, not because the individual thereby treats himself unjustly, but because he does an injustice to the community. It is only by metaphor that a man may be called unjust to himself, an expression which means that the relation between one part of him and another part of him is analogous to the unjust relation between persons.

Wisdom, Prudence and Continence

The ensuing discussion of intellectual virtue requires some remarks on the soul. We distinguish in the rational part, that which knows, concerned with the unchanging; and that which reasons, concerned with the changing. Our intellects and our propensions—not our sense-perceptions, which are shared with animals—guide our actions and our apprehension of truth. Attraction and repulsion, in correspondence with affirmation and denial, combine to form right choice; the practical—as opposed to the pure—reason having an external object, and being a motive power.

There are five modes of attaining truth: (1) Concerning things unalterable, defined as demonstrative science; (2) concerning the making of things changeable, art; (3) concerning the doing—not making—of things changeable, prudence; (4) intuitive reason, the basis of demonstrative science; (5) wisdom, the union of intuitive reason and science.

Wisdom and prudence are the two virtues of the intellect. Wisdom implies intuitive reason, which grasps undemonstrable first principles; it is concerned with the interests not of the moment, the individual, or the locality. Whereas prudence is concerned precisely with these; it is essentially practical. Wisdom cannot be identified with statesmanship; which, again, is not the same as prudence—which applies to the self, and to the family, as well as to the State; it differs from wisdom as requiring experience.

Wisdom, knowledge of the ultimate bases, is equally without practical bearing for those who have acquired a right habit and for those who have not; just as a knowledge of medical theory is of no use to the average man. But being an activity of the soul, *ipso facto*, it conduces to happiness. The general conclusion is that what we have called "prudence" shows the means to the end which the moral virtues aim at. It is not a moral virtue, but the moral virtues accord with it. Both are necessary to the achievement of goodness.

We come now to a second group of qualities, concerned with conduct. We have dealt with the virtues and their opposing vices. We pass by the infra-human and the supra-human bestiality and holiness; but have still to deal with Continence and its contrasted qualities, which are concerned with the passions.

In the popular view, continence, self-control, is adherence to our formed judgment. Incontinence is yielding to passion where we know it to be wrong, and may be indulged in the pursuit of vengeance, honor, or gain. A number of *prima facie* contradictions are started out of the popular views. We find that a man does not act against complete knowledge or knowledge of which he is fully conscious. The knowledge may, so to speak, be there, but is in abeyance, a condition which is palpably exemplified in a drunken man. Now, incontinence is concerned with pleasures, which are necessary—as for sustenance of life—and unnecessary but, *per se,* desirable, as honor. Incontinence is a term applied only by analogy in the case of the latter; its proper concern—as with the moral vice, which we call intemperance—is with the former. It implies, however, violent desire, which intemperance does not. We have examples of such desires in a morbid or diseased form, species of mania; but here again the term incontinence is only applied by analogy. Its legitimate application, in short, is restricted to the normal.

Incontinence in respect of anger is not so bad as in respect of desire. It is often constitutional, it is in itself painful, and it is not wanton, being in all three points unlike the other. What we spoke of as bestiality is more horrible than vice or incontinence, as being inhuman; but it does less harm. Incontinence means transgressing the ordinary standards in respect of pleasure and pain. Such transgression, when of set purpose, and not followed by repentance—consequently, incurable—is the moral vice of intemperance; which, being characterized by the absence of violent desire, is worse than incontinence. The latter is open, and is curable. The confusion between the two is due to their issuing in like acts; the passionate impulse is temporary; it is not a formed habit of wrong choice.

Continence is acting on conviction in resistance to passion; not merely sticking to any and every opinion, which is really rather more like incontinence. The other extreme, of actual apathy, is rare. Continence differs from temperance, as implying resistance to strong desires; whereas temperance implies that such desires are not active. Prudence—but not the acuteness which is sometimes confused with prudence—is incompatible with incontinence, which is least curable when the outcome of weakness.

Here it becomes necessary to make some inquiry as to Pleasure and Pain. Some maintain that pleasure is never good, some that it is partly good and partly not; some that it is good, but not the best. But it cannot be bad *per se*, since it may be defined as the unimpeded activity of a formed faculty. Pleasure, as such, is not a hindrance to any activity, but its fulfillment; *e.g.*, the pleasure of speculative inquiry does not hinder it. As a matter of fact, everyone does pursue pleasure; the denial that it is good results from thinking of it as meaning only bodily pleasures. And even they are not evil, but only the excessive pursuit of them. As to pleasure being fleeting, that is only because circumstances vary. The pleasure of the unchanging would be permanent.

Friendship

A quality rendered as "Friendship" [though the Greek and English terms are not identical in content] now comes under examination. It is a relation to some other person or persons without which life is hardly worth living. Some account for it on the principle of "like to like," others on the opposite theory. Now, lovableness comes of goodness, or pleasantness, or usefulness. Love is not bestowed on the inanimate, and it must be mutual; it is to be distinguished from goodwill or devotion, which need not be reciprocated.

Genuine friendship must be based on goodness; what rests on pleasantness (as with the young), or on utility (as with the old), is only to be recognized conventionally as friendship. In perfection it cannot subsist without perfect mutual knowledge, and only between the good; hence it is not possible for anyone to have many real friends. Of the conventional forms, that which is born of intellectual sympathy is more enduring than what springs from sexual attraction; while what comes of utility is quite accidental. The former may develop into genuine friendship if there be virtue in both parties. Companionship is a necessary condition, in any case.

Variants of friendship, however, may subsist between unequals, as between parents and children, princes and subjects, men and women, where there is a difference in the character of the affection of the two parties. A certain degree of inequality—though we cannot lay down the limitation—makes "friendship" a misnomer. One would not desire the actual apotheosis of a friend, because that would take him out of reach; it would end friendship. Friendship lies rather in the active loving than in being loved, though most people are more anxious to be loved than to love.

Every form of social community—typified in the State—involves relationships into which friendship enters. The relationships in the family correspond to those in states; monarch to subjects as father to children, tyrant to subjects as master to slaves; autocratic rule to that of the husband, oligarchic rule to that of the wife; what we call Timocracy to the fraternal relation, and Democracy to the entirely unregulated household. In some kinds of association, friendship takes the form of *esprit de corps.* It may be seen that quarrels arise most readily in those friendships between equals which are based upon interest, and in friendships between unequals.

Friendship is a kind of exchange—equal between equals, and proportional between unequals; a repayment. This suggests various questions as to priority of claim—*e.g.*, between paying your father's ransom and repaying a loan, both being in a sort the repayment of a debt. No fixed law can be laid down—*i.e.* it cannot be said that one obligation at all times and in all circumstances overrides all others.

The dissolution of friendship is warranted when one party has become depraved, since he has changed from being the person who was the object of friendship. But he should not be given up while there is hope of restoring his character. Again, if one develops a great superiority, friendship proper cannot persist—at least, in its first form. Our relations with a friend are much like those with our own selves; the true friend is a sort of *alter ego.* Friendship is not to be identified with goodwill, though the latter is a condition precedent; we may feel goodwill, but not friendship, towards a person we have never seen or spoken to. Unanimity of feeling—not as to facts, but as to ends and means—is a sort of equivalent to friendship in the body politic. The reason why conferring a benefit creates more affection than receiving it seems to be that the benefactor feels himself the maker of the other; we all incline to love what we produced—as parents their children, or the artist his own creations.

Self-love is wrong in a sense—the usual sense in which the term is used, of giving priority to oneself in the acquisition of material pleasures. But the seeking of the noblest things for oneself is really self-love, and may involve giving others, especially friends, the priority in respect of desirable things—even to resigning to another the opportunity of doing a noble deed. In this higher sense, self-love is praiseworthy.

The good man is self-sufficing, but friends are desirable, if not actually necessary to him, as giving scope for the exercise of beneficent activities, not as conferring benefits upon him. Besides, man's highest activities must be exercised not in isolation, but as a member of society, and such life lacks completeness if without friends. Finally, friendship attains its most complete realization where comradeship is complete; that is to say, in a common life.

Conclusion

We must revert once more to the question of Pleasure and Pain. To say that pleasure is not good is absurd; he who does so stultifies himself by his own acts. Eudoxus thought it was *the* good, his opinion being the weightier because of his temperateness.

It is desired for its own sake; its opposite is admittedly undesirable. But since it may be added to other good things, it cannot be *the* good: though to say that what every one desires is not good at all is folly. That it is not "a quality," or that it is "indeterminate," are irrelevant arguments, both statements applying to what are admittedly among "goods." The doctrine that it is a process, again, will not hold water. Pleasure is a thing complete; whereas a process is complete at no moment unless it be that of its termination. It is the completion of its appropriate activity; not in the sense that a habit makes the activity complete, but as its accompaniment and complement. Continuous it is not, just as the activity is not. It is not the complete life, but is inseparable from it. Pleasures, however, differ specifically and in value, as do the qualities with whose activities they are associated. The pleasures proper to men are those associated with the activities proper to man as man, those shared with other animals being so only in a less degree.

It remains to recapitulate the sum of our conclusions regard-

ing Happiness. It is not a habit, but lies in the habitual activities—desirable in and for themselves not as means—exercised
deliberately, excluding mere amusement. Man's highest faculty
being intelligence, its activity is his highest happiness—contemplation—constant, sufficient, and sought not as a means,
but as an end.

This kind of happiness belongs to the gods also. Exclusively
human, but below the other, is the fulfillment of the moral life,
conditioned by human society, and more affected by environ-
ments and material wants. For contemplative activity, the
barest material needs suffice. But this does not of itself induce
the moral life, being apart from conduct. To induce morality,
not only knowledge, but the right habit of action—which does
not follow from knowledge and may be implanted without it—
is absolutely necessary. Compulsion may successfully establish
the habit where argument might fail. Compulsion, therefore, is
the proper course for the State to take.

Saint Augustine

(c. 354–430)

From

THE CITY OF GOD

The Origin of the Two Cities

I write, dear Marcellinus, of that most glorious City of God, both in her present pilgrimage and life by faith, and in that fixed and everlasting seat which she awaits in patience. I write to defend her against those who place their gods above her Founder—a great and arduous work, but God is my aid. I well know what power a writer needs who would show the proud how great is the virtue of humility. For the law of our King and Founder is this: "God is against the proud but gives grace to the humble"; but the swollen and insolent soul loves herein to usurp the divine Majesty, and itself "to spare the subject and subdue the proud." Wherefore I may not pass over in silence that earthly city also, enslaved by its lust of empire.

For it is from this City of the World that those enemies have arisen, against whom we have to defend the City of God; Romans, spared by the barbarians on Christ's account, are haters of the name of Christ. The shrines of the martyrs and the basilicas of the apostles received, in the devastation of the city, not their own people only, but every fugitive; and the fury and greed of the invaders were quenched at these holy thresholds. Yet with thankless arrogance and impious frenzy these men, who took refuge under that Name in order that they might enjoy the light of fugitive years, perversely oppose it now, that they may languish in sempiternal gloom.

Never has it been known, in so many wars as are recorded from before the foundation of Rome to the present day, that an enemy, having reduced any city, should have spared those who had fled to the temples of their gods; not even the Romans themselves, whose moderation in victory has so often been justly praised, have respected the sanctuary of vanquished deities.

The devastation and massacre and pillage and conflagrations of the sack of Rome were nothing new. But this one thing was new and unheard of—these savages became suddenly so mild as to set apart spacious basilicas and to fill them with people on whom they had mercy; no one might be killed therein nor any dragged from thence. Who does not see that this is due to the name of Christ and to a Christian age? Who can deny that these sanguinary hordes were bridled by Him who had said: "I will visit their sins with the rod, but will not take my mercy from them?"

All natures, because they exist and therefore have their manner and species and a certain peace with themselves, are good; and when they are in the places belonging to the order of nature, they preserve the being which they have received.

The truest cause of the felicity of the good angels is to be found in this, that they adhere to Him who supremely is; and the cause of the misery of bad angels lies in this, that they have turned away from Him who supremely is, to themselves, who have not supreme being. This vice has no other name but pride, which is the beginning of every sin. They refused to preserve their strength for Him, and so threw away that in which all their greatness consisted. It is vain to seek for an efficient cause for the bad will; we have to do, not with anything efficient, but with a deficiency. The mere defection from that which supremely is to things which are on a lower grade of being is to begin to have a bad will.

Now God founded mankind, not as the angels, so that even did they sin they should not die; but in such a way that did they obey, they should enter, without death, on a blessed eternity; but, did they disobey, they should suffer the most just penalty, both of body and of soul. For though the human soul is truly said to be immortal, yet is there a sense in which it dies when God forsakes it.

Only because they had begun inwardly to be evil did the first of mankind fall into overt disobedience. A bad will had preceded the bad action, and of that bad will the beginning was pride, or the appetite for an inordinate rank. To lift oneself up is in itself to be cast down and to fall. Wherefore humility is most highly of all things commended in and to the City of God, and in Christ her King; but the contrary vice of arrogance especially rules her adversary, the devil, and this is unquestionably the great difference by which the two cities are divided, and the society of the pious from the society of the impious. Thus two loves have founded two cities, the love of Self extending to contempt of God has made the City of the World; the love of God extending to contempt of Self has made the Heavenly City.

The Growth of the Cities

This whole universal time or age, in which the dying give way and the newborn succeed them, is the scene and history of those two cities which are our theme. The City of the World, which lasts not forever, has its good here below, and rejoices in it with such joy as is possible. The objects of its desire are not otherwise than good, and itself is the best of the good things of earth. It desires an earthly peace for lower ends, makes wars to gain this peace, wins glorious victories, and when victory crowns a just cause, who shall not acclaim the wished-for peace? These things are good indeed, and unquestionably are the gifts of God. But if, neglecting the better things, which belong to the supernal city, they covet these lower ends as if there were none higher, misery must inevitably follow.

All men, indeed, desire peace; but while the society which does not live by faith seeks its peace in the temporal advantages of the present life, that which lives by faith awaits the promised blessings, and makes use of earthly and temporal things only as pilgrims do. The earthly city seeks its peace in a harmony of the wills of men with respect to the things of this life. And the heavenly city also, or, rather, that part of it which travels in this mortality, must use that earthly peace while mortality remains. Living a captive life in the midst of the earthly city, it does not hesitate to respect its laws. Since this mortality is common to both cities, there is a concord between them in the things that belong to it. Only, the heavenly city cannot have common laws of religion with the earthly city, but has been forced to dissent, and to suffer hatred and the storms of persecution.

Therefore, this heavenly city, a pilgrim upon earth, calls out citizens from all peoples and collects a pilgrim society of all tongues, careless what differences there may be in manners, laws and institutions by which earthly peace is achieved and maintained, destroying none of these, but rather serving and fulfilling them. Even the celestial city, therefore, uses the earthly peace, and uses it as a means to the heavenly peace; for that alone can be called the peace of a rational creature which consists in a harmonious society devoted to the enjoyment of God and one another in God.

As for that uncertainty with regard to everything, which characterizes the New Academy, the City of God detests all such doubting as a form of madness, since she has the most certain knowledge of those things which she understands by mind and reason, however that knowledge may be limited by our corruptible body. She believes also the evidence of the senses, which the mind uses through the body, for he is miserably deceived who regards them as untrustworthy. She believes also the holy Scriptures, which we call canonical.

It is no matter to the City of God what dress the citizen wears, or what manner of life he follows, so long as it is not contrary to the Divine commands; so that she does not compel the philosophers, who become Christians, to change their habit or their means of life, which are no hindrance to religion, but only their false opinions. As for these three kinds of life, the contemplative, the active, and that which partakes of both qualities, although a man living in faith may adopt any of them, and therein reach eternal reward, yet the love of truth and the duties of charity alike must have their place. One may not so give himself to contemplation as to neglect the good of his neighbor, nor be so deeply immersed in action as to neglect the contemplation of God. In leisure we ought to delight, not in an empty inertia. but in the inquisition or discovery of truth, in such a way that each may make progress without envying the attainments of another. In action we ought to seek neither the honors of this life nor power, since all that is under the sun is vanity; but only the work itself, which our situation enables us to do, and to do it rightly and serviceably.

According to the definitions which Scipio used in Cicero's *Republic*, there never really existed a Roman republic. For he briefly defines a republic as the estate of the people—"res publica" as "res populi," and defines the people as a multitudinous assemblage, united by consent to law and by community of advantage. So, then, where justice is not, there can be no people; and if no people, then no estate of the people, but only of a confused multitude unworthy of the name of a people. Where no justice is, there is no commonwealth. Now, justice is a virtue distributing unto everyone his due. Where, then, is the justice of the man who deserts the true God and gives himself over to unclean demons? Is this giving everyone his due?

But if we define a people in another way, and consider it as an assemblage of rational beings united by unanimity as to the objects of their love, then, in order to ascertain the character of a people, we must ascertain what things they love. Whatever it loves, so long as it is an assemblage of rational creatures and not a herd of cattle, and is agreed as to the objects of its love, it is truly a people, though so much the better as its concord lies in better things, and so much the worse as its concord lies in inferior things. According to this definition, then, the Roman people is indeed a people, and its estate is a commonwealth. But what things that people has loved in its earlier and later times, and how it fell into bloody seditions and into social and civil wars, breaking and corrupting that concord which is the health of a people—of these things history is witness. Yet I would not on that account deny it the name of a people, nor its estate the name of a republic, so long as there remains some assemblage of rational persons associated by unanimity with regard to the objects of love. But in general, whatever be the nation in question, whether Athens, Egypt, Babylon, or Rome, the city of the ungodly—refusing obedience to the commandment of God that no sacrifice should be offered but to Him alone—is without true justice.

For though there may be an apparent mastery of the soul over the body, and of reason over vices, yet if soul and reason do not serve God as He has commanded, they can have no true dominion over the body and its passions. How can the mind which is ignorant of the true God, and instead of obeying Him is prostituted to impure demons, be true mistress of the body and the vices? Nay, the very virtues which it appears to itself to possess, by which it rules the body and the vices in order that it may obtain and guard the objects which it desires, being undirected to God, are rather vices than virtues. For as that which makes flesh to live is not flesh but above it, so that which

enables man to live in blessedness is not of man, but above
him.

The Destiny of the Just

Who is able to tell of the creation, with its beauty and utility,
which God has set before the eyes of man, though here condemned to labor and sorrow? The innumerable loveliness of
sky, earth and sea, the abundance and wonder of light, the sun,
moon and stars, the shade of trees, the colors and fragrance of
flowers, the multitude of birds of varied hue and song, the many
forms of animals, of which the smallest are more wonderful
than the greatest, the works of bees more amazing than the vast
bodies of whales—who shall describe them?

What shall those rewards, then, be? What will God give
them whom He has predestined to life, having given such great
things to those whom He has predestined to death? What in
that blessed life will He lavish upon those for whom He gave
His Son to death? What will the state of man's spirit be when it
has become wholly free from vice; yielding to none, enslaved
by none, warring against none, but perfectly and wholly at
peace with itself?

Who can say, or even imagine, what degrees of glory shall
there be given to the degrees of merit? Yet we cannot doubt that
there will be degrees; and that in that blessed city no one in
lower place shall envy his superior; for no one will wish to be
that which he has not received, though bound in closest concord with him who has received. Together with his reward, each
shall have the gift of contentment, so as to desire no more than
he has. There we shall rest and see, we shall see and love, we
shall love and praise. For what other end have we, but to reach
the kingdom of which there is no end?

Saint Thomas Aquinas
(c. 1225–1274)

From

SUMMA THEOLOGICA

Whether God Can Move the Created Will?

Objection 1. It would seem that God cannot move the created will. For whatever is moved from without, is forced. But the will cannot be forced. Therefore it is not moved from without. Therefore it cannot be moved by God.

Obj. 2. Further, God cannot make two contradictories to be true at the same time. But this would follow if He moved the will; for to be voluntarily moved means to be moved from within, and not by another. Therefore God cannot move the will.

Obj. 3. Further, movement is attributed to the mover rather than to the one moved; and so homicide is not ascribed to the stone, but to the thrower. Therefore, if God moves the will, it follows that voluntary actions are not imputed to man for reward or blame. But this is false. Therefore God does not move the will.

On the contrary, It is written (*Phil.* II 13): *It is God who worketh in us both to will and to accomplish.*

I answer that, Just as the intellect is moved by the object and by the giver of the power of understanding, as was stated above, so the will is moved by its object, which is the good, and by Him who creates the power of willing. Now the will can be moved by any good as its object, but by God alone is it moved sufficiently and efficaciously. For nothing can move a movable thing sufficiently unless the active power of the mover surpasses or at least equals the potentiality of the movable thing. Now the potentiality of the will extends to the universal good, for its object is the universal good, just as the object of the intellect is universal being. But every created good is some particular good, and God alone is the universal good. Therefore He alone fills the capacity of the will, and moves it sufficiently as its object. In like manner, the power of willing is caused by God alone. For to will is nothing but to be inclined towards the object of the will, which is the universal good. But to incline towards the universal good belongs to the first mover, to whom the ultimate end is proportioned; just as in human affairs to him that presides over the community belongs the directing of his subjects to the common weal. Therefore in both ways it belongs to God to move the will; but especially in the second way by an interior inclination of the will.

Reply Obj. 1. A thing moved by another is forced if it is moved against its natural inclination. But if it is moved by another which gives to it its natural inclination, it is not forced. Thus, a heavy body, made to move downward by that which produced it, is not forced. In like manner God, while moving the will, does not force it, because He gives the will its own natural inclination.

Reply Obj. 2. To be moved voluntarily is to be moved from within, that is, by an interior principle. But this interior principle may be caused by an exterior principle; and so to be moved from within is not repugnant to being moved by another.

Reply Obj. 3. If the will were so moved by another as in no way to be moved from within itself, the act of the will would not be imputed for reward or blame. But since its being moved by another does not prevent its being moved from within itself, as we have stated, it does not thereby forfeit the motive for merit or demerit.

Whether God Works in Every Agent?

Objection 1. It would seem that God does not work in every agent. For we must not attribute any insufficiency to God. If therefore God works in every agent, He works sufficiently in each one. Hence it would be superfluous for the created agent to work at all.

Obj. 2. Further, the same work cannot proceed at the same time from two sources, just as neither can one and the same movement belong to two movable things. Therefore if the creature's operation is from God operating in the creature, it cannot at the same time proceed from the creature; and so no creature works at all.

Obj. 3. Further, the maker is the cause of the operation of the thing made, as giving it the form whereby it operates. Therefore, if God is the cause of the operation of the things made by Him, this would be inasmuch as He gives them the power of operating. But this is in the beginning, when He makes them. Thus it seems that God does not operate any further in the operating creature.

On the contrary, It is written (*Isa.* xxvi 12): *Lord, Thou hast wrought all our works in us.*

I answer that, Some have understood God to work in every agent in such a way that no created power has any effect in things, but that God alone is the immediate cause of everything wrought; for instance, that it is not fire that gives heat, but God in the fire, and so forth. But this is impossible. First, because the order of cause and effect would be taken away from created things, and this would imply a lack of power in the Creator; for it is due to the power of the cause, that it bestows active power on its effect. Secondly, because the operative powers which are seen to exist in things would be bestowed on things to no purpose, if things produced nothing through them. Indeed, all things created would seem, in a way, to be purposeless, if they lacked an operation proper to them; since the purpose of everything is its operation. For the less perfect is always for the sake of the more perfect. Consequently, just as the matter is for the sake of the form, so the form which is the first act is for the sake of its operation, which is the second act; and thus operation is the end of the creature. We must therefore understand that God works in things in such a manner that things have also their proper operation.

In order to make this clear, we must observe that of the four causes matter is not a principle of action, but the subject that receives the effect of action. On the other hand, the end, the agent and the form are principles of action, but in a certain order. For the first principle of action is the end which moves the agent, the second is the agent, and the third is the form of that which the agent applies to action (although the agent also acts through its own form). This may be clearly seen in things made by art. For the craftsman is moved to action by the end, which is the thing wrought, for instance a chest or a bed, and he applies to action the axe which cuts because it is sharp.

Thus then does God work in every agent, according to these three things. First, as an end. For since every operation is for the sake of some good, real or apparent, and since nothing is good, either really or apparently, except in so far as it participates in a likeness to the highest good, which is God, it follows that God Himself is the cause of every operation as its end. Again, it is to be observed that where there are several agents in order, the second always acts in virtue of the first; for the first agent moves the second to act. And thus all agents act in virtue of God Himself; and so, He is the cause of action in every agent. Thirdly, we must observe that God not only moves things to operate, as it were applying their forms and powers to operation, just as the workman applies the ax to cutting (who nevertheless did not himself give the ax its form), but He also gives created agents their forms and preserves them in being. Therefore He is the cause of action not only by giving the form which is the principle of action, as the generator is said to be the cause of movement in things heavy and light, but also as conserving the forms and powers of things; just as the sun is said to be the cause of the manifestation of colors, inasmuch as it gives and conserves the light by which colors are made manifest. And since the form of a thing is within the thing, and all the more so, as it approaches nearer to the first and universal cause; and because in all things God Himself is properly the cause of universal being which is innermost in all things—it follows that God works intimately in all things. For this reason in Holy Scripture the operations of nature are attributed to God as operating in nature, according to *Job* x 11: *Thou hast clothed me with skin and flesh: Thou hast put me together with bones and sinews.*

Reply Obj. 1. God works sufficiently in things as a first cause, but it does not follow from this that the operation of secondary agents is superfluous.

Reply Obj. 2. One action does not proceed from two agents of the same order. But nothing hinders the same action from proceeding from a primary and a secondary agent.

Reply Obj. 3. God not only gives things their forms, but He also conserves them in being, and applies them to act, and is moreover the end of every action, as was explained above.

Whether God Can Do Anything Outside the Established Order of Nature?

Objection 1. It would seem that God cannot do anything outside the established order of nature. For Augustine says: *God, the Maker and Creator of each nature, does nothing against nature.* But that which is outside the natural order seems to be against nature. Therefore God can do nothing outside the natural order.

Obj. 2. Further, as the order of justice is from God, so is the order of nature. But God cannot do anything outside the order of justice, for then He would be doing something unjust. Therefore He cannot do anything outside the order of nature.

Obj. 3. Further, God established the order of nature. Therefore, if God does anything outside the order of nature, it would seem that He is changeable; which cannot be said.

On the contrary, Augustine says: *God sometimes does things which are contrary to the wonted course of nature.*

I answer that, From each cause there results a certain order to its effects, since every cause is a principle; and so, according to the multiplicity of causes, there results a multiplicity of orders, subject one to the other, just as cause is subject to cause. Hence, a higher cause is not subject to a cause of a lower order, but conversely. An example of this may be seen in human affairs. On the father of a family depends the order of the household; which order is contained in the order of the city; which order again depends on the ruler of the city; while this last order depends on that of the king, by whom the whole kingdom is ordered.

If, therefore, we consider the order of things according as it depends on the first cause, God cannot do anything against this order; for, if He did so, He would act against His foreknowledge, or His will, or His goodness. But if we consider the order of things according as it depends on any secondary cause, thus God can do something outside such order. For He is not subject to the order of secondary causes, but, on the contrary, this order is subject to Him, as proceeding from Him, not by a natural necessity, but by the choice of His own will; for He could have created another order of things. Therefore God can do something outside this order created by Him, when He chooses—for instance, by producing the effects of secondary causes without them, or by producing certain effects to which secondary causes do not extend. So Augustine says: *God acts against the wonted course of nature, but by no means does He act against the supreme law; because He does not act against Himself.*

Reply Obj. 1. In natural things something may happen outside this natural order, in two ways. It may happen by the action of an agent which did not give them their natural inclination, as, for example, when a man moves a heavy body upwards, which does not owe to him its natural inclination to move downwards. Now this would be against nature. It may also happen by the action of the agent on whom the natural inclination depends, and this is not against nature, as is clear in the ebb and flow of the tide, which is not against nature, although it is against the natural movement of water, which is moved downward; for it is owing to the influence of a heavenly body, on which the natural inclination of lower bodies depends. Therefore since the order of nature is given to things by God, if He does anything outside this order, it is not against nature. Hence Augustine says: *That is natural to each thing which is caused by Him from whom is all limit, number and order in nature.*

Reply Obj. 2. The order of justice arises by relation to the first cause, which is the rule of all justice; and that is why God can do nothing against such an order.

Reply Obj. 3. God fixed a certain order in things in such a way that at the same time He reserved to Himself whatever He intended to do otherwise than by a particular cause. So when He acts outside this order, He does not change.

Whether Whatever God Does Outside the Natural Order Is Miraculous?

Objection 1. It would seem that not everything which God does outside the natural order of things is miraculous. For the creation of the world and of souls, and the justification of the unrighteous, are done by God outside the natural order; for these effects are not accomplished by the action of any natural cause. Yet these things are not called miracles. Therefore not everything that God does outside the natural order is a miracle.

Obj. 2. Further, a miracle is *something difficult, which sel-dom occurs, surpassing the faculty of nature, and going so far beyond our hopes as to compel our astonishment.* But some things outside the order of nature are not arduous, for they occur in small things, such as the recovery of some precious stone or the healing of the sick. Nor are they of rare occur-rence, since they happen frequently; as when the sick were placed in the streets, to be healed by the shadow of Peter (*Acts* v 15). Nor do they surpass the ability of nature; as when people are cured of a fever. Nor are they beyond our hopes, since we all hope for the resurrection of the dead, which nevertheless will be outside the course of nature. Therefore not all things that are outside the course of nature are miraculous.

Obj. 3. Further, the term *miracle* is derived from admiration. Now admiration concerns things manifest to the senses. But sometimes things happen outside the order *of* nature which are not manifest to the senses; as when the Apostles were endowed with knowledge without studying or being taught. Therefore not everything that occurs outside the order of nature is miraculous.

On the contrary, Augustine says: *Where God does anything against that order of nature which we know and are accustomed to observe, we call it a miracle.*

I answer that, The term *miracle* is derived from admiration, which arises when an effect is manifest, whereas its cause is hidden; as when a man sees an eclipse without knowing its cause, as the Philosopher says in the beginning of his *Metaphysics.* Now the cause of a manifest effect may be known to one, but unknown to others. Hence a thing is wonderful to one man, and not at all to others; as an eclipse is to a rustic, but not to an astronomer. Now a miracle is so called as being full of wonder, in other words, as having a cause absolutely hid-den from all. This cause is God. Therefore those things which God does outside the causes which we know are called mira-cles.

Reply Obj. 1. Creation, and the justification of the unright-eous, though done by God alone, are not, properly speaking, miracles, because they are not of a nature to proceed from any other cause; so they do not occur outside the order of nature, since they do not belong to the capacity of nature.

Reply Obj. 2. An arduous thing is called a miracle, not because of the excellence of the thing wherein it is done, but because it surpasses the ability of nature. So, too, a thing is called unusual, not because it does not often happen, but because it is outside the usual natural course of things. Furthermore, a thing is said to be above the ability of nature, not only by reason of the substance of the thing done, but also because of the manner and order in which it is done. Again, a miracle is said to go beyond the hope *of nature,* not above the hope *of grace,* which hope comes from faith, whereby we believe in the future resurrection.

Reply Obj. 3. The knowledge of the Apostles, although not manifest in itself, yet was made manifest in its effect, from which it was shown to be wonderful.

Niccolò Machiavelli

(1469–1527)

From

THE PRINCE

Of Princedoms Won by Merit

All states and governments are either republics or princedoms. Princedoms are either hereditary or new. Hereditary states are maintained with far less difficulty than new states, but in new princedoms difficulties abound.

And first if the princedom be joined on to ancient dominions of the prince, so as to form a mixed princedom, rebellion is a danger; for men are always ready to change masters. When a state rebels and is again got under it will not afterwards be lost so easily; for the prince will use the rebellion as a pretext to make himself more secure.

Such new states when they are of the same province and tongue as the ancient dominions of the prince are easily retained. It is enough to have rooted out the line of the reigning prince. But where the language and usages differ the difficulty is multiplied. One expedient is for the prince himself to dwell in the new state, as the Turk has done in Greece. Another is to send colonies into one or two places which may become keys to the province; for the cost of troops is far greater. In such provinces, moreover, the prince should always make himself the protector of his weaker neighbors, without adding to their strength; but should humble the great, and never suffer a formidable stranger to acquire influence, as was the rule with the Romans. Whereas King Louis of France has in Italy done the direct opposite in every single respect. In especial we may draw from the French king's actions the general axiom, which never or rarely errs, that "he who is the cause of another's greatness is himself undone."

Now, all princedoms are governed in one or two ways: either by a sole prince served by ministers, or by a prince with barons who hold their rank not by favor but by right of descent. The Turk is an example of the first, the French king of the second. A state of the first kind is difficult to win, but when won is easily held, since the prince's family may be easily rooted out; but in such a state as France you may gain an entry, but to hold your ground afterwards is difficult, since you cannot root out the barons.

Hence we need not wonder at the ease wherewith Alexander was able to lay a firm hold on Asia, albeit he died before he had well entered on possession; since the dominion of Darius was of the same character as that of the Turk.

When the newly acquired state has hitherto lived under its own laws and in freedom there are three ways of holding it. The first is to destroy it; the second to reside in it; the third to leave it under its own laws, choosing for its governors from the inhabitants such as will be friendly to you. But the safest course is either to destroy it or to go and live in it.

Where the prince himself is new, either merit or good fortune is implied, and if we consider the most excellent examples, such as Moses, Cyrus, Romulus, and the like, we shall see that they owed to fortune nothing beyond the opportunity which they seized. Those who, like these, come to the princedom by virtuous paths acquire with difficulty, but keep with ease. Their difficulties arise because they are of necessity innovators. If, then, they have force of their own to employ they seldom fail. Hence it comes that all armed prophets have been victorious and all unarmed prophets have been destroyed; as was the case with Savonarola.

Of Princedoms Won Otherwise than by Merit

Those who rise to princedom by mere good fortune have much trouble to maintain themselves; some lack both the knowledge and the power to do so. Yet even if such a one be of great parts, he may lose what he has won, like Cesare Borgia.

It was impossible for the duke to aggrandize himself unless the states of Italy were thrown into confusion so that he might safely make himself master of some part of them. This was made easy for him as concerned Romagna by the conduct of the French and Venetians. The next step was to weaken the factions

of the Orsini and the Colonnesi. Having scattered the
Colonnesi, the Orsini were so won over as to be drawn in their
simplicity into his hands at Sinigaglia. Having thus disposed of
the leaders, he set about ingratiating himself with the population of Romagna and Urbino. He first set over the country a
stern ruler to restore order. This end being accomplished, that
stern but unpopular ruler was beheaded.

Next, as a new pope might be dangerous, he set himself to
exterminate the kindred of those lords whom he had despoiled
of their possessions, to win over the Roman nobility, and to
secure a majority among the cardinals. But before the duke had
completely consolidated his power his father, Pope Alexander
VI, died. Even so, the skill with which he had laid the foundations of his power must have resulted in success had he not
himself been almost at death's door at that critical moment. The
one mistake he made was in the choice of the new pope, Julius
II, and this error was the cause of his ultimate downfall.

A man may rise, however, to a princedom by paths of
wickedness and crime; that is, not precisely by either merit or
fortune. We may take as example first Agathocles the Sicilian.
To slaughter fellow citizens, to betray friends, to be devoid of
honor, pity, and religion cannot be counted as merit. But the
achievements of Agathocles can certainly not be ascribed to
fortune. We cannot, therefore, attribute either to fortune or to
merit what he accomplished without either. For a modern
instance we may consider Oliverotto of Fermo, who seized upon
that town by a piece of monstrous treachery and merciless
butchery; yet he established himself so firmly and so formida-
bly that he could not have been unseated had he not let himself
be overreached by Cesare Borgia.

Our lesson from these examples is that on seizing a state the
usurper should make haste to inflict what injuries he must at
one stroke, and afterwards win men over by benefits.

Next is the case of those who are made princes by the favor of
their countrymen, which they owe to what may be termed a fortunate astuteness. If he be established by the favor of the people,
to secure them against the oppression of the nobles his position
is stronger than if he owe it to the nobles; but in either case it is
the people whom he must conciliate, and this I affirm in spite of
the old saw, "He who builds on the people builds on mire."

A prince who cannot get together an army fit to take the field against any assailant should keep his city strongly fortified, taking no heed of the country outside, for then he will not be readily attacked, and if he be it will be difficult to maintain a siege longer than it may be resisted.

Merit, or good fortune, are needed to acquire ecclesiastical princedoms, but not to maintain them, for they are upheld by the authority of religion. It is due to the policy of the Popes Alexander VI and Julius II that the temporal power of the pope has become so great; and from his holiness Pope Leo we may hope that as his predecessors made the papacy great with arms he will render it still greater and more venerable by his benignity and other countless virtues.

Of Maintaining a Princedom

A prince must defend his state with either his own subjects or mercenaries, or auxiliaries. Mercenaries are utterly untrustworthy; if their captain be not an able man the prince will probably be ruined, whereas if he be an able man he will be seeking a goal of his own. This has been perpetually exemplified among the cities and states of Italy which have sought to maintain themselves by taking foreigners into their pay.

But he who would deprive himself of every chance of success should have recourse to auxiliaries; that is, to the troops of a foreign potentate. For these are far more dangerous than mercenary arms, bringing ruin with them ready-made. The better such troops are the more dangerous they are. From Hiero of Syracuse to Cesare Borgia, princes have become powerful in proportion as they could dispense with such aid and place their dependence upon national troops.

A prince, then, who would be powerful should have no care or thought but for war, lest he lose his dominions. If he be ignorant of military affairs he can neither be respected by the soldiers nor trust them. Therefore, he must both practice and study this art. For the practice, the chase in many respects provides an excellent training both in knowledge of the country and in vigor of the body. As to study, a prince should read histories, note the actions of great men, and examine the causes of their victories and defeats; seeking to imitate those who have been renowned.

Anyone who would act up to a perfect standard of goodness
in everything must be ruined among so many who are not good.
It is essential therefore for a prince to have learnt how to be
other than good, and to use, or not to use, his goodness as
necessity requires.

It may be a good thing to be reputed liberal, but liberality
without the reputation of it is hurtful. Display necessitates the
imposition of taxes, whereby the prince becomes hateful;
whereas through parsimony his revenue will be sufficient.
Hence we have seen no princes accomplish great results save
those who have been accounted miserly.

Every prince should desire to be accounted merciful, not
cruel; but a new prince cannot escape a name for cruelty, for he
who quells disorder by a few signal examples will, in the end,
be the more merciful.

Men are less careful how they offend him who makes himself
loved than him who makes himself feared; yet should a prince
inspire fear in such a fashion that, if he do not win love, he may
escape hate; remembering that men will sooner forget the slay-
ing of their father than the loss of their patrimony.

Princes who set little store by their word, but have known
how to overreach men by their cunning, have accomplished
great things, and in the end got the better of those who trusted
to honest dealing. The prince must be a lion, but he must also
know how to play the fox. He who wishes to deceive will never
fail to find willing dupes. The prince, in short, ought not to quit
good courses if he can help it, but should know how to follow
evil courses if he must.

A prince must avoid being despised as well as being hated;
therefore courage, wisdom, and strength must be apparent in
all his actions. Against such a one conspiracy is difficult. That
prince is wise who devolves on others those matters that entail
responsibility, and may therefore make him odious either to the
nobles or to the commons, but reserves to himself the matters
that relate to grace and favor.

What I have said is not contradicted by the history of the
Roman emperors; for they had to choose between satisfying the
soldiers and satisfying the people. It was imperative that at any
cost they should maintain control of the soldiery, which scarce
any of them could do without injustice to the people. If we

examine their histories in detail we shall find that they fully
bear out the principles I have laid down.

But in our time the standing armies of princes have not the
same power as the armies of the Roman empire, and except
under the Turk and the Soldan it is more needful to satisfy the
people than the soldiery.

Of Artifices

A new prince will never disarm his subjects, but will rather
arm them, at least in part. For thus they become his partisans,
whereas without them he must depend on mercenaries.

But a prince who adds a new state to his old possessions
should disarm its inhabitants, relying on the soldiers of his own
ancient dominions. Some have fostered feuds among their new
subjects in order to keep them weak, but such a policy rarely
proves useful in the end. The prince who acquires a new state
will gain more strength by winning over and trusting those who
were at first opposed to him than by relying on those who were
at first his friends. The prince who is more afraid of his subjects
than of strangers ought to build fortresses, while he who is more
afraid of strangers than of his subjects should leave them alone.
On the whole, the best fortress you can have is in not being
hated by your subjects.

Nothing makes a prince so well thought of as to undertake
great enterprises and give striking proofs of his capacity.
Ferdinand of Aragon, in our own time, has become the foremost
king in Christendom. If you consider his achievements, you
will find them all great and some extraordinary. First he made
war on Grenada, and this was the foundation of his power.
Under the cloak of religion, with what may be called pious cruelty, he cleared his kingdom of the Moors; under the same pretext he made war on Africa, invaded Italy, and finally attacked
France; while his subjects, occupied with these great actions,
had neither time nor opportunity to oppose them.

The prince whose ministers are at once capable and faithful
may always be accounted wise, since he must be one who can
discern the merits and demerits of his servant. For which dis-
cernment this unfailing rule may be laid down: When you see a
minister thinking more of himself than of you, and in all his

actions seeking his own ends, that man can never be a minister you can trust. To retain a good minister the prince will bind him to himself by benefits. Above all, he will avoid being deceived by flatterers, and while he consults his counselors should reflect and judge for himself. A prince who is not wise himself cannot be well advised by others.

The Italian princes who in our own times have lost their dominions have either been deficient in respect of arms, or have had the people against them, or have not known how to secure themselves against the nobles. As to the influence of fortune, it may be the case that she is the mistress of one half of our actions, but leaves the control of the other half to ourselves. That prince will prosper most whose mode of acting best adapts itself to the character of the times; so that at one time a cautious temperament, and at another an impetuous temperament, will be the more successful.

Now, at this time the whole land of Italy is without a head, without order, beaten, spoiled, torn in pieces, overrun, and abandoned to destruction in every shape. She prays God to send someone to rescue her from these barbarous cruelties; she is eager to follow anyone who could undertake the part of a deliverer; nor does this seem too hard a task for you, the Magnificent Lorenzo of the illustrious house of Medici. The cause is just; we have before us unexampled proofs of Divine favor. Everything has concurred to promote your greatness. What remains to be done must be done by you, for God will not do everything Himself.

René Descartes
(1596–1650)

From
DISCOURSE ON METHOD

The Aim of this Discourse

Good sense or reason must be better distributed than anything else in the world, for no man desires more of it than he already has. This shows that reason is by nature equal in all men. If there is diversity of opinion, this arises from the fact that we conduct our thought by different ways, and consider not the same things. It does not suffice that the understanding be good—it must be well applied.

My mind is no better than another's, but I have been lucky enough to chance on certain ways, which have led me to a certain method by means of which it seems to me that I may by degrees augment my knowledge to the modest measure of my intellect and my length of days. I shall be very glad to make plain in this discourse the paths I have followed, and to picture my life so that all may judge of it, and by the setting forth of their opinions may furnish me with yet other means of improvement.

It is my design not to teach the method which each man ought to follow for the right guidance of his reason, but only to show in what manner I have tried to conduct my own.

I had been nourished on letters from my infancy, but as soon as I had finished the customary course of study, I found myself hampered by so many doubts and errors that I seemed to have reaped no benefits, except that I had observed more and more of my ignorance. Yet I was at one of the most celebrated schools in Europe, and I was not held inferior to my fellow-students, some of whom were destined to take the place of our masters; nor did our age seem less fruitful of good wits than any which had gone before. Though I did not cease to esteem the studies of the schools, I began to think that I had given enough time to

languages, enough also to ancient books, their stories and their
fables; for when a man spends too much time in traveling
abroad he becomes a stranger in his own country; and so, when
he is too curious concerning what went on in past ages, he is
apt to remain ignorant of what is taking place in his own day. I
set a high price on eloquence, and I was in love with poetry;
above all, I rejoiced in mathematics, but I knew nothing of its
true use.

I revered our theology, but, since the way to heaven lies open
to the ignorant no less than to the learned, and the revealed
truths which lead thither are beyond our intelligence, I did not
dare to submit them to my feeble reasonings.

In philosophy there is no truth which is not disputed, and
which, consequently, is not doubtful; and, as to the other sciences, they all borrow their principles from philosophy.
Therefore, I entirely gave up the study of letters, and employed
the rest of my youth in traveling, being resolved to seek no
other science than that which I might find within myself, or in
the Great Book of the World.

Here the best lesson that I learned was not to believe too
firmly anything of which I had learnt merely by example and
custom; and thus little by little was delivered from many errors
which are liable to obscure the light of nature, and to diminish
our capacity of hearing reason. Finally, I resolved one day to
study myself in the same way, and in this it seems to me I succeeded much better than if I had never departed from either my
country or my books.

The Intellectual Crisis

Being in Germany, on my way to rejoin the army after the coro-
nation of the Emperor [Ferdinand II], I was lying at an inn
where, in default of other conversation, I was at liberty to entertain my own thoughts. Of these, one of the first was that often
there is less perfection in works which are composite than in
those which issue from a single hand. Such was the case with
buildings, cities, states; for a people which has made its laws
from time to time to meet particular occasions will enjoy a less
perfect polity than a people which from the beginning has
observed the constitution of a far-sighted legislator. This is

very certain, that the estate of true religion, which God alone has ordained, must be incomparably better guided than any other. And again, I considered that as, during our childhood, we had been governed by our appetites and our tutors, which are often at variance, which neither of them perhaps always gave us the best counsel, it is almost impossible that our judgments should be so pure and so solid as they would have been if we had had the perfect use of our reason from the time of our birth, and had never been guided by anything else.

Hence, as regarded the opinions that I had received into my belief, I thought that, as a private person may pull down his own house to build a finer, so I could not do better than remove them therefrom in order to replace them by sounder, or, after I should have adjusted them to the level of reason, to establish the same once more.

When I was younger I had studied logic, analytical geometry, and algebra. Of these, I found that logic served rather for explaining things we already know; while of geometry and algebra, the former is so tied to the consideration of figures that it cannot exercise the understanding without wearying the imagination, and the latter is so bound down to certain rules and ciphers that it has been made a confused and obscure art which hampers the mind instead of a science which cultivates it. And as a state is better governed which has but few laws, and those laws strictly observed, I believed that I should find sufficient four precepts which follow.

The first was never to accept anything as true when I did not recognize it clearly to be so—that is to say, carefully to avoid precipitation and prejudice, but to include in my opinions nothing beyond that which should present itself so clearly and distinctly to my mind that I might have no occasion to doubt it.

The second was to divide up the difficulties which I should examine into as many parts as possible, and as should be required for their better solution.

The third was to conduct my thoughts in order, by beginning with the simplest objects and those most easy to know, so as to mount little by little, by stages, to the most complex knowledge, even supposing an order among things which did not naturally stand in an order of antecedent and consequent.

And the last was to make everywhere enumerations so complete, and surveys so wide, that I should be sure of omitting nothing.

Exact observation of these precepts gave me such facility in unraveling the questions comprehended in geometrical analysis and in algebra, that in two or three months not only did I find my way through many which I had formerly accounted too hard for me, but, towards the end, I seemed to be able to determine, in those which were new to me, by what means and to what extent it was possible to resolve them. And so I promised myself that I would apply my system with equal success to the difficulties of other sciences; but since their principles must all be borrowed from philosophy, in which I found no certain principles of its own, I thought that before all else I must try to establish some therein. By way of preparation (for I was then but twenty-three years old) I must root up from my mind my previous bad opinion of it, and must practice my method in order that I might be confirmed in it more and more.

A Rule of Life

Meanwhile I must have a rule of life as a shelter while my new house was in building, and this consisted of three or four maxims.

The first was to conform myself to the laws and customs of my country, and to hold to the religion in which, by God's grace, I had been brought up; guiding myself, for the rest, by the least extreme opinions of the most intelligent. Among extremes I counted all promises by which a man curtails anything of his liberty; for I should have deemed it a grave fault against good sense if, because I approved something in a given moment, I had bound myself to accept it as good for ever after.

My second maxim was to follow resolutely even doubtful opinions when sure opinions were not available, just as the traveler, lost in some forest, had better walk straight forward, though in a chance direction; for thus he will arrive, if not precisely at the place where he desires to be, at least probably at a better place than the middle of a forest.

My third maxim was to endeavor always to conquer myself rather than fortune, and to change my desires rather than the order of the world, and in general to bring myself to believe that there is nothing wholly in our power except our thoughts. And

I believe that herein lay the secret of those philosophers who, in the days of old, could withdraw from the domination of fortune, and, despite pain and poverty, challenge the felicity of their gods.

Finally, after looking out upon the divers occupations of men, I pondered that I could do no better than persevere in that which I had chosen—so deep was my content in discovering every day by its means truths which seemed to me important, yet were unknown to the world.

Having thus made myself sure of these maxims, and having set them apart together with the verities of faith, I judged that for the rest of my opinions I might set freely to work to divest myself of them. For nine years, therefore, I went up and down the world a spectator rather than an actor. These nine years slipped away before I had begun to seek for the foundations of any philosophy more certain, nor perhaps should I have dared to undertake the quest had it not been put about that I had already succeeded.

"I Think, Therefore I Am"

I had long since remarked that in matters of conduct it is necessary sometimes to follow opinions known to be uncertain, as if they were not subject to doubt; but, because now I was desirous to devote myself to the search after truth, I considered that I must do just the contrary, and reject as absolutely false everything concerning which I could imagine the least doubt to exist.

Thus, because our senses sometimes deceive us I would suppose that nothing is such as they make us to imagine it; and because I was as likely to err as another in reasoning, I rejected as false all the reasons which I had formerly accepted as demonstrative; and finally considering that all the thoughts we have when awake can come to us also when we sleep without any of them being true, I resolved to feign that everything which had ever entered into my mind was no more truth than the illusion of my dreams.

But I observed that, while I was thus resolved to feign that everything was false, I who thought must of necessity be somewhat; and remarking this truth—*"I think, therefore I am"*—was

so firm and so assured that all the most extravagant suppositions of the skeptics were unable to shake it, I judged that I
could unhesitatingly accept it as the first principle of the philosophy I was seeking. I could feign that there was no world, I
could not feign that I did not exist. And I judged that I might
take it as a general rule that the things which we conceive very
clearly and very distinctly are all true, and that the only difficulty lies in the way of discerning which those things are that
we conceive distinctly.

After this, reflecting upon the fact that I doubted, and that
consequently my being was not quite perfected (for I saw that
to *know* is a greater perfection than to *doubt*), I bethought me to
inquire whence I had learned to think of something more perfect than myself; and it was clear to me that this must come
from some nature which was in fact more perfect. For other
things I could regard as dependencies of my nature if they were
real, and if they were not real they might proceed from nothing—that is to say, they might exist in me by way of defect. But
it could not be the same with the idea of a being more perfect
than my own; for to derive it from nothing was manifestly
impossible; and, because it is no less repugnant that the more
perfect should follow and depend upon the less perfect than
that something should come forth out of nothing, I could not
derive it from myself.

It remained, then, to conclude that it was put into me by a
nature truly more perfect than was I, and possessing in itself all
the perfections of what I could form an idea—in a word, by
God. To which I added that, since I knew some perfections
which I did not possess, I was not the only being who existed,
but that there must of necessity be some other being, more perfect, on whom I depended, and from whom I had acquired all
that I possessed; for if I had existed alone and independent of
all other, so that I had of myself all this little whereby I partic-
ipated in the Perfect Being, I should have been able to have in
myself all those other qualities which I knew myself to lack,
and so to be infinite, eternal, immutable, omniscient,
almighty—in fine, to possess all the perfections which I could
observe in God.

Proposing to myself the geometer's subject matter, and then
turning again to examine my idea of a Perfect Being, I found
that existence was comprehended in that idea just as, in the

idea of a triangle is comprehended the notion that the sum of
its angles is equal to two right angles; and that consequently it
is as certain that God, this Perfect Being, is or exists, as any
geometrical demonstration could be.

That there are many who persuade themselves that there is a
difficulty in knowing Him is due to the scholastic maxim that
there is nothing in the understanding which has not first been
in the senses; where the ideas of God and the soul have never
been.

Than the existence of God all other things, even those which
it seems to a man extravagant to doubt, such as his having a
body, are less certain. Nor is there any reason sufficient to
remove such doubt but such as presupposes the existence of
God. From His existence it follows that our ideas or notions,
being real things, and coming from God, cannot but be true in
so far as they are clear and distinct. In so far as they contain
falsity, they are confused and obscure, there is in them an element of mere negation (*elles participant du néant*); that is to
say, they are thus confused in us because we ourselves are not
all perfect. And it is evident that falsity or imperfection can no
more come forth from God than can perfection proceed from
nothingness. But, did we not know that all which is in us of the
real and the true comes from a perfect and infinite being, however clear and distinct our ideas might be, we should have no
reason for assurance that they possessed the final perfection—
truth.

Reason instructs us that all our ideas must have some foundation of truth, for it could not be that the All-Perfect and the
All-True should otherwise have put them into us; and because
our reasonings are never so evident or so complete when we
sleep as when we wake, although sometimes during sleep our
imagination may be more vivid and positive, it also instructs us
that such truth as our thoughts have will assuredly be in our
waking thoughts rather than in our dreams.

Why I Do Not Publish "The World"

I have always remained firm in my resolve to assume no other
principle than that which I have used to demonstrate the existence of God and of the soul, and to receive nothing which did
not seem to me clearer and more certain than the demonstra-

tions of the philosophers had seemed before; yet not only have I found means of satisfying myself with regard to the principal difficulties which are usually treated of in philosophy, but also I have remarked certain laws which God has so established in nature, and of which He has implanted such notions in our souls, that we cannot doubt that they are observed in all which happens in the world.

The principal truths which flow from these I have tried to unfold in a treatise ("On the World, or on Light"), which certain considerations prevent me from publishing. This I concluded three years ago, and had begun to revise it for the printer when I learned that certain persons to whom I defer had disapproved an opinion on physics published a short time before by a certain person [Galileo, condemned by the Roman Inquisition in 1633], in which opinion I had noticed nothing prejudicial to religion; and this made me fear that there might be some among my opinions in which I was mistaken.

I now believe that I ought to continue to write all the things which I judge of importance, but ought in no wise to consent to their publication during my life. For my experience of the objections which might be made forbids me to hope for any profit from them. I have tried both friends and enemies, yet it has seldom happened that they have offered any objection which I had not in some measure foreseen; so that I have never, I may say, found a critic who did not seem to be either less rigorous or less fair-minded than myself.

Whereupon I gladly take this opportunity to beg those who shall come after us never to believe that the things which they are told come from me unless I have divulged them myself; and I am in nowise astonished at the extravagances attributed to those old philosophers whose writings have not come down to us. They were the greatest minds of their time, but have been ill-reported. Why, I am sure that the most devoted of those who now follow Aristotle would esteem themselves happy if they had as much knowledge of nature as he had, even on the condition that they should never have more! They are like ivy, which never mounts higher than the trees which support it, and which even comes down again after it has attained their summit. So at least, it seems to me, do they who, not content with knowing all that is explained by their author, would find in him the solution also of many difficulties of which he says nothing, and of which, perhaps, he never thought.

Yet their method of philosophizing is very convenient for those who have but middling minds, for the obscurity of the distinctions and principles which they employ enables them to speak of all things as boldly as if they had knowledge of them, and sustain all they have to say against the most subtle and skillful without there being any means of convincing them; wherein they seem to me like a blind man who, in order to fight on equal terms with a man who has his sight, invites him into the depths of a cavern. And I may say that it is to their interest that I should abstain from publishing the principles of the philosophy which I employ, for so simple and so evident are they that to publish them would be like opening windows into their caverns and letting in the day. But if they prefer acquaintance with a little truth, and desire to follow a plan like mine, there is no need for me to say to them any more in this discourse than I have already said.

For if they are capable of passing beyond what I have done, much rather will they be able to discover for themselves whatever I believe myself to have found out; besides which, the practice which they will acquire in seeking out easy things and thence passing to others which are more difficult, will stead them better than all my instructions.

But if some of the matters spoken about at the beginning of the "Dioptrics" and the "Meteors" [published with the *Discourse on Method*] should at first give offense because I have called them " suppositions," and have shown no desire to prove them, let the reader have patience to read the whole attentively, and I have hope that he will be satisfied.

The time remaining to me I have resolved to employ in trying to acquire some knowledge of nature, such that we may be able to draw from it more certain rules for medicine than those which up to the present we possess. And I hereby declare that I shall always hold myself more obliged to those by whose favor I enjoy my leisure undisturbed than I should be to any who should offer me the most esteemed employments in the world.

John Locke
(1632–1704)

From

AN ESSAY CONCERNING HUMAN UNDERSTANDING

The Nature of Simple Ideas

"Idea" being that term which, I think, serves best to stand for whatsoever is the object of the understanding, I have used it to express whatever is meant by phantasm, notion, species, or whatever it is the mind can be employed about in thinking. Let us, then, suppose the mind to be, as we say, white paper void of all characters—without any ideas. Whence comes it by that vast store which the busy and boundless fancy of man has painted on it with an almost endless variety? To this, I answer in one word—Experience; in that all our knowledge is founded, and from that it ultimately derives itself.

Let anyone examine his own thoughts and thoroughly search his understanding, and then let him tell me whether of all the original ideas he has there are any other than of the objects of his senses, or of the observations of his mind considered as objects of his reflection. Though the qualities that affect our senses are, in the things themselves, so united and blended that there is no separation, no distance between them, yet it is plain the ideas they produce in the mind enter by the senses simple and unmixed. For, though the sight and touch often take in from the same object at the same time different ideas, yet the simple ideas thus united in the same subject are as perfectly distinct as those that come in by different senses; the coldness and hardness which a man feels in a piece of ice being as distinct ideas in the mind as the smell and whiteness of a lily, and each of them being in itself uncompounded, contains nothing but one uniform appearance, or conception, in the mind, and is not distinguishable into different ideas.

When the understanding is once stored with these simple ideas, it has the power to repeat, compare, and unite them even to an almost infinite variety, and so can make at will new complex ideas. But it is not in the power of any most exalted wit or enlarged understanding, by any quickness or variety of thought, to invent or frame one new simple idea in the mind, nor to destroy those that are there. I would have anyone try to fancy any taste which had never affected his palate, or frame the idea of a scent he had never smelt; and when he can do this, I will also conclude that a blind man hath ideas of colors and a deaf man true, distinct notions of sound.

There are some ideas which have admittance only through one sense which is peculiarly adapted to receive them. Thus, light and colors come in only by the eye, all kinds of noises by the ear, the tastes and smells by the nose and palate. The most considerable of those belonging to the touch are heat, cold, and solidity—which is the idea that belongs to the body, whereby we conceive it to fill space.

Simple ideas of divers senses are the ideas of space or extension, figure, rest, and motion, for these make perceivable impressions both on the eyes and touch, and we can receive and convey into our minds the ideas of the extension, figure, motion, and rest of bodies both by seeing and feeling.

The mind, receiving the ideas mentioned in the foregoing from without, when it turns its view inward upon itself and observes its own actions about those ideas it has, takes from thence other ideas which are as capable to be the objects of its contemplation as any of those it received from foreign things. The two great and principal actions of the mind which are most frequently considered, and which are so frequent that everyone that pleases may take notice of them in himself, are these two—Perception or Thinking, and Volition or Will. The power of thinking is called the Understanding, and the power of volition is called the Will. And these two powers, or abilities, in the mind are denominated Faculties. Some of the modes of these simple ideas of reflection are remembrance, discerning, reasoning, judging, knowledge, faith.

It has, further, pleased our wise Creator to annex to several objects and to the ideas which we receive from them, as also to several of our thoughts, a concomitant pleasure, and that in several objects to several degrees, that those faculties which He has endowed us with might not remain wholly idle and unemployed by us. Pain has the same efficacy and use to set us on work that pleasure has, we being as ready to employ our faculties to avoid that as to pursue this.

Existence and unity are two other ideas that are suggested to the understanding by every object without and every idea within. Power, also, is another of those simple ideas which we receive from sensation and reflection; and, besides these, there is succession.

Nor let anyone think these too narrow bounds for the capacious mind of man to expatiate in, which takes its flight farther than the stars and cannot be confined by the limits of the world, that extends its thoughts often even beyond the utmost expansion of matter and makes excursions into that incomprehensible inane. Nor will it be so strange to think these few simple ideas sufficient to employ the quickest thought or largest capacity if we consider how many words may be made out of the various composition of twenty-four letters; or if, going one step farther, we will but reflect on the variety of combinations that may be made with barely one of the above-mentioned ideas, *viz.*, number, whose stock is inexhaustible. And what a large and immense field doth extension alone afford the mathematicians!

Of Idea-Producing Qualities

The power to produce any idea in our mind I call Quality of the subject wherein that power is. Qualities are, first, such as are utterly inseparable from the body in what state soever it be. These I call original or primary qualities, which I think we may observe to produce simple ideas in us, *viz.*, solidity, extension, figure, motion or rest, and number.

Secondly, such qualities which in truth are nothing in the objects themselves, but powers to produce various sensations in us by their primary qualities, *i.e.*, by the bulk, figure, texture, and motion of their insensible parts. These secondary qualities are colors, sounds, tastes, etc. From whence I think it is easy to draw this observation: that the ideas of primary qualities of bodies are resemblances of them, but the ideas produced in us by the secondary qualities have no resemblance in them at all.

If anyone will consider that the same fire that at one distance produces in us the sensation of warmth does, at a nearer approach, produce in us the far different sensation of pain, let him bethink himself what reason he has to say that his idea of warmth, which was produced in him by fire, is actually in the fire; and his idea of pain, which the same fire produced in him in the same way, is not in the fire. The particular bulk, number, figure, and motion of the parts of fire or snow are really in them, whether anyone's senses perceive them or not; and, therefore, they may be called real qualities, because they really exist in those bodies. But light, heat, whiteness, or coldness are no more really in them than sickness or pain is in manna. Take away the sensation of them; let not the eyes see light or colors, nor the ears hear sounds; let the palate not taste, nor the nose smell; and all colors, tastes, odors, and sounds, as they are such particular ideas, vanish and cease, and are reduced to their causes, *i.e.*, bulk, figure, and motion of parts.

Various Faculties of the Mind

What perception is everyone will know better by reflecting on what he does himself when he sees, hears, feels, etc., or thinks, than by any discourse of mine. This is certain, that whatever alterations are made in the body, if they reach not the mind, whatever impressions are made on the outward parts, if they are not taken notice of within, there is no perception.

We ought further to consider concerning perception, that the ideas we receive by sensation are often in grown people altered by the judgment without our taking any notice of it. When we set before our eyes a round globe of any uniform color—*e.g.*, gold, alabaster, or jet—it is certain that the idea thereby imprinted in our mind is of a flat circle variously shadowed with several degrees of light and brightness coming to our eyes. But we having by use been accustomed to perceive what kind of appearances convex bodies are wont to make in us, what alterations are made in the reflections of light by the difference of the sensible figures of bodies, the judgment presently, by an habitual custom, alters the appearances into their causes; so that from that which is truly a variety of shadow or color collecting the figure, it makes it pass for a mark of figure, and frames to itself the perception of a convex figure and a uniform color, when the idea we receive from thence is only a plane variously colored, as is evident in painting. Perception, then, is the first operation of our intellectual faculties, and the inlet of all knowledge into our minds.

The next faculty of the mind whereby it makes a further progress towards knowledge is that which I call Retention, or the keeping of those simple ideas which from sensation or reflection it hath received. This is done, first, by keeping the idea which is brought into it for some time actually in view, which is called Contemplation. The other way of retention is the power to revive again in our minds those ideas which after imprinting have disappeared, or have been, as it were, laid aside out of sight; and thus we do when we conceive heat or light, yellow or sweet, the object being removed. This is memory, which is, as it were, the storehouse of our ideas.

Another faculty we may take notice of in our minds is that of Discerning, and distinguishing between the several ideas it has. It is not enough to have a confused perception of something in general. Unless the mind had a distinct perception of different objects and their qualities, it would be capable of very little knowledge, though the bodies that affect us were as busy about us as they are now, and the mind were continually employed in thinking. On this faculty of distinguishing one thing from another depends the evidence and certainty of several even very general propositions which have passed for innate truths, because men, overlooking the true cause why those propositions find universal assent, impute it wholly to native uniform impressions; whereas it, in truth, depends upon this clear discerning faculty of the mind, whereby it perceives two ideas to be the same or different.

The comparing of ideas one with another is the operation of the mind upon which depends all that large tribe of ideas comprehended under relations. The next operation is composition, whereby the mind puts together several simple ideas and combines them into complex ones.

The use of words being to stand as outward marks of our internal ideas, and those ideas being taken from particular things, if every particular idea that we take in should have a distinct name, names must be endless. To prevent this, the mind makes the particular ideas received from particular objects to become general, which is done by considering them as they are in the mind, and such appearances separate from all other existences, and from the circumstances of real existence, as time, place, or any other concomitant ideas. This is called Abstraction, whereby ideas taken from particular being become general representatives of all of the same kind. Thus, the same color being observed today in chalk or snow which the mind yesterday received from milk, it considers that that appearance alone makes it a representative of all of that kind; and having given it the name "whiteness," it by that sound signifies the same quality wheresoever imagined or met with; and thus universals, whether ideas or terms, are made.

As the mind is wholly passive in the reception of all its simple ideas, so it exerts several acts of its own, whereby, out of its simple ideas, as the materials and foundations of the rest the others are framed. And I believe we shall find, if we observe the originals of our notions, that even the most abstruse ideas, how remote soever they may seem from sense, or from any operation of our minds, are yet only such as the understanding frames to itself, by repeating and joining together ideas that it had either from objects of sense or from its own operations about them; so that even those large and abstract ideas are derived from sensation or reflection, being no other than what the mind may and does attain by the ordinary use of its own faculties.

Knowledge of the Existence of Other Things

It is the actual receiving of ideas from without that gives us notice of the existence of other things, and makes us know that something does exist at that time without us which causes that idea in us, though perhaps we neither know nor consider how it does it. And this, though not so certain as our own intuitive knowledge, or as the deductions of our reason employed about the clear abstract ideas of our own minds, yet deserves the name of knowledge.

It is plain that those perceptions are produced by exterior causes affecting our senses for the following reasons.

Because those that want the organs of any sense never can have the ideas belonging to that sense produced in their minds.

Because sometimes I find I cannot avoid having those ideas produced in my mind; for as when my eyes are shut, or the windows fast, I can at pleasure recall to my mind the ideas of light or the sun which former sensations have lodged in my memory; so I can at pleasure lay by that idea and take into my view that of a rose or taste of sugar. But if I turn my eyes at noon towards the sun, I cannot avoid the ideas which the light or sun produces in me. There is nobody who does not perceive the difference in himself contemplating the sun as he has an idea of it in his memory and actually looking upon it; and, therefore, he has certain knowledge that they are not both memory or the actions of his mind and fancies only within him, but that actual seeing has a cause without.

Add to this that many of those ideas are produced with pain, which afterwards we remember without the least offense.

Lastly, our senses bear witness to the truth of each other's report concerning the existence of sensible things without us.

Jean Jacques Rousseau
(1712–1778)

From
THE SOCIAL CONTRACT

The Terms of the Contract

My object is to discover whether, in civil polity, there is any legitimate and definite canon of government, taking men as they are, and laws as they might be. In this inquiry I shall uniformly try to reconcile that which is permitted by right with that which is prescribed by interest so as to avoid the clash of justice with utility.

Man is born free, and yet is everywhere in fetters. He is governed, obliged to obey laws. What is it that legitimizes the subjection of men to government? I think I can solve the problem.

It is not merely a matter of force; force is only the power of the strongest, and must yield when a greater strength arises; there is here no question of right, but simply of might. But social order is a sacred right that serves as a base for all others. This right, however, does not arise from nature; it is founded, therefore, upon conventions. It is necessary, then, to know what these conventions are.

The explanation of social order is not to be found in the family tie, since, when a child grows up it escapes from tutelage; the parents' right to exercise authority is only temporary. Nor can government be based on servitude. An individual man may sell his liberty to another for sustenance; but a nation cannot sell its liberty—it does not receive sustenance from its ruler, but on the contrary sustains him. A bargain in which one party gains everything and the other loses everything is plainly no bargain at all, and no claim of right can be founded on it. But even supposing that a people could thus give up its liberty to a ruler, it must be a people before it does so. The gift is a civil act, which presupposes a public deliberation. Before, then, we examine the act by which a people chooses a king, it would be well to examine the act by which a people becomes a people; for this act, which necessarily precedes the other, must be the true foundation of society.

Let it be assumed that the obstacles which prejudice the conservation of man in a state of nature have prevailed by their resistance over the forces which each individual is able to employ to keep himself in that state. The primitive condition can then no longer exist; mankind must change it or perish.

The problem with which men are confronted under these circumstances may be stated as follows—"To find a form of association that defends and protects with all the common force the person and property of each partner, and by which each partner, uniting himself with all the rest, nevertheless obeys only himself, and remains as free as heretofore." This is the fundamental problem to which the Social Contract affords a solution.

The clauses of this contract are determined by the nature of the act in such a manner that the least modification renders them of no effect; so that, even when they have not been formally stated, they are everywhere the same, everywhere tacitly acknowledged; and if the compact is violated, everyone returns forthwith to his natural liberty.

The essence of the pact is the total and unreserved alienation by each partner of all his rights to the community as a whole. No individual can retain any rights that are not possessed equally by all other individuals without the contract being thereby violated. Again, each partner, by yielding his rights to the community, yields them to no individual, and thus in his relations with individuals he regains all the rights he has sacrificed.

The compact, therefore, may be reduced to the following terms—"each of us places in common his person and all his power under the supreme direction of the general will; and we receive each member as an indivisible part of the whole."

By this act is created a moral and collective body, composed of as many members as the society has voices, receiving from this same act its unity, its common "I," its life, and its will. This body is the Republic, called by its members the state, the state when passive, the sovereign when active, a power in its relations with similar bodies. The partners are collectively called the people; they are citizens, as participants in the sovereign authority, and subjects as under obligation to the laws of the state.

The sovereign, then, is the general will; and each individual finds himself engaged in a double relationship—as a member of the sovereign. To the general will each partner must, by the terms of the contract, submit himself, without respect to his private inclinations. If he refuses to submit, the sovereign will compel him to do so; which is as much as to say, that it will force him to be free; for in the supremacy of the general will lies the only guarantee to each citizen of freedom from personal dependence.

By passing, through the compact, from the state of nature to the civil state, man substitutes justice for instinct in his conduct, and gives to his actions a morality of which they were formerly devoid. What man loses by the contract is his natural liberty, and an illimitable right to all that tempts him and that he can obtain; what he gains is civil liberty, and a right of secure property in all that he possesses.

I shall conclude this chapter with a remark which should serve as a basis for the whole social system; it is that in place of destroying natural liberty, the fundamental pact substitutes a moral and legitimate equality for the natural physical inequality between men, and that, while men may be unequal in strength and talent, they are all made equal by convention and right.

The Sovereign and the Laws

The first and most important consequence of the principles above established is that only the general will can direct the forces of the state towards the aim of its institutions, which is the common good; for if the antagonism of particular interests has rendered necessary the establishment of political societies, it is the accord of these interests that has rendered such societies possible.

I maintain, then, that sovereignty, being the exercise of the general will, cannot be alienated, and that the sovereign, which is simply a collective being, cannot be represented save by itself; it may transfer its power, but not its will.

For the same reason that sovereignty is inalienable, it is

indivisible. For the will is either general or it is not. If it is general, it is, when declared, an act of the people, and becomes law; if it is not general, it is, when declared, merely an act of a particular person or persons, not of the sovereign.

The general will is infallible; but the deliberations of the people are not necessarily so. The people may be, and often are, deceived. Particular interests may gain an advantage over general interests, and in that case the rival particular interests should be allowed to destroy each other, so that the true general interest may prevail. In order to secure the clear expression of the general will, there should be no parties or groups within the state; if such groups exist, they should be multiplied in number, so that no one party should get the upper hand.

While, under the contract, each person alienates his power, his goods, and his liberty, he only alienates so much of these as are of concern to the community; but it belongs to the sovereign to determine what is of concern to the community and what is not.

Whatsoever services a citizen owes to the state, he owes them directly the sovereign demands them; but the sovereign, on its part, must not charge its citizens with any obligations useless to the community; for, under the law of reason, nothing is done without cause, anymore than under the law of nature. The general will, let it be repeated, tends always to public utility, and is intrinsically incapable of demanding services not useful to the public.

A law is an expression of a general will, and must be general in its terms and import. The sovereign cannot legislate for part of the individuals composing the state, for if it did so the general will would enter into a particular relation with particular people, and that is contrary to its nature. The law may thus confer privileges, but must not name the persons to whom the privileges are to belong. It may establish a royal government, but must not nominate a king. Any function relating to an individual object does not appertain to the legislative power. As a popular assembly is not always enlightened, though the general will when properly ascertained, must be right—the service of a wise legislator is necessary to draw up laws with the sovereign's approval.

The legislator, if he be truly wise, will not begin by writing down laws very good in the abstract, but will first look about to see whether the people for whom he intends them is capable of upholding them. He must bear in mind many considerations—the situation of the country—the nature of the soil—the density of the population—the national history, occupations, and aptitudes.

Among these considerations one of the most important is the area of the state. As nature has given limits to the stature of a normal man, beyond she makes only giants or dwarfs, there are also limits beyond which a state is, in the one direction, too large to be well-governed, and, in the other, too small to maintain itself. There is in every body politic a maximum of force which cannot be exceeded, and from which the state often falls away by the process of enlarging itself. The further the social bond is extended, the slacker it becomes; and, in general, a small state is proportionately stronger than a large one.

It is true that a state must have a certain breadth of base for the sake of solidity, and in order to resist violent shocks from without. But, on the other hand, administration becomes more troublesome with distance. It increases in burdensomeness, moreover, with the multiplication of degrees. Each town, district, and province, has its administration, for which the people must pay. Finally, overwhelming everything, is the remote central administration. Again the government in a large state has less vigor and swiftness than in a smaller one; the people have less affection for their chiefs, their country, and for each other—since they are, for the most part, strangers to each other. Uniform laws are not suitable for diverse provinces. Yet diverse laws among people belonging to the same state, breed weakness and confusion, for a healthy and well-knit constitution, in brief, it is wiser to count upon the vigor that is born of good government than upon the resources supplied by greatness of territory.

The greatest good of all, which should be the aim of every system of legislation, may, on investigation, be reduced to two main objects, *liberty* and *equality*: liberty, because all dependence of individuals on other individuals is so much force taken away from the body of the state; equality, because without it liberty cannot exist.

But these general objects of every good institution should be regulated in every country in accord with its situation and the character of its inhabitants. Nations with rich territories, for example, should be led to devote themselves to agriculture; manufacturing industry should be left to sterile lands. That which renders the constitution of the state genuinely solid and endurable is the judicious adaptation of laws to natural conditions. A conflict between the two tends to destruction; but when the laws are in sympathy with the natural conditions, when they keep in touch with them, and improve them, the state should prosper.

The Government

Every free action has two causes which concur to produce it: one of them the will that determines upon the act, the other the power that performs it. In the political body, one must distinguish between these two—the legislative power and the executive power. The executive power cannot belong to the sovereign, inasmuch as executive acts are particular acts, aimed at individuals, and therefore, as already explained, outside the sovereign's sphere. Public force, then, requires an agent to apply it, according to the direction of the general will. This is the government, erroneously confounded with the sovereign, of which it is only the minister. It is an intermediary body, established between subject and sovereign for their mutual correspondence, charged with the execution of the laws and the maintenance of civil and political liberty.

The magistrates who form the government may be numerous, or may be few; and, generally speaking, the fewer the magistrates the stronger the government. A magistrate has three wills: his personal will, his will as one of the governors, and his will as a member of the sovereign. The last named is the weakest, the first named the most powerful. If there is only one governor, the two stronger wills are concentrated in one man; with a few governors, they are concentrated in few men; when the government is in the hands of all the citizens, the second will is obliterated, and the first widely distributed, and the government is consequently weak. On the other hand, where there are many governors, the government will be more readily kept in correspondence with the general will. The duty of the legislator is to hit the happy medium at which the government, while not failing in strength, is yet properly submissive to the sovereign.

The sovereign may, in the first place, entrust the government to the whole people, or the greater part of them; this form is called democracy. Or it may be placed in the hands of a minority, in which case it is called the aristocracy. Or it may be concentrated in the hands of a single magistrate, from whom all the others derive their power; this is called monarchy.

It may be urged, on behalf of democracy, that those who make the laws know better than anybody how they should be interpreted and administered. But it is not right that the makers of the laws should execute them, nor that the main body of the people should turn its attention from general views to particular objects. Nothing is more dangerous than the influence of private interests on public affairs. A true democracy, in the rigorous sense of the term, never has existed and never will. A people composed of gods would govern itself democratically. A government so perfect is unsuited to men.

There are three forms of aristocracy: natural, elective, and hereditary. The first is only adapted to simple people; the third is the worst of all governments; the second is the best of all. By the elective method, probity, sagacity, experience, and all other sources of preference and public esteem afford guarantees that the community will be wisely governed.

The first defect of monarchy is that it is to the interests of the monarch to keep the people in a state of misery and weakness, so that they may be unable to resist his power. Another is that under a monarchy the posts of honor are occupied by bunglers and rascals who win their promotion by petty court intrigue. Again, an elective monarchy is a cause of disorder whenever a king dies; and a hereditary monarchy leaves the character of the king to chance, which, as everything tends to deprive of justice and reason a man trained to supreme rule, generally goes astray.

The question as to whether there is any sign by which we can tell whether a people is well or ill governed readily admits of a solution. What is the surest token of the preservation and prosperity of a political community? It is to be found in the population. Other things being equal, the government under which, without extrinsic devices, without naturalization, without colonies, the citizens increase and multiply, is infallibly the best. Calculators, it is therefore your affair; count, measure, compare.

As particular wills strive unceasingly against the general will, so the government makes a continual attack upon the sovereign. If the government is able, by its efforts, to usurp the sovereignty, then the social contract is broken; the citizens, who have by right been thereby restored to their natural liberty, may be forced to obey the usurper, but are under no other obligation to do so.

Since the sovereign has no power except its legislative authority, it only acts by laws; and since the laws are simply the authentic acts of the general will, the sovereign cannot act save when the people are assembled. It is essential that there should be definitely fixed periodic assemblies of the people that cannot be abolished or delayed, so that on the appointed day the people would be legitimately convoked by the law, without need of any formal summons.

I may be asked, how are the citizens of a large state composed of many communities, to hold frequent meetings? I reply that it is useless to quote the disadvantages of large states to one who considers that all states ought to be small. But how are small states to defend themselves against large ones? By confederation, after the manner of the Greek and ancient times, and the Dutch and Swiss in times more modern.

But between the sovereign authority and arbitrary government there is sometimes introduced a middle power of which I ought to speak. As soon as the public service ceases to be the main interest of the citizens, as soon as they prefer to serve their purses rather than themselves, the state is nearing its ruin. The weakening of patriotism, the activity of private interests, the immensity of states, conquests, and the abuse of government, have led to the device of deputies or representatives of the people in the national assemblies. But sovereignty cannot be represented, even as it cannot be alienated; it consists essentially in the general will, and the will is not ascertainable by representation; it is either itself, or something else; there is no middle course. A law not ratified by the people in person is no law at all. The English people believes itself free, but it greatly deceives itself; it is not so, except during the election of members of parliament. As soon as they are elected, it is enslaved, it is nothing.

How are we to conceive the act by which the government is instituted? The first process is the determination of the sovereign, that the government shall assume such and such a form; this is the establishment of a law. The second process is the nomination by the people of those to whom the government is to be entrusted; this is not a law, but a particular act, a function of government.

How, then, can we have an act of government before the government exists? How can the people, who are only sovereigns or subjects, become magistrates under certain circumstances? Here we discover one of those astonishing properties of the body politic, by which it reconciles operations apparently contradictory; for the process is accomplished by a sudden conversion from sovereignty to democracy, so that, with no sensible change, and simply by a new relation of all to all, the citizens become magistrates, pass from general to parti-acts, and from the law to its execution. In this manner the English House of Commons resolves itself into committee, and thus becomes a simple commission of the sovereign court which it was a moment before; afterwards reporting to itself, as House of Commons, as to its proceedings in the form of a committee.

It is a logical sequence of the Social Contract that in the assemblies of the people the voice of the majority prevails. The only law requiring unanimity is the contract itself. But how can a man be free and at the same time compelled to submit to laws to which he has not consented? I reply that when a law is proposed in the popular assembly, the question put is not precisely whether the citizens approve or disapprove of it, but whether it conforms or not to the general will. The minority, then, simply have it proved to them that they estimated the general will wrongly. Once it is declared, they are as citizens participants in it, and as subjects they must obey it.

Civil Religion

Religion, in its relation to society, can be divided into two kinds—the religion of the man, and that of the citizen. The first, without temples, without altars, without rites, limited to the

inner and private worship of the Supreme God, and to the eternal duties of morality, is the pure and simple religion of the
Evangel, the true theism. The other, established in one country
only, gives that country its own gods, its own tutelary patrons; it
has its own dogmas and ritual, and all foreigners are deemed to
be infidels. Such were all the religions of the primitive peoples.

There is a third and more eccentric kind of religion, which,
giving men two legislations, two chiefs, two countries, imposes
upon them contradictory duties, and forbids them from being at
the same time devotees and patriots. Such is the religion of the
Llamas; such is the religion of the Japanese; such is Roman
Christianity.

Politically considered, all these kinds have their defects.
The third is so manifestly bad that one need waste no time upon
it. That which breaks social unity is worthless. The second is
good, in that it inculcates patriotism, makes it a religious duty
to serve the state. But it is founded on error and falsehood, and
renders its adherents superstitious, intolerant, and cruel. The
first, the religion of man, or Christianity, is a sublime and true
religion by which men, children of one god, acknowledge each
other as brethren, and the society that unites them does not dissolve even with death. But Christianity of itself is not calculated to strengthen a nation; it teaches submissiveness, and dis-
courages patriotic pride.

Now it is of prime importance to the state that each citizen
should have a religion which teaches him to love his duty; but
the state is only concerned with religion so far as it teaches
morality and the duty of man towards his neighbor. Beyond
that, the sovereign has nothing to do with a man's religious
opinions.

There should, therefore, be a purely civil profession of faith,
the articles of which are to be fixed by the sovereign, not precisely as religious dogmas, but as sentiments of sociability,
without which it is impossible for a man to be a good citizen or
a faithful subject. Without being able to compel anybody to
believe the articles, the sovereign could banish from the state
anybody who did not believe them; it can banish him, not as
impious, but as unsociable, as incapable of sincerely loving
laws and justice. If anyone, having publicly accepted these
dogmas, should act as if he did not believe them, he should be

punished with death; he would have committed the greatest of crimes, that of lying against the laws.

The dogmas of the civil religion should be simple, few, precise, without explanations or commentaries. The existence of a powerful, wise, benevolent, provident, and bountiful Deity, the life to come, the happiness of the just, the punishment of the wicked, the sanctity of the social contract, and the laws; these are the positive dogmas. As for negative dogmas, I limit them to one; I would have every good citizen forswear intolerance in religion.

After having laid down the true principles of political rights, and sought to place the state upon its proper basis, it should remain to support it by its external relations—international law, commerce, and so on. But this forms a new aim too vast for my limited view; I have had to fix my eyes on objects nearer at hand.

Adam Smith
(1723–1790)

From

WEALTH OF NATIONS

Labor and Its Produce

The division of labor has been the chief cause of improvement in the productiveness of labor. For instance, the making of a single pin involves eighteen separate operations, which are entrusted to eighteen separate workmen; and the result is, that whereas one man working alone could only make perhaps twenty pins in a day, several men working together, on the principle of division of labor, can make several thousands of pins per man in one day. Division of labor, in a highly developed state of society, is carried into almost every practical art; and its great benefits depend upon the increase of dexterity in each workman, upon the saving of time otherwise lost in passing from one kind of work to another, and finally, upon the use of many labor-saving machines, which is made possible by the division of labor.

This division of labor, from which so many advantages are derived, is not originally the effect of any human wisdom which foresees and intends the opulence to which it gives rise; it is rather the gradual result of the propensity, in human nature, to barter and exchange one thing for another. The power of exchanging their respective produce makes it possible for one man to produce only bread, and for another to produce only clothing. The extent to which the division of labor can be carried is therefore limited by the extent of the market. There are some sorts of industry, even of the lowest kind, which can be carried on nowhere but in a great town; a porter, for example, cannot find employment and subsistence in a village. In the highlands of Scotland every farmer must be butcher, baker, and brewer for his own family.

As water-carriage opens a more extensive market to every

kind of industry than is afforded by land-carriage, it is on the sea coast and on the banks of navigable rivers, that industry begins to subdivide and improve itself, and it is not till long afterwards that these improvements extend to the inland parts. It was thus that the earliest civilized nations were grouped round the coasts of the Mediterranean Sea, and the extent and easiness of its inland navigation was probably the chief cause of the early improvement of Egypt.

As soon as the division of labor is well established, every man becomes in some measure a merchant, and the society becomes a commercial society; and the continual process of exchange leads inevitably to the origin of money. In the absence of money or a general medium of exchange, society would be restricted to the cumbersome method of barter. Every man therefore would early endeavor to keep by him, besides the produce of his own industry, a certain quantity of some commodity such as other people will be likely to take in exchange for the produce of their particular industries. Cattle, for example, have been widely used for this purpose in primitive societies, and Homer speaks of a suit of armor costing a hundred oxen.

But the durability of metals, as well as the facility with which they can be subdivided, has led to their employment, in all countries, as the means of exchange; and in order to obviate the necessity of weighing portions of the metals at every purchase, as well as to prevent fraud, it has been found necessary to affix a public stamp upon certain quantities of the metals commonly used to purchase goods. The value of commodities thus comes to be expressed in terms of coinage.

But labor is the real measure of the exchangeable value of all commodities; the value of any commodity to the person who possesses it is equal to the quantity of labor which it enables him to purchase or to command. What is bought with money or with goods is purchased by labor as much as what we acquire by the toil of our own body. Labor alone, never varying in its own value, is alone the ultimate and real standard by which the value of all commodities can at all times and in all places be estimated and compared. It is their real price; money is their nominal price only. Equal quantities of labor will at distant times be purchased more nearly with equal quantities of corn, the subsistence of the laborer, than with equal quantities of gold, or of any other commodity.

Several elements enter into the price of commodities. In a nation of hunters, if it costs twice the labor to kill a beaver which it costs to kill a deer, one beaver will be worth two deer. But if the one kind of labor be more severe than the other, some allowance will naturally be made for this superior hardship; and thirdly, if one kind of labor requires an uncommon degree of dexterity and ingenuity, it will command a higher value than that which would be due to the time employed in it. So far, the whole produce of labor belongs to the laborer.

But as soon as stock has accumulated in the hands of particular persons, some of them will employ it in setting to work industrious workmen, whom they will supply with materials and subsistence, in order to make a profit by the sale of their work. The profits of stock are not to be regarded as the wages of a particular sort of labor, the labor of inspection and direction; for they are regulated altogether by the value of the stock employed, and are greater or smaller in proportion to the extent of this stock.

There is in every society or neighborhood an ordinary or average rate both of wages and profit in every different employment of labor and stock; and this rate is regulated partly by the general circumstances of the society, its richness or poverty, and partly by the peculiar nature of each employment. There is also in every society or neighborhood an ordinary or average rate of rent, which is regulated too by the general circumstances of the society or neighborhood in which the land is situated, and partly by the natural or improved fertility of the land. What we may call the natural price of any commodity depends upon these natural rates of wages, profit and rent, at the place where it is produced. But its market price may be above, below, or identical with its natural price, and depends upon the proportion between the supply and the demand.

Nature, Accumulation, and
Employment of Stock

When the stock which a man possesses is no more than sufficient to maintain him for a few days or weeks, he seldom thinks
of deriving any revenue from it; but when he possesses enough
to maintain him for months or years, he endeavors to derive a
revenue from the greater part of it. The part of his stock from
which he expects to derive revenue is called his capital.

There are two ways in which capital may be employed so as
to yield a profit to its employer. First, it may be employed in
raising, manufacturing, or purchasing goods, and selling them
again with a profit; this is circulating capital. Secondly, it may
be employed in the improvement of land, or in the purchase of
machines and instruments; and this capital, which yields a
profit from objects which do not change masters, is called fixed
capital.

The general stock of any country or society is the same as
that of all its inhabitants or members, and is therefore divided
into the same three portions, each of which has a different
function. The first is the portion which is reserved for immediate consumption, and so affords no revenue or profit. The second is the fixed capital, which consists of

(a) all useful machines and instruments of trade which facilitate and abridge labor;

(b) all profitable buildings, which procure a revenue, not
only to their owner, but also to the person who rents them, such
as shops, warehouses, farmhouses, factories, etc.;

(c) the improvements of land, and all that has been laid out
in clearing, draining, enclosing, manuring, and reducing it into
the condition most proper for culture; and

(d) the acquired and useful abilities of all the inhabitants or
members of the society, for the acquisition of such talents, by
the maintenance of the learner during his education or appren-
ticeship, costs a real expense, which is a capital fixed in his
person.

The third and last of the three portions into which the general stock of the society naturally divides itself is the circulating capital, which affords a revenue only by changing masters.
It includes

(a) all the money by means of which all the other three are circulated and distributed to their proper consumers;

(b) all the stock of provisions which are in the possession of the butcher, farmer, corn-merchant, etc., and from the sale of which they expect to derive a profit;

(c) all the materials, whether altogether rude, or more or less manufactured, for clothes, furniture and building, which are not yet made up into any of these shapes, but remain in the hands of the growers, manufacturers and merchants; and

(d) all the work which is made up and completed, but is not yet disposed of to the proper consumers.

The substitution of paper in the place of gold and silver money replaces a very expensive instrument of commerce by one much less costly, and sometimes equally convenient. Circulation comes to be carried on by a new wheel, which it costs less both to erect and to maintain than the old one. The effect of the issue of large quantities of bank notes in any country is to send abroad the gold, which is no longer needed at home, in order that it may seek profitable employment. It is not sent abroad for nothing, but is exchanged for foreign goods of various kinds in such a way as to add to the revenue and profits of the country from which it is sent; unless, indeed, it is spent abroad on such goods as are likely to be consumed by idle people who produce nothing.

The Progress of Opulence in Different Nations

The greatest commerce of every civilized society is that carried on between the inhabitants of the town and those of the country. It consists in the exchange of rude for manufactured produce, either immediately, or by the intervention of money, or of some sort of paper which represents money. The country supplies the town with the means of subsistence, and the materials for manufacture. The town repays this supply by sending back a part of the manufactured produce to the inhabitants of the country. The town, in which there neither is nor can be any reproduction of substances, may very properly be said to gain its whole subsistence from the country. And in how great a degree the country is benefited by the commerce of the town may be seen from a comparison of the cultivation of the lands in the neighborhood of any considerable town with that of those which lie at some distance from it.

As subsistence is, in the nature of things, prior to conveniency and luxury, so the rural industries which procure the former must be prior to the urban industries which minister to the latter. The greater part of the capital of every growing society is therefore first directed to agriculture, afterwards to manufactures, and last of all to foreign commerce. But this natural order of things has, in all the modern states of Europe, been in many respects entirely inverted. The foreign commerce of some of their cities has given rise to their finer manufactures, and manufactures and foreign commerce together have given birth to the principal improvements of agriculture. The manners and customs which the nature of their original government introduced, and which remained after that government was greatly altered, necessarily forced them into this unnatural and retrograde order.

In the ancient state of Europe, after the fall of the Roman Empire, agriculture was greatly discouraged by several causes. The rapine and violence which the barbarians exercised against the ancient inhabitants interrupted the commerce between the towns and the country; the towns were deserted and the country was left uncultivated. The western provinces of Europe sank into the lowest state of poverty, and the land, which was mostly uncultivated, was engrossed by a few great proprietors.

These lands might in the natural course of events have been soon divided again, and broken into small parcels by succession or by alienation; but the law of primogeniture hindered their division by succession, and the introduction of entails prevented their being divided by alienation. These hindrances to the division and consequently to the cultivation of the land were due to the fact that land was considered as the means not of subsistence merely, but of power and protection. In those disorderly times, every great landlord was a sort of petty prince.

Unfortunately these laws of primogeniture and entail have continued long after the circumstances which gave rise to them have disappeared. Unfortunately, because it seldom happens that a great landlord is a great improver. To improve land with profit requires an exact attention to small savings and small gains, of which a man born to a great fortune is seldom capable. And if little improvement was to be expected from the great proprietors, still less was to be hoped for from those who occupied the land under them. In the ancient state of Europe, the occupiers of land were all tenants at will, and practically slaves. To these succeeded a kind of farmers known at present in France by the name of "metayers," whose produce was divided equally between the proprietor and the farmer, after setting aside what was judged necessary for keeping up the stock, which still belonged to the landlord. To these, in turn, succeeded, though by very slow degrees, farmers properly so called, who cultivated the land with their own stock, paying a fixed rent to the landlord, and enjoying a certain degree of security of tenure. And every improvement in the position of the actual cultivation of the soil is attended by a corresponding improvement of the land and of its cultivation.

After the fall of the Roman Empire the inhabitants of cities and towns were not more favored than those of the country. The towns were inhabited chiefly by tradesmen and mechanics, who were in those days of servile, or nearly servile condition. Yet the townsmen arrived at liberty and independence much earlier than the country population; their towns became "free burghs," and were erected into commonalties or corporations, with the privilege of having magistrates and a town council of their own, of making bylaws for their own government and of building walls for their own defense. Order and good government, and the liberty and security of individuals, were thus established in cities at a time when the occupiers of land in the country were exposed to every sort of violence.

The increase and riches of commercial and manufacturing towns thenceforward contributed to the improvement and cultivation of the countries to which they belonged, in three different ways. First, by affording a great and ready market for the rude produce of the country. Secondly, the wealth acquired by the inhabitants of cities was employed in purchasing uncultivated lands and in bringing them under cultivation; for merchants are ambitious of becoming country gentlemen, and when they do so, are generally the best of all improvers. And lastly, commerce and manufactures gradually introduced order and good government, and with them the liberty and security of individuals, among the inhabitants of the country.

The Mercantile System

From the mistaken theory that wealth consists in money, or in gold and silver, there has arisen an erroneous and harmful system of political economy and of legislation in the supposed interests of manufacture, of commerce, and of the wealth of nations. A rich country is supposed to be a country abounding in money; and all the nations of Europe have consequently studied, though to little purpose, every possible means of accumulating gold and silver in their respective countries. For example, they have at times forbidden, or hindered by heavy duties, the export of these metals. But all these attempts are vain; for on the one hand, when the quantity of gold and silver imported into any country exceeds the effectual demand, no vigilance can prevent their exportation; and on the other hand, if gold and silver should fall short in a country, there are more expedients for supplying their place than that of any other commodity. The real inconvenience which is commonly called "scarcity of money" is not a shortness in the medium of exchange, but is a weakening and diminution of credit, due to over-trading. Money is part of the national capital, but only a small part and always the most unprofitable part of it.

The principle of the "commercial system" or "mercantile system" is, that wealth consists in money, or in gold and silver. It is an utterly untrue principle. But once it had been established in general belief that wealth consists in gold and silver, and that these metals can be brought into a country which has no mines only by the "balance of trade," that is to say, by exporting to a greater value than it imports, it necessarily became the great object of political economy to diminish as much as possible the importation of foreign goods for home consumption, and to increase as much as possible the exportation of the produce of domestic industry. Its two great engines for enriching the country, therefore, were restraints upon importation and encouragements to exportation.

The restraints upon importation were of two kinds: first, restraints upon the importation of such foreign goods for home consumption as could be produced at home, from whatever country they were imported; and secondly, restraints upon the importation of goods of almost all kinds from those particular countries with which the balance of trade was supposed to be

disadvantageous. These different restraints consisted sometimes in high duties, and sometimes in absolute prohibitions.

Exportation was encouraged sometimes by drawbacks, sometimes by bounties, sometimes by advantageous treaties of commerce with sovereign states, and sometimes by the establishment of colonies in distant countries. The above two restraints,
and these four encouragements to exportation, constitute the
six principal means by which the commercial or mercantile
system proposes to increase the quantity of gold and silver in
any country by turning the balance of trade in its favor.

The entire system, in all its developments, is a fallacious
and an evil one. It is not difficult to determine who have been
the contrivers of this whole mercantile system: not the consumers, whose interest has been entirely neglected; but the
producers, and especially the merchants and manufacturers,
whose interest has been so carefully attended to. It remains to
be said, also, that the "agricultural system," which represents
the produce of land as the sole source of the revenue and
wealth of every country, and as therefore justifying a special
protection of it, is as fallacious and as harmful as the other.

The Revenue of the Sovereign or Commonwealth

The first duty of the sovereign, that of protecting the society
from the violence and invasion of other independent societies,
can be performed only by means of a military force. This may
be effected either by obliging all the citizens of the military
age, or a certain number of them, to join in some measure the
trade of a soldier to whatever other trade or profession they may
happen to carry on; or by maintaining a certain number of citizens in the constant practice of military exercises, thus rendering the trade of a soldier a particular trade, separate from
all others. In the former case a militia is formed, in the latter a
standing army; and of the two, the second is by far the more
powerful, as it is also the more expensive.

The second duty of the sovereign, that of protecting, as far as
possible, every member of the society from the injustice or
oppression of every other member of it, or the duty of establishing an exact administration of justice, requires an increasing expenditure corresponding to the advance and development
of the society.

Public works and public institutions are a third cause of expenditure on the part of sovereign or commonwealth; and have two principal objects—that of facilitating the commerce of the society and that of promoting the instruction of the people. Roads, bridges, canals, are examples of the former; schools, universities, established Churches are examples of the latter. And among other expenses of the sovereign or commonwealth we must include the expenses of supporting the dignity of the sovereign.

The funds or sources of revenue which peculiarly belong to the sovereign or commonwealth consist either in stock or in land; but being quite insufficient to meet the public expenditure they are supplemented by taxation. Every tax is finally paid from rent, profit or wages, or from all of them indifferently; and the chief principle to be observed in taxation is, that the subjects of the State ought to contribute towards the support of the government, as nearly as possible, in proportion to their respective abilities—that is, in proportion to the revenue which they respectively enjoy under the protection of the State. The tax which each individual is bound to pay ought to be certain and not arbitrary, every tax ought to be levied at the time or in the manner in which it is most likely to be convenient for the contributor to pay it; and finally, every tax ought to be so contrived as to take out and to keep out of the pockets of the people as little as possible over and above what it brings into the public treasury of the State.

Immanuel Kant

(1724–1804)

From

THE CRITIQUE OF PURE REASON

Knowledge Transcendental: Aesthetic

Experience is something of which we are conscious. It is the first result of our comprehension, but it is not the limit of our understanding, since it stimulates our faculty of reason, but does not satisfy its desire for knowledge. While all our knowledge may begin with sensible impressions or experience, there is an element in it which does not rise from this source, but transcends it. That knowledge is transcendental which is occupied not so much with mere outward objects as with our manner of knowing those objects, that is to say, with our *a priori* concepts of them. All our knowledge is either *a priori* or *a posteriori*. That is *a posteriori* knowledge which is derived from sensible experience as including sensible impressions or states; while *a priori* knowledge is that which is not thus gained, but consists of whatever is universal or necessary. A complete "Transcendental Philosophy" would be a systematic exposition of all that is *a priori* in human knowledge, or of "all the principles of pure reason." But a "Critique of Pure Reason" cannot include all this. It can do little more than deal with the synthetic element or quality in *a priori* knowledge, as distinguished from the analytic element.

We perceive objects through our sensibility which furnishes us, as our faculty of receptivity, with those intuitions that become translated into thought by means of the understanding. This is the origin of our conceptions, or ideas. I denominate as matter that which in a phenomenon corresponds to sensation; while I call form that quality of matter which presents it in a perceived order. Only matter is presented to our minds *a posteriori;* as to form, this must inevitably exist in the mind *a priori*, and therefore it can be considered apart from all sensation.

Pure representation, entirely apart from sensation, in a transcendental signification, forms the pure intuition of the mind, existing in it as a mere form of sensibility. Transcendental esthetic is the science of all the principles of sensibility. But transcendental logic is the science of the principles of pure thought. In studying the former we shall find that there are two pure forms of sensuous intuition, namely, space and time.

Are space and time actual entities? Or are they only relations of things? Space is simply the form of all the phenomena of external senses; that is, it is the subjective condition of the sensibility under which alone external intuition is possible. Thus, the form of all phenomena may exist *a priori* in the soul as a pure intuition previous to all experience. So we can only speak of space and of extended objects from the standpoint of human reason. But when we have abstracted all the forms perceived by our sensibility, there remains a pure intuition which we call space. Therefore our discussion teaches us the objective validity of space with regard to all that can appear before us externally as an object; but equally the subjective ideality of space, with regard to things if they are considered in themselves by our reason, that is, without; taking into account the nature of our sensibility.

Time is not empirically conceived of; that is, it is not experimentally apprehended. Time is a necessary representation on which all intuitions are dependent, and the representation of time to the mind is thus given *a priori*. In it alone can phenomena be apprehended. These may vanish, but time cannot be put aside.

Time is not something existing by itself independently, but is the formal condition *a priori* of all phenomena. If we deduct our own peculiar sensibility, then the idea of time disappears indeed, because it is not inherent in any object, but only in the subject which perceives that object. Space and time are essential *a priori* ideas, and they are the necessary conditions of all particular perceptions. From the latter and their objects we can, in imagination, without exception, abstract; from the former we cannot.

Space and time are therefore to be regarded as the necessary *a priori* pre-conditions of the possibility and reality of all phenomena. It is clear that transcendental aesthetic can obtain

only these two elements, space and time, because all other concepts belong to the senses and pre-suppose experience, and so
imply something empirical. For example, the concept of motion
presupposes something moving, but in space regarded alone
there is nothing that moves; therefore, whatever moves must be
recognized by experience, and is a purely empirical datum.

Transcendental Logic

Our knowledge is derived from two fundamental sources of the
consciousness. The first is the faculty of receptivity of impressions; the second, the faculty of cognition of an object by means
of these impressions or representations, this second power
being sometimes styled spontaneity of concepts. By the first, an
object is given to us; by the second it is thought of in the mind.
Thus intuition and concepts constitute the elements of our
entire knowledge, for neither intuition without concepts, nor
concepts without intuition, can yield any knowledge whatever.
Hence arise two branches of science, aesthetic and logic, the
former being the science of the rules of sensibility; the latter,
the science of the rules of the understanding.

Logic can be treated in two directions: either as logic of the
general use of the understanding, or of some particular use of
it. The former includes the rules of thought, without which
there can be no use of the understanding; but it has no regard
to the objects to which the understanding is applied. This is
elementary logic. But logic of the understanding in some particular use includes rules of correct thought in relation to special classes of objects; and this latter logic is generally taught
in schools as preliminary to the study of science.

Thus, general logic takes no account of any of the contents
of knowledge, but is limited simply to the consideration of the
forms of thought. But we are constrained by anticipation to
form an idea of a logical science which has to deal not only with
pure thought but also has to determine the origin, validity, and
extent of the knowledge to which intuitions relate, and this science might be styled transcendental logic.

In transcendental aesthetic we isolated the faculty of sensibility. So in transcendental logic we isolate the understanding,
concentrating our consideration on that element of thought
which has its source simply in the understanding. But tran-

scendental logic must be divided into transcendental analytic and transcendental dialectic. The former is a logic of truth, and is intended to furnish a canon of criticism. When logic is used to judge not analytically, but to judge synthetically of objects in general, it is called transcendental dialectic, which serves as a protection against sophistical fallacy.

ANALYTIC OF PURE CONCEPTS

The understanding may be defined as the faculty of judging. The function of thought in a judgment can be brought under four heads, each with three subdivisions.

1. Quantity of judgments: Universal, particular, singular.
2. Quality: Affirmative, negative, infinite.
3. Relation: Categorical, hypothetical, disjunctive.
4. Modality: Problematical, assertory, apodictic [above contradiction].

If we examine each of these forms of judgment we discover that in every one is involved some peculiar idea which is its essential characteristic. Thus, a singular judgment, in which the subject of discourse is a single object, involves obviously the special idea of oneness, or unity. A particular judgment, relating to several objects, implies the idea of plurality, and discriminates between the several objects. Now, the whole list of these ideas will constitute the complete classification of the fundamental conceptions of the understanding, regarded as the faculty which judges, and these may be called categories.

1. Of Quantity: Unity, plurality, totality.
2. Of Quality: Reality, negation, limitation.
3. Of Relation: Substance and accident, cause and effect, action and reaction.
4. Of Modality: Possibility—impossibility, existence—nonexistence, necessity—contingence.

These, then, are the fundamental, primary, or native conceptions of the understanding, which flow from, or constitute the mechanism of, its nature; are inseparable from its activity; and are hence, for human thought, universal and necessary, or *a priori*. These categories are "pure" conceptions of the understanding, inasmuch as they are independent of all that is contingent in sense.

TRANSCENDENTAL DIALECTIC

A distinction is usually made between what is immediately known and what is only inferred. It is immediately known that in a figure bounded by three straight lines there are three angles, but that these angles together are equal to two right angles is only inferred. In every syllogism is first a fundamental proposition; secondly, another deduced from it; and, thirdly, the consequence.

In the use of pure reason its concepts, or transcendental ideas, aim at unity of all conditions of thought. So all transcendental ideas may be arranged in three classes; the first containing the unity of the thinking subject; the second, the unity of the conditions of phenomena observed; the third, the unity of the objective conditions of thought.

This classification becomes clear if we note that the thinking subject is the object-matter of psychology; while the system of all phenomena (the world) is the object-matter of cosmology; and the Being of all Beings (God) is the object-matter of theology.

Hence we perceive that pure reason supplies three transcendental ideas, namely, the idea of a transcendental science of the soul (*psychologia rationalis*); of a transcendental science of the world (*cosmologia rationalis*); and, lastly, of a transcendental science of God (*theologia transcendentalis*). It is the glory of transcendental idealism that by it the mind ascends in the series of conditions till it reaches the unconditioned, that is, the principles. We thus progress from our knowledge of self to a knowledge of the world, and through it to a knowledge of the Supreme Being.

The Antinomies of Pure Reason

Transcendental reason attempts to reconcile conflicting assertions. There are four of these antinomies, or conflicts.

FIRST ANTINOMY. Thesis. The world has a beginning in time, and is also limited in regard to space. Proof. Were the world without a time-beginning we should have to ascribe a present limit to that which can have no limit, which is absurd. Again, were the world not limited in regard to space, it must be conceived as an infinite whole, yet it is impossible thus to conceive it.

Antithesis. The world has neither beginning in time, nor

limit in space, but in both regards is infinite. Proof. The world must have existed from eternity, or it could never exist at all. If we imagine it had a beginning, we must imagine an anterior time when nothing was. But in such time the origin of anything is impossible. At no moment could any cause for such a beginning exist.

SECOND ANTINOMY. Thesis. Every composite substance in the world is composed of simple parts. This thesis seems scarcely to require proof. No one can deny that a composite substance consists of parts, and that these parts, if themselves composite, must consist of others less composite, till at length we come, by compulsion of thought, to the conception of the absolutely simple as that wherein the substantial consists.

Antithesis. No composite thing in the world consists of simple parts, and nothing simple exists anywhere in the world. Proof. Each simple part implied in the thesis must be in space. But this condition is a positive disproof of their possibility. A simple substance would have to occupy a simple portion of space; but space has no simple parts. The supposition of such a part is the supposition, not of space, but of the negation of space. A simple substance, in existing and occupying any portion of space, must contain a real multiplicity of parts external to each other, *i.e.*, it must contradict its own nature, which is absurd.

THIRD ANTINOMY. Thesis. The causality of natural law is insufficient for the explanation of all the phenomena of the universe. For this end another kind of causality must be assumed, whose attribute is freedom. Proof. All so-called natural causes are effects of preceding causes, forming a regressive series of indefinite extent, with no first beginning. So we never arrive at an adequate cause of any phenomenon. Yet natural law has for its central demand that nothing shall happen without such a cause.

Antithesis. All events in the universe occur under the exclusive operation of natural laws, and there is no such thing as freedom. Proof. The idea of a free cause is an absurdity. For it contradicts the very law of causation itself, which demands that every event shall be in orderly sequence with some preceding event. Now, free causation is such an event, being the active beginning of a series of phenomena. Yet the action of the supposed free cause must be imagined as independent of all connection with any previous event. It is without law or reason, and would be the blind realization of confusion and lawlessness. Therefore transcendental freedom is a violation of the law of causation, and is in conflict with all experience. We must of necessity acquiesce in the explanation of all phenomena by the operation of natural law, and thus transcendental freedom must be pronounced a fallacy.

FOURTH ANTINOMY. Thesis. Some form of absolutely necessary existence belongs to the world, whether as its part or as its cause. Proof. Phenomenal existence is serial, mutable, consistent. Every event is contingent upon a preceding condition. The conditioned pre-supposes, for its complete explanation, the unconditioned. The whole of past time, since it contains the whole of all past conditions, must of necessity contain the unconditioned or also "absolutely necessary."

Antithesis. There is no absolutely necessary existence, whether in the world as its part, or outside of it as its cause. Proof. Of unconditionally necessary existence within the world there can be none. The assumption of a first unconditioned link in the chain of cosmical conditions is self-contradictory. For such link or cause, being in time, must be subject to the law of all temporal existence, and so be determined—contrary to the original assumption—by another link or cause before it.

The supposition of an absolutely necessary cause of the world, existing without the world, also destroys itself. For, being outside the world, it is not in time. And yet, to act as a cause, it must be in time. This supposition is therefore absurd.

The theses in these four antinomies constitute the teaching of philosophical dogmatism. The antitheses constitute doctrines of philosophical empiricism.

Criticism of the Chief Arguments for the Existence of God

The ontological argument aims at asserting the possibility of conceiving the idea of an *ens realissimum*, of being possessed of all reality. But the idea of existence and the fact of existence are two very different things. Whatever I conceive, or sensibly imagine, I necessarily conceive as though it were existing Though my pocket be empty, I may conceive it to contain a "hundred thalers." If I conceive them there, I can only conceive them as actually existing there. But, alas, the fact that I am under this necessity of so conceiving by no means carries with it a necessity that the coins should really be in my pocket. That can only be determined by experience.

The cosmological argument contends that if anything exists, there must also exist an absolutely necessary being. Now, at least I myself exist. Hence there exists an absolutely necessary being. The argument coincides with that by which the thesis of the fourth antinomy is supposed. The objections to it are summed up in the proof of the antithesis of the fourth antinomy. As soon as we have recognized the true conception of causality, we have already transcended the sensible world.

The physico-theological or teleological argument is what is often styled the argument from design. It proceeds not from general, but particular experience. Nature discloses manifold signs of wise intention and harmonious order, and these are held to betoken a divine designer. This argument deserves always to be treated with respect. It is the oldest and clearest of all proofs, and best adapted to convince the reason of the mass of mankind. It animates us in our study of nature. And it were not only a cheerless, but an altogether vain task to attempt to detract from the persuasive authority of this proof. There is naught to urge against its rationality and its utility.

All arguments, however, to prove the existence of God must, in order to be theoretically valid, start from specifically and exclusively sensible or phenomenal data, must employ only the conceptions of pure physical science, and must end with demonstrating in sensible experience an object congruous with, or corresponding to, the idea of God. But this requirement cannot be met, for, scientifically speaking, the existence of an absolutely necessary God cannot be either proved or disproved. Hence room is left for faith in any moral proofs that may present themselves to us, apart from science. With this subject ethics, the science of practice or of practical reason, will have to deal.

From

THE CRITIQUE OF PRACTICAL REASON

Analytic of Practical Reason

Practical principles are propositions containing a general determination of the will. They are maxims, or subjective propositions, when expressing the will of an individual; objective, when they are valid expressions of the will of rational beings generally.

Practical principles which presuppose an object of desire are empirical, or experimental, and supply no practical laws. Reason, in the scope of a practical law, influences the will not by the medium of pleasure or pain. All rational beings necessarily wish for happiness, but they are not all agreed either as to the means to attain it, or as to the objects of their enjoyment of it. Thus, subjective practical principles can only be reckoned as maxims, never as law.

A rational being ought not to conceive that his individual maxims are calculated to constitute universal laws, and to become the basis of universal legislation. To discover any law which would bring all men into harmony is absolutely impossible.

One of the problems of practical reason is to find the law which can necessarily determine the will, assuming that the will is free. The solution of this problem is to be found in action according to the moral law. We should so act that the maxim of our will can always be valid as a principle of universal legislation. Experience shows how the moral consciousness determines freedom of the will.

Suppose that someone affirms of his inclination for sensual pleasure that he cannot possibly resist temptation to indulgence. If a gallows were erected at the place where he is tempted, on which he should be hanged immediately after satiating his passions, would he not be able to control his inclination? We need not long doubt what would be his answer.

But ask him, if his sovereign commanded him to bear false witness against an honorable man, under penalty of death, whether he would hold it possible to conquer his love of life.

He might not venture to say what he would choose, but he would certainly admit that it is possible to make choice. Thus, he judges that he can choose to do a thing because he is conscious of moral obligation, and he thus recognizes for himself a freedom of will of which, but for the moral law, he would never have been conscious.

We obtain the exact opposite of the principle of morality if we adopt the principle of personal private happiness as the determining motive of the will. This contradiction is not only logical, but also practical. For morality would be totally destroyed were not the voice of reason as clear and penetrating in relation to the will, even to the most ordinary men.

If one of your friends, after bearing false witness against you, attempted to justify his base conduct by enumerating the advantages which he had thus secured for himself and the happiness he had gained, and by declaring that thus he performed a true human duty, you would either laugh him to scorn or turn from him in horror. And yet, if a man acts for his own selfish ends, you have not the slightest objection to such behavior.

MORALITY AND HAPPINESS

The maxim of self-love simply advises; the law of morality commands. There is a vast difference between what we are advised and what we are obliged to do. No practical laws can be based on the principle of happiness, even on that of universal happiness, for the knowledge of this happiness rests on merely empirical or experimental data, every man's ideas of it being conditioned only on his individual opinion. Therefore, this principle of happiness cannot prescribe rules for all rational beings.

But the moral law demands prompt obedience from everyone, and thus even the most ordinary intelligence can discern what should be done. Everyone has power to comply with the dictates of morality, but even with regard to any single aim it is not easy to satisfy the vague precept of happiness. Nothing could be more absurd than a command that everyone should make himself happy, for one never commands anyone to do what he inevitably wishes to do. Finally, in the idea of our practical reason, there is something which accompanies the viola-

tion of a moral law—namely, its demerit, with the consciousness that punishment is a natural consequence. Therefore,
punishment should be connected in the idea of practical reason
with crime, as a consequence of the crime, by the principles of
moral legislation.

ANALYSIS OF PRINCIPLES

The practical material principles of determination constituting
the basis of morality may be thus classified.

1. Subjective

External: Education; the civil constitution. Internal: Physical
feeling; moral feeling.

2. Objective

Internal: Perfection. External: Will of God.

The subjective elements are all experimental, or empirical,
and cannot supply the universal principle of morality, though
they are expounded in that sense by such writers as Montaigne,
Mandeville, Epicurus, and Hutcheson.

But the objective elements, as enunciated and expounded by
Wolf and the Stoics, and by Crusius and other theological
moralists, are founded on reason, for absolute perfection as a
quality of things (that is, God Himself) can only be thought of
by rational concepts.

The conception of perfection in a practical sense is the adequacy of a thing for various ends. As a human quality (and so
internal) this is simply talent, and what completes it is skill.
But supreme perfection in substance, that is, God Himself, and
therefore external (considered practically), is the adequacy of
this being for all purposes. All these principles above classified
are material, and so can never furnish the supreme moral law.
For even the Divine will can supply a motive in the human
mind because of the expectation of happiness from it.

Therefore, the formal practical principle of the pure reason
insists that the mere form of a universal legislation must constitute the ultimate determining principle of the will. Here is

the only possible practical principle which is sufficient to furnish categorical imperatives, that is, practical laws which make action a duty.

It follows from this analytic that pure reason can be practical. It can determine the will independently of all merely experimental elements.

There is a remarkable contrast between the working of the pure speculative reason and that of the pure practical reason. In the former—as was shown in the treatise on that subject—a pure, sensible intuition of time and space made knowledge possible, though only of objects of the senses.

On the contrary, the moral law brings before us a fact absolutely inexplicable from any of the data of the world of sense. And the entire range of our theoretical use of reason indicates a pure world of understanding, which even positively determines it, and enables us to know something of it—namely, a law.

We must observe the distinction between the laws of a system of nature to which the will is subject, and of a system of nature which is subject to the will. In the former, the objects cause the ideas which determine the will; in the latter, the objects are caused by the will. Hence, causality of the will has its determining principle exclusively in the faculty of pure reason, which may, therefore, also be called a pure practical reason.

The moral law is a law of the causality through freedom, and therefore of the possibility of a super-sensible system of nature. It determines the will by imposing on its maxim the condition of a universal legislative form, and thus it is able for the first time to impart practical reality to reason, which otherwise would continue to be transcendent when seeking to proceed speculatively with its ideas.

Thus the moral law induces a stupendous change. It changes the transcendent use of reason into the immanent use. And in result reason itself becomes, by its ideas, an efficient cause in the field of experience.

HUME AND SKEPTICISM

It may be said of David Hume that he initiated the attack on pure reason. My own labors in the investigation of this subject were occasioned by his skeptical teaching, for his assault made them necessary. He argued that without experience it is impossible to know the difference between one thing and another; that is, we can know *a priori*, and, therefore, the notion of a cause is fictitious and illusory, arising only from the habit of observing certain things associated with each in succession of connections.

On such principles we can never come to any conclusion as to causes and effects. We can never predict a consequence from any of the known attributes of things. We can never say of any event that it must *necessarily* have followed from another; that is, that it must have had an antecedent cause. And we could never lay down a rule derived even from the greatest number of observations. Hence we must trust entirely to blind chance, abolishing all reason, and such a surrender establishes skepticism in an impregnable citadel.

Mathematics escaped Hume, because he considered that its propositions were analytical, proceeding from one determination to another, by reason of identity contained in each. But this is not really so, for, on the contrary, they are synthetical, the results depending ultimately on the assent of observers as witnesses to the universality of propositions. So Hume's empiricism leads inevitably to skepticism even in this realm.

My investigations led me to the conclusion that the objects with which we are familiar are by no means things in themselves, but are simply phenomena, connected in a certain way with experience. So that without contradiction they cannot be separated from that connection. Only by that experience can they be recognized. I was able to prove the objective reality of the concept of cause in regard to objects of experience, and to demonstrate its origin from pure understanding, without experimental or empirical sources.

Thus, I first destroyed the source of skepticism, and then the resulting skepticism itself. And thus was subverted the thorough doubt as to whatever theoretic reason claims to perceive, as well as the claim of Hume that the concept of causality involved something absolutely unthinkable.

GOOD AND EVIL

By a concept of practical reason, I understand the representation to the mind of an object as an effect possible to be produced through freedom. The only objects of practical reason are *good* and *evil*. For by "good" we understand an object necessarily abhorred, the principle of reason actuating the mind in each case.

In the common use of language we uniformly distinguish between the "good" and the "pleasant," the "evil" and the "unpleasant," good and evil being judged by reason alone. The judgment on the relation of means to ends certainly belongs to reason. But "good" or "evil" always implies only a reference to the "will," as resolved by the law of reason, to make something its object.

Thus good and evil properly relate to actions, not to personal sensations. So, if anything is to be reckoned simply good or evil, it can only be so estimated by the way of acting. Hence, only the maxim of the will, and consequently the person himself, can be called good or evil, not the thing itself.

The Stoic was right, even though he might be laughed at, who during violent attacks of gout exclaimed, "Pain, I will never admit that thou art an evil!" What he felt was indeed what we call a bad thing; but he had no reason to admit that any evil attached thereby to himself, for the pain did not in the least detract from his personal worth, but only from that of his condition. If a single lie had been on his conscience it would have humiliated his soul; but pain seemed only to elevate it, when he was not conscious of having deserved it as a punishment for any unjust deed.

The rule of judgment subject to the laws of pure practical reason is this: Ask yourself whether if the action you propose were to happen by a natural system of law, of which you were yourself a part, you could regard it as possible by your own will? In fact, everyone does decide by this rule whether actions are morally good or evil.

Dialectic of Practical Reason

THE IMMORTALITY OF THE SOUL

Pure practical reason postulates the immortality of the soul, for reason in the pure and practical sense aims at the perfect good (*summum bonum*), and this perfect good is only possible on the supposition of the soul's immortality. It is the moral law which determines the will, and, in this will, the perfect harmony of the mind with the moral law, is the supreme condition of the *summum bonum*. The principle of the moral destination of our nature—that only by endless progress can we come into full harmony with the moral law—is of the greatest use, not only for fortifying the speculative reason, but also with respect to religion. In default of this, either the moral law is degraded from its holiness, being represented as indulging our convenience, or else men strain after an unattainable aim, hoping to gain absolute holiness of will, thus losing themselves in fanatical theosophic dreams utterly contradicting self-knowledge.

For a rational, but finite, being the only possibility is an endless progression from the lower to the higher degrees of perfection. The Infinite Being, to whom the time-condition is nothing, sees in this endless succession the perfect harmony with the moral law.

THE EXISTENCE OF GOD

The pure practical reason must also postulate the existence of God as the necessary condition of the attainment of the *summum bonum*. As the perfect good can only be promoted by accordance of the will with the moral law, so also this *summum bonum* is possible only through the supremacy of an Infinite Being possessed of causality harmonizing with morality. But the postulate of the highest derived good (sometimes denominated the best world) coincides with the postulate of a highest original good, or of the existence of God.

We now perceive why the Greeks could never solve their problem of the possibility of the *summum bonum,* because they made the freedom of the human will the only and all-sufficient ground of happiness, imagining there was no need for the existence of God for that end. Christianity alone affords an idea of the *summum bonum* which answers fully to the requirement of practical reason. That idea is the Kingdom of God.

The holiness which the Christian law requires makes essential an infinite progress. But just for that very reason it justifies in man the hope of endless existence. And it is only from an Infinite Supreme Being, morally perfect, holy, good, and with an omnipotent will, that we can hope, by accord with His will, to attain the *summum bonum,* which the moral law enjoins on us as our duty to seek ever to attain.

The moral law does not enjoin on us to render ourselves happy, but instructs us how to become worthy of happiness. Morality must never be regarded as a doctrine of happiness, or direction how to become happy, its province being to inculcate the rational condition of happiness, not the means of attaining it. God's design in creating the world is not primarily the happiness of the rational beings in it, but the *summum bonum,* which super-adds another condition to that desire of human beings, namely, the condition of deserving such happiness. That is to say, the morality of rational beings is a condition which alone includes the rule by observing which they can hope to participate in happiness at the hand of an all-wise Creator.

The highest happiness can only be conceived as possible under conditions harmonizing with the divine holiness. Thus they are right who make the glory of God the chief end of creation. For beyond all else that can be conceived, that glorifies God which is the most estimable thing in the whole world, honor for His command and obedience to His law, when to this is added His glorious design to crown so beauteous an order of things with happiness corresponding.

CONCLUSION

Two things fill the mind with ever new and increasing wonder and awe—the starry heavens above me, and the moral law within me. I need not search for them, and vaguely guess concerning them, as if they were veiled in darkness or hidden in the infinite altitude. I see them before me, and link them immediately with the consciousness of my existence. The former begins from the spot I occupy in the outer world of sense, and enlarges my connection with it to a boundless extent with worlds upon worlds and systems of systems.

The second begins from my invisible self, my personality, and places me in a truly infinite world traceable only by the understanding, with which I perceive I am in a universal and necessary connection, as I am also thereby with all those visible worlds.

This view infinitely elevates my value as an intelligence by my personality, in which the moral law reveals to me a life independent of the animal and even the whole material world, and reaching by destiny into the infinite.

But though admiration may stimulate inquiry, it cannot compensate for the want of it. The contemplation of the world, beginning with the most magnificent spectacle possible, ended in astrology; and morality, beginning with the noblest attribute of human nature, ended in superstition. But after reason was applied to careful examination of the phenomena of nature a clear and unchangeable insight was secured into the system of the world. We may entertain the hope of a like good result in treating of the moral capacities of our nature by the help of the moral judgment of reason.

Thomas Paine
(1737–1809)

From

THE RIGHTS OF MAN

Among the incivilities by which nations or individuals provoke or irritate each other, Mr. Burke's pamphlet in the French revolution is an extraordinary instance. There is scarcely an epithet of abuse in the English language with which he has not loaded the French nation and the National Assembly. Considered as an attempt at political argument, his work is a pathless wilderness of rhapsodies, in which he asserts whatever he pleases without offering either evidence or reasons for so doing.

With his usual outrage, he abuses the Declaration of the Rights of Man published by the National Assembly as the basis of the French constitution. But does he mean to deny that man has any rights? If he does, then he must mean that there are no such things as rights anywhere; for who is there in the world but man? But if Mr. Burke means to admit that man has rights, the question then will be: What are those rights and how came man by them originally?

The error of those who reason by precedents drawn from antiquity respecting the rights of man is that they do not go far enough into antiquity; they stop in some of the intermediate stages, and produce what was then done as a rule for the present day. Mr. Burke, for example, would have the English nation submit themselves to their monarchs forever, because an English Parliament did make such a submission to William and Mary, not only on behalf of the people then living, but on behalf of their heirs and posterities—as if any parliament had the right of binding and controlling posterity, or of commanding for ever how the world should be governed. If antiquity is to be authority, a thousand such authorities may be produced, successively contradicting each other; but if we proceed on, we shall at last come out right; we shall come to the time when man came from the hand of his Maker. What was he then? Man! Man was his high and only title, and a higher cannot be given him.

All histories of creation agree in establishing one point, the unity of man, by which I mean that men are all of one degree, and that all men are born equal, and with equal natural rights. These natural rights are the foundation of all their civil rights.

A few words will explain this: Natural rights are those which appertain to man in right of his existence. Of this kind are the rights of the mind, and also those rights of acting as an individual for his own happiness, which are not injurious to the natural rights of others. Civil rights are those which appertain to man in right of his being a member of society. Every civil right has for its foundation some natural right pre-existing in the individual, but to the enjoyment of which his individual power is not, in all cases, sufficiently competent. Of this kind are all those which relate to security and protection.

It follows, then, that the power produced from the aggregate of natural rights, imperfect in power in the individual, cannot be applied to invade the natural rights which are retained in the individual, and in which the power to execute is as perfect as the right itself.

Let us now apply these principles to governments. These may all be comprehended under three heads: First, superstition; secondly, power; thirdly, the common interest of society and the common rights of man.

When a set of artful men pretended to hold intercourse with the Deity, as familiarly as they now march up the backstairs in European courts, the world was completely under the government of superstition. This sort of government lasted as long as this sort of superstition lasted.

After these, a race of conquerors arose, whose government, like that of William the Conqueror, was founded in power. Governments thus established last as long as the power to support them lasts; but, that they might avail themselves of every engine in their favor, they united fraud to force, and set up an idol which they called *Divine Right,* and which twisted itself afterwards into an idol of another shape, called *Church and State.* The key of St. Peter and the key of the treasury became quartered on one another, and the wondering cheated multitude worshipped the invention.

We have now to review the governments which arise out of society. If we trace government to its origin, we discover that governments must have arisen either *out* of the people or over the people. In those which have arisen out of the people, the individuals themselves, each in his own personal and sovereign right, have entered into a compact with each other to produce a government; and this is the only mode in which governments have a right to arise.

This compact is the constitution, and a constitution is not a thing in name only, but in fact. Wherever it cannot be produced in a visible form, there is none. A constitution is a thing antecedent to government, and a government is only its creature. The constitution of a country is not the act of its government, but of the people constituting its government.

Can, then, Mr. Burke produce the English constitution? He cannot, for no such thing exists, nor ever did exist. The English government is one of those which arose out of a conquest, and not out of society, and consequently it arose over the people; and though it has been much modified since the time of William the Conqueror, the country has never yet regenerated itself, and is therefore without a constitution.

France and England Compared

I now proceed to draw some comparisons between the French constitution and the governmental usages in England.

The French constitution says that every man who pays a tax of sixty sous per annum (2s. 6d., English) is an elector. What will Mr. Burke place against this? Can anything be more limited, and at the same time more capricious, than the qualifications of electors are in England?

The French constitution says that the National Assembly shall be elected every two years. What will Mr. Burke place against this? Why, that the nation has no right at all in the case, and that the government is perfectly arbitrary with respect to this point.

The French constitution says there shall be no game laws, and no monopolies of any kind. What will Mr. Burke say to this? In England, game is made the property of those at whose expense it is not fed; and with respect to monopolies, every chartered town is an aristocratical monopoly in itself, and the qualification of electors proceeds out of these monopolies. Is this freedom? Is this what Mr. Burke means by a constitution?

The French constitution says that to preserve the national representation from being corrupt no member of the National Assembly shall be an officer of the government, a placeman, or a pensioner. What will Mr. Burke place against this? I will whisper his answer: "Loaves and Fishes." Ah! this government of loaves and fishes has more mischief in it than people have yet reflected on. The English Parliament is supposed to hold the national purse in trust for the nation. But if those who vote the supplies are the same persons who receive the supplies when voted, and are to account for the expenditure of those supplies to those who voted them, it is themselves accountable to themselves, and the comedy of errors concludes with the pantomime of hush. Neither the ministerial party nor the opposition will touch upon this case. The national purse is the common hack which each mounts upon. They order these things better in France.

The French constitution says that the right of war and peace is in the nation. Where else should it reside but in those who are to pay the expense? In England this right is said to reside in a metaphor shown at the Tower for sixpence or a shilling a head.

It may with reason be said that in the manner the English nation is represented it signifies not where the right resides, whether in the crown or in the parliament. War is the common harvest of all those who participate in the division and expenditure of public money in all countries. In reviewing the history of the English Government, an impartial bystander would declare that taxes were not raised to carry on wars, but that wars were raised to carry on taxes.

The French constitution says, "There shall be no titles"; and, of consequence, "nobility" is done away, and the peer is exalted into man.

Titles are but nicknames, and every nickname is a title. The thing is perfectly harmless in itself, but it marks a sort of foppery in the human character which degrades it. If no mischief had annexed itself to the folly of titles, they would not have been worth a serious and formal destruction. Let us, then, examine the grounds upon which the French constitution has resolved against having a house of peers in France.

Because, in the first place, aristocracy is kept up by family tyranny and injustice, due to the unnatural and iniquitous law of primogeniture.

Secondly, because the idea of hereditary legislators is as inconsistent as that of hereditary judges or hereditary juries; and as absurd as an hereditary mathematician, or an hereditary wise man; and as ridiculous as an hereditary poet-laureate.

Thirdly, because a body of men, holding themselves accountable to nobody, ought not to be trusted by anybody.

Fourthly, because it is continuing the uncivilized principle of government founded in conquest, and the base idea of man having property in man, and governing him by personal right.

The French constitution hath abolished or renounced toleration and intolerance also, and hath established universal right of conscience.

Toleration is not the opposite of intolerance, but is the counterfeit of it. Both are despotisms. The one assumes to itself the right of withholding liberty of conscience, and the other of granting it. Who art thou, vain dust and ashes! by whatever name thou art called, whether a king, a bishop, a church, or a state, a parliament, or anything else, that obtrudest thine insignificance between the soul of man and its Maker? Mind thine own concerns. If he believes not as thou believest, it is a proof that thou believest not as he believes, and there is no earthly power can determine between you.

The opinions of men with respect to government are changing fast in all countries. The revolutions of America and France have thrown a beam of light over the world, which reaches into men. Ignorance is of a peculiar nature; once dispelled, it is impossible to re-establish it. It is not originally a thing of itself, but is only the absence of knowledge; and though man may be kept ignorant, he cannot be made ignorant.

When we survey the wretched condition of man, under the monarchical and hereditary systems of government, dragged from his home by one power, or driven by another, and impoverished by taxes more than by enemies, it becomes evident that these systems are bad, and that a general revolution in the principle and construction of governments is necessary.

And it is not difficult to perceive, from the enlightened state of mankind, that hereditary governments are verging to their decline, and that revolutions on the broad basis of national sovereignty and government by representation are making their way in Europe; it would be an act of wisdom to anticipate their approach and produce revolutions by reason and accommodation, rather than commit them to the issue of convulsions.

The Old and New Systems

The danger to which the success of revolutions is most exposed is in attempting them before the principles on which they proceed, and the advantages to result from them are sufficiently understood. Almost everything appertaining to the circumstances of a nation has been absorbed and confounded under the general and mysterious word government. It may, therefore, be of use in this day of revolutions to discriminate between those things which are the effect of government, and those which are not.

Great part of that order which reigns among mankind is not the effect of government. It has its origin in the principles of society and the natural constitution of man. The mutual dependence and reciprocal interest which man has upon man, and all the parts of civilized community upon each other, create that great chain of connection which holds it together. In fine, society performs for itself almost everything which is ascribed to government, which is no farther necessary than to supply the few cases to which society and civilization are not conveniently competent.

The more perfect civilization is, the less occasion has it for government, because the more does it regulate its own affairs, and govern itself. All the great laws of society are laws of nature. They are followed and obeyed because it is the interest of the parties to do so, and not on account of any formal laws their governments may impose. But how often is the natural propensity to society disturbed or destroyed by the operations of government! When the latter, instead of being ingrafted on the principles of the former, assumes to exist for itself, and acts by partialities of favor and oppression, it becomes the cause of the mischiefs it ought to prevent.

It is impossible that such governments as have hitherto existed in the world would have commenced by any other means than a total violation of every principle, sacred and moral. The obscurity in which the origin of all the present old governments is buried implies the iniquity and disgrace with which they began. What scenes of horror present themselves in contemplating the character and reviewing the history of such governments! If we would delineate human nature with a baseness of heart and hypocrisy of countenance that reflection would shudder at and humanity disown, they are kings, courts, and cabinets that must sit for the portrait. Man, naturally as he is, with all his faults about him, is not up to the character.

Government on the old system is an assumption of power, for the aggrandizement of itself; on the new a delegation of power for the common benefit of society. The one now called the old is hereditary, either in whole or in part, and the new is entirely representative. It rejects all hereditary government:

First, as being an imposition on mankind.

Secondly, as inadequate to the purposes for which government is necessary.

All hereditary government is in its nature tyranny. To inherit a government is to inherit the people, as if they were flocks and herds. Kings succeed each other, not as rationals, but as animals. It signifies not what their mental or moral characters are. Monarchical government appears under all the various characters of childhood, decrepitude, dotage; a thing at nurse, in leading-strings, or in crutches. In short, we cannot conceive a more ridiculous figure of government than hereditary succession. By continuing this absurdity, man is perpetually in contradiction with himself; he may accept for a king, or a chief magistrate, or a legislator a person whom he would not elect for a constable.

The representative system takes society and civilization for its basis; nature, reason, and experience for its guide. The original simple democracy was society governing itself without the aid of secondary means. By ingrafting representation upon democracy we arrive at a system of government capable of embracing and confederating all the various interests and every extent of territory and population; and that also with advantages as much inferior to hereditary government, as the republic of letters is to hereditary literature.

Considering government in the only light in which it should be considered, that of a national association, it ought to be constructed as not to be disordered by any accident happening among the parts, and, therefore, no extraordinary power should be lodged in the hands of any individual. Monarchy would not have continued so many ages in the world had it not been for the abuses it protects. It is the master-fraud which shelters all others. By admitting a participation of the spoil, it makes itself friends; and when it ceases to do this it will cease to be the idol of courtiers.

One of the greatest improvements that have been made for the perpetual security and progress of constitutional liberty is the provision which the new constitutions make for occasionally revising, altering, and amending them. The best constitutions that could now be devised consistently with the condition of the present moment, may be far short of that excellence which a few years may afford. There is a morning of reason rising upon man on the subject of governments that has not appeared before. Just emerging from such a barbarous condition, it is too soon to determine to what extent of improvement government may yet be carried. For what we can foresee, all Europe may form but one great republic, and man be free of the whole.

The Reform of England

As it is necessary to include England in the prospect of general reformation, it is proper to inquire into the defects of its government. It is only by each nation reforming its own, that the whole can be improved and the full benefit of reformation enjoyed.

When in countries that are called civilized we see age going to the workhouse and youth to the gallows something must be wrong in the system of government. Why is it that scarcely any are executed but the poor? The fact is a proof, among other things, of a wretchedness in their condition. Bred up without morals, and cast upon the world without a prospect, they are the exposed sacrifice of vice and legal barbarity.

The first defect of English government I shall mention is the evil of those Gothic institutions, the corporation towns. As one of the houses of the English Parliament is, in a great measure, made up of elections from these corporations, and as it is unnatural that a pure stream should flow from a foul fountain, its vices are but a continuation of the vices of its origin. A man of moral honor and good political principles cannot submit to the mean drudgery and disgraceful arts by which such elections are carried.

I proceed in the next place to the aristocracy. The house of peers is simply a combination of persons in one common interest. No better reason can be given why a house of legislation should be composed entirely of men whose occupation consists in letting landed property, than why it should be composed of brewers, of bakers, or any other separate class of men. What right has the landed interest to a distinct representation from the general interest of the nation? The only use to be made of its power is to ward off the taxes from itself, and to throw the burden upon such articles of consumption by which itself would be least affected.

I proceed to what is called the crown. It signifies a nominal office of a million sterling a year, the business of which consists in receiving the money. Whether the person be wise or foolish, sane or insane, a native or a foreigner, matters not. The hazard to which this office is exposed in all countries is not from anything that can happen to the man, but from what may happen to the nation—the danger of its coming to its senses.

I shall now turn to the matter of lessening the burden of taxes. The amount of taxation now levied may be taken in round numbers at £17,000,000, nine millions of which are appropriated to the payment of interest on the national debt, and eight millions to the current expenses of each year.

All circumstances taken together, arising from the French revolution, from the approaching harmony of the two nations, the abolition of court intrigue on both sides, and the progress of knowledge in the science of governing, the annual expenditure might be put back to one million and a half—half a million each for Navy, Army, and expenses of government.

Three hundred representatives fairly elected are sufficient for all the purposes to which legislation can apply. They may be divided into two or three houses, or meet in one, as in France. If an allowance of £500 per annum were made to each representative, the yearly cost would be £15,000. The expense of the official departments could not reasonably exceed £425,000. All revenue officers are paid out of the moneys they collect, and therefore are not in this estimation.

Taking one million and a half as a sufficient peace establishment for all the honest purposes of government, there will remain a surplus of upwards of six millions out of the present current expenses. How is this surplus to be disposed of?

The first step would be to abolish the poor rates entirely, and in lieu thereof to make a remission of taxes to the poor of double the amount of the present poor rates—*viz.*, four millions annually out of the surplus taxes. This money could be distributed so as to provide £4 annually per head for the support of children of poor families, and to provide also for the cost of education of over a million children; to give annuities of £10 each for the aged poor over sixty, and of £6 each for the poor over fifty; to give donations of £1 each on occasions of births in poor families, and marriages of the poor; to make allowances for funeral expenses of persons traveling for work, and dying at a distance from their friends; and to furnish employment for the casual poor of the metropolis, where modes of relief are necessary that are not required in the country.

Of the sum remaining after these deductions, half a million should be spent in pensioning disbanded soldiers and in increasing the pay of the soldiers who shall remain. The burdensome house and window tax, amounting to over half a million annually, should be taken off. There yet remains over a million surplus, which might be used for special purposes, or applied to relief of taxation as circumstances require.

For the commutation tax there should be substituted an estate tax rising from 3d. in the pound on the first £500 to 20s. in the pound on the twenty-third £1,000. Every thousand beyond the twenty-third would thus produce no profit but by dividing the estate, and thereby would be extirpated the overgrown influence arising from the unnatural law of primogeniture.

Of all nations in Europe there is none so much interested in the French revolution as England. Enemies for ages, the opportunity now presents itself of amicably closing the scene and joining their efforts to reform the rest of Europe. Such an alliance, together with that of Holland, could propose with effect a general dismantling of all the navies in Europe, to a certain proportion to be agreed upon. This will save to France and England at least two million sterling annually to each, and their relative force would be in the same proportion as it is now. Peace, which costs nothing, is attended with infinitely more advantage than any victory with all its expense.

Never did so great an opportunity offer itself to England, and to all Europe, as is produced by the two revolutions of America and France. By the former, freedom has a national champion in the western world, and by the latter in Europe. When another nation shall join France, despotism and bad government will scarcely dare to appear. The present age will hereafter merit to be called the Age of Reason, and the present generation will appear to the future as the Adam of a new world.

Thomas Jefferson
(1743–1826)

THE DECLARATION OF INDEPENDENCE

When, in the course of human events, it becomes necessary for one people to dissolve the political bands which have connected them with another, and to assume among the powers of the earth the separate and equal station to which the laws of nature and of nature's God entitle them, a decent respect to the opinions of mankind requires that they should declare the causes which impel them to the separation.

We hold these truths to be self-evident: that all men are created equal; that they are endowed by their Creator with inherent and inalienable rights; that among these are life, liberty, and the pursuit of happiness; that to secure these rights, governments are instituted among men, deriving their just powers from the consent of the governed; that whenever any form of government becomes destructive of these ends, it is the right of the people to alter or to abolish it, and to institute new government, laying its foundation on such principles, and organizing its powers in such form, as to them shall seem most likely to effect their safety and happiness. Prudence, indeed, will dictate that governments long established should not be changed for light and transient causes; and accordingly all experience hath shown that mankind are more disposed to suffer while evils are sufferable, than to right themselves by abolishing the forms to which they are accustomed. But when a long train of abuses and usurpations, begun at a distinguished period and pursuing invariably the same object, evinces a design to reduce them under absolute despotism, it is their right, it is their duty to throw off such government, and to provide new guards for their future security. Such has been the patient sufferance of these colonies; and such is now the necessity which constrains them to expunge their former systems of government. The history of the present king of Great Britain is a history of unremitting injuries and usurpations, among which appears no solitary fact to contradict the uniform tenor of the rest, but all have in direct object the establishment of an absolute tyranny over these states. To prove this, let facts be submitted to a candid world for the truth of which we pledge a faith yet unsullied by falsehood.

He has refused his assent to laws the most wholesome and necessary for the public good.

He has forbidden his governors to pass laws of immediate and pressing importance, unless suspended in their operation till his assent should be obtained; and, when so suspended, he has utterly neglected to attend to them.

He has refused to pass other laws for the accommodation of large districts of people, unless those people would relinquish the right of representation in the legislature, a right inestimable to them, and formidable to tyrants only.

He has called together legislative bodies at places unusual, uncomfortable, and distant from the depository of their public records, for the sole purpose of fatiguing them into compliance with his measures.

He has dissolved representative houses repeatedly and continually for opposing with manly firmness his invasions on the rights of the people.

He has refused for a long time after such dissolutions to cause others to be elected, whereby the legislative powers, incapable of annihilation, have returned to the people at large for their exercise, the state remaining, in the meantime, exposed to all the dangers of invasion from without and convulsions within.

He has endeavored to prevent the population of these states; for that purpose obstructing the laws for naturalization of foreigners, refusing to pass others to encourage their migrations hither, and raising the conditions of new appropriations of lands.

He has suffered the administration of justice totally to cease in some of these states, refusing his assent to laws for establishing judiciary powers.

He has made our judges dependent on his will alone for the tenure of their offices, and the amount and payment of their salaries.

He has erected a multitude of new offices, by a self-assumed power, and sent hither swarms of new officers to harass our people and eat out their substance.

He has kept among us in times of peace standing armies and ships of war without the consent of our legislatures.

He has affected to render the military independent of, and superior to, the civil power.

He has combined with others to subject us to a jurisdiction foreign to our constitutions and unacknowledged by our laws, giving his assent to their acts of pretended legislation for quartering large bodies of armed troops among us; for protecting them by a mock trial from punishment for any murders which they should commit on the inhabitants of these states; for cutting off our trade with all parts of the world; for imposing taxes on us without our consent; for depriving us of the benefits of trial by jury; for transporting us beyond seas to be tried for pretended offenses; for abolishing the free system of English laws in a neighboring province, establishing therein an arbitrary government, and enlarging its boundaries, so as to render it at once an example and fit instrument for introducing the same absolute rule into these states; for taking away our charters, abolishing our most valuable laws, and altering fundamentally the forms of our governments; for suspending our own legislatures, and declaring themselves invested with power to legislate for us in all cases whatsoever.

He has abdicated government here withdrawing his governors, and declaring us out of his allegiance and protection.

He has plundered our seas, ravaged our coasts, burnt our towns, and destroyed the lives of our people.

He is at this time transporting large armies of foreign mercenaries to complete the works of death, desolation, and tyranny already begun with circumstances of cruelty and perfidy unworthy the head of a civilized nation.

He has constrained our fellow citizens taken captive on the high seas, to bear arms against their country, to become the executioners of their friends and brethren, or to fall themselves by their hands.

He has endeavored to bring on the inhabitants of our frontiers, the merciless Indian savages, whose known rule of warfare is an undistinguished destruction of all ages, sexes, and conditions of existence.

He has incited treasonable insurrections of our fellow citizens, with the allurements of forfeiture and confiscation of our property.

He has waged cruel war against human nature itself, violating its most sacred rights of life and liberty in the persons of a distant people who never offended him, captivating and carrying them into slavery in another hemisphere, or to incur miserable death in their transportation thither. This piratical warfare, the opprobrium of infidel powers, is the warfare of the Christian king of Great Britain. Determined to keep open a market where men should be bought and sold, he has prostituted his negative for suppressing every legislative attempt to prohibit or to restrain this execrable commerce. And that this assemblage of horrors might want no fact of distinguished die, he is now exciting those very people to rise in arms among us, and to purchase that liberty of which he has deprived thereby murdering the people on whom he also obtruded them: thus paying off former crimes committed against the liberties of one people, with crimes which he urges them to commit against the lives of another.

In every stage of these oppressions we have petitioned for redress in the most humble terms: our repeated petitions have been answered only by repeated injuries.

A prince whose character is thus marked by every act which may define a tyrant is unfit to be the ruler of a people who mean to be free. Future ages will scarcely believe that the hardiness of one man adventured, within the short compass of twelve years only, to lay a foundation so broad and so undisguised for tyranny over a people fostered and fixed in principles of freedom.

Nor have we been wanting in attentions to our British brethren. We have warned them from time to time of attempts by their legislature to extend a jurisdiction over these our states. We have reminded them of the circumstances of our emigration and settlement here, no one of which could warrant so strange a pretension; that these were effected at the expense of our own blood and treasure, unassisted by the wealth or the strength of Great Britain; that in constituting indeed our several forms of government, we had adopted one common king, thereby laying a foundation for perpetual league and amity with them; but that submission to their Parliament was no part of our constitution, nor ever in idea, if history may be credited; and, we appealed to their native justice and magnanimity as well as to the ties of our common kindred to disavow these usurpations which were likely to interrupt our connection and correspondence. They too have been deaf to the voice of justice and of consanguinity, and when occasions have been given them, by the regular course of their laws, of removing from their councils the disturbers of our harmony, they have, by their free election, reestablished them in power. At this very time too, they are permitting their chief magistrate to send over not only soldiers of our common blood, but Scots and foreign mercenaries to invade and destroy us. These facts have given the last stab to agonizing affection, and manly spirit bids us to renounce forever these unfeeling brethren. We must endeavor to forget our former love for them, and hold them as we hold the rest of mankind, enemies in war, in peace friends. We might have been a free and a great people together; but a communication of grandeur and of freedom, it seems, is below their dignity. Be it so, since they will have it. The road to happiness and to glory is open to us, too. We will tread it apart from them, and acquiesce in the necessity which denounces our eternal separation.

We, therefore, the representatives of the United States of America in General Congress assembled, do, in the name and by the authority of the good people of these states, reject and renounce all allegiance and subjection to the kings of Great Britain and all others who may hereafter claim by, through, or under them; we utterly dissolve all political connection which may heretofore have subsisted between us and the people or Parliament of Great Britain; and finally we do assert and declare these colonies to be free and independent states, and that as free and independent states, they have full power to levy war, conclude peace, contract alliances, establish commerce, and to do all other acts and things which independent states may of right do.

And for the support of this declaration, we mutually pledge to each other our lives, our fortunes, and our sacred honor.

Georg Wilhelm Friedrich Hegel
(1770–1831)

From

THE PHILOSOPHY OF HISTORY

In the East Began History

Universal or world-history travels from east to west, for Europe is absolutely the end of history, Asia the beginning. The history of the world has an east in an absolute sense, for, although the earth forms a sphere, history describes no orbit round it, but has, on the contrary, a determinate orient—*viz.*, Asia. Here rises the outward visible sun, and in the west it sinks down; here also rises the sun of self-consciousness. The history of the world is a discipline of the uncontrolled natural will, bringing it into obedience to a universal principle and conferring a subjective freedom. The East knew, and to this day knows, freedom only for one; the Greek and Roman world knew that some are free; the German world knows that all are free. The first political form, therefore, that we see in history is despotism; the second democracy and aristocracy; and the third monarchy.

The first phase—that with which we have to begin—is the East. Unreflected consciousness—substantial, objective, spiritual existence—forms the basis; to which the subjective will first sustains a relation in the form of faith, confidence, obedience. In the political life of the East we find realized national freedom, developing itself without advancing to subjective freedom. It is the childhood of history. In the gorgeous edifices of the Oriental empires we find all national ordinances and arrangements, but in such a way that individuals remain as mere accidents. These revolve round a center, round the sovereign, who as patriarch stands (not as despot, in the sense of the Roman imperial constitution) at the head. For he has to enforce the moral and substantial; he has to uphold those essential ordinances which are already established; so that what among us belongs entirely to subjective freedom, here proceeds from the entire and general body of the state.

The glory of the Oriental conception is the one individual as the substantial being to which all belongs, so that no other individual has a separate existence, or mirrors himself in his subjective freedom. All the riches of imagination and nature are appropriated to that dominant existence in which subjective freedom is essentially merged; the latter looks for its dignity not in itself but in the absolute object. All the elements of a complete state—even subjectivity—may be found there, but not yet harmonized with the grand substantial being. For outside the one power—before which nothing can maintain an independent existence—there is only revolting caprice, which, beyond the limits of the central power, moves at will without purpose or result.

Accordingly we find the wild herds breaking out from the upland, falling upon the countries in question and laying them waste, or settling down in them and giving up their wild life; but in all cases lost resultlessly in the central substance.

This phase of substantiality, since it has not taken up its antithesis into itself and overcome it, directly divides itself into two elements. On the one side we see duration, stability—empires belonging, as it were, to mere Space (as distinguished from Time); unhistorical history, as, for example, in China, the state based on the family relation. Yet the states in question, without undergoing any change in themselves, or in the principle of their existence, are constantly changing their opinion towards each other. They are in ceaseless conflict, which brings on rapid destruction. The opposing principle of individuality enters into these conflicting relations; but it is itself as yet only unconscious, merely natural universality—light which is not yet the light of the personal soul. This history, too, is for the most part really unhistorical, for it is only the repetition of the same majestic ruin.

The new element which, in the shape of bravery, prowess, magnanimity, occupies the place of the previous despotic pomp goes through the same cycle of decline and subsidence. And this subsidence, therefore, is not really such; for through all this restless change no advance has been made. History passes at this point—and only outwardly, that is, without connection with the previous phase—to Central Asia. To carry on the comparison with the individual man, this would be the boyhood of history, no longer manifesting the repose and trustfulness of the child, but boisterous and turbulent.

Greece, Rome and Christianity

The Greek world may, then, be compared to the season of adolescence, for here we have individualities shaping themselves. This is the second main principle in human history. Morality is, as in Asia, a principle, but it is morality impressed on individuality, and consequently denoting the free volition of individuals. Here, then, is the union of the moral with the subjective will, or the kingdom of beautiful freedom, for the idea is united with a plastic form. It is not yet regarded abstractly, but intimately bound up with the real, as in a beautiful work of art; the sensible bears the stamp and expression of the spiritual. The kingdom is consequently true harmony; it is a world of the most charming but perishable, or quickly passing, bloom; it is the natural, unreflecting observance of what is becoming—not yet true morality; The individual will of the subject adopts without reflection the conduct and habit prescribed by justice and the laws. The individual is, therefore, in unconscious unity with the idea—the social weal.

The third phase is the realm of abstract universality (in which the social aim absorbs all individual aims); it is the Roman state, the severe labors of the manhood of history. For true manhood acts neither in accordance with the caprice of a despot nor in obedience to a graceful caprice of its own. It works for a general aim, one in which the individual perishes and realizes his own private object only in that general aim. The state begins to have an abstract existence and to develop itself for a definite object, in accomplishing which its members have indeed a share, but not a complete and concrete one (calling their whole being into play). Free individuals are sacrificed to the severe demands of the national ends, to which they must surrender themselves in this service of abstract generalization. The Roman state is not a repetition of such a state of individuals as was the Athenian *polis*. The geniality and joy of soul that existed there have given place to harsh and rigorous toil. The interest of history is detached from individuals.

But when, subsequently, in the historical development, individuality gains the ascendant, and the breaking up of the community into its component atoms can be restrained only by external compulsion, then the subjective might of individual despotism comes forward to play its part. The individual is led to seek consolation for the loss of his freedom in exercising and developing his private rights. In the next place, the pain inflicted by despotism begins to be felt, and spirit, driven back into its utmost depths, leaves the godless world, seeks for a harmony in itself, and begins now an inner life—a complete concrete subjectivity, which at the same time possesses a substantiality that is not grounded in mere external existence.

Within the soul, therefore, arises the spiritual solution of the struggle, in the fact that the individual personality, instead of following its own capricious choice, is purified and elevated into universality—a subjectivity that of its own free will adopts principles tending to the good of all, reaches, in fact, a divine personality. To the worldly empire this spiritual one wears a predominant aspect of opposition, as the empire of subjectivity that has attained to the knowledge of itself—itself in its essential nature—the empire of spirit in its full sense.

The Christian community found itself in the Roman world, but as it was secluded from this state, and did not hold the emperor for its absolute sovereign, it was the object of persecution. Then was manifested its inward liberty in the steadfastness with which sufferings were borne. As regards its relation to the truth, the fathers of the Church built up the dogma, but a chief element was furnished by the previous development of philosophy. Just as Philo found a deeper import shadowed forth in the Mosaic record and idealized what he considered the bare shell of the narrative, so also did the Christians treat their records.

It was through the Christian religion that the absolute idea of God, in its true conception, attained consciousness. Here man, too, finds himself comprehended in his true nature, given in the specific conception of "the Son." Man, finite when regarded for himself, is yet at the same time the image of God and a fountain of infinity in himself. Consequently he has his true home in a super-sensuous world—an infinite subjectivity, gained only by a rupture with mere natural existence and volition. This is religious self-consciousness.

The first abstract principles are won by the instrumentality of the Christian religion for the secular state. First, under

Christianity slavery is impossible; for man as man—in the
abstract essence of his nature—is contemplated in God; each
unit of mankind is an object of the grace of God and of the
divine purpose. Utterly excluding all specialty, therefore, man,
in and for himself—in his simple quality of man—has infinite
value; and this infinite value abolishes, *ipso facto,* all particularity attaching to birth or country.

The other, the second principle, regards the subjectivity of
man in its bearing on chance. Humanity has this sphere of free
spirituality in and for itself, and everything else must proceed
from it. The place appropriated to the abode and presence of
the Divine Spirit—the sphere in question—is spiritual subjectivity, and is constituted the place in which all contingency is
amenable. It follows, thence, that what we observe among the
Greeks as a form of customary morality cannot maintain its
position in the Christian world. For that morality is spontaneous, unreflected wont; while the Christian principle is independent subjectivity—the soil on which grows the True.

Now, an unreflected morality cannot continue to hold its
ground against the principle of subjective freedom. Now the
principle of absolute freedom in God makes its appearance.
Man no longer sustains the relation of dependence, but of
love—in the consciousness that he is a partaker in the Divine
existence.

The Germanic World

The German world appears at this point of development—the
fourth phase of world history. The old age of nature is weakness; but this of spirit is its perfect maturity and strength, in
which it returns to unity with itself, but in its fully developed
character as spirit.

The Greeks and Romans had reached maturity within ere
they directed their energies outwards. The Germans, on the
contrary, began with self-diffusion, deluging the world, and
breaking down in their course the hollow political fabrics of the
civilized nations. Only then did their development begin, kin-
dled by a foreign culture, a foreign religion, polity, and legislation. The process of culture they underwent consisted in taking
up foreign elements into their own national life.

The German world took up the Roman culture and religion in their completed form. The Christian religion which it adopted had received from councils and fathers of the Church—who possessed the whole culture, and in particular the philosophy of the Greek and Roman world—a perfected dogmatic system. The Church, too, had a completely developed hierarchy. To the native tongue of the Germans the Church likewise opposed one perfectly developed—the Latin. In art and philosophy a similar alien influence predominated. The same principle holds good in regard to the form of the secular sovereignty. Gothic and other chiefs gave themselves the name of Roman patricians. Thus, superficially, the German world appears to be a continuation of the Roman. But there dwelt in it an entirely new spirit—the free spirit which reposes on itself.

The three periods of this world will have to be treated accordingly.

The first period begins with the appearance of the German nations in the Roman Empire. The Christian world presents itself as Christendom—one mass of which, the spiritual and the secular, form only different aspects. This epoch extends to Charlemagne. In the second period the Church develops for itself a theocracy and the state a feudal monarchy. Charlemagne had formed an alliance with the Holy See against the Lombards and the factions of the nobles in Rome. A union thus arose between the spiritual and the secular power, and a kingdom of heaven on earth promised to follow in the wake of this conciliation. But just at this time, instead of a spiritual kingdom of heaven, the inwardness of the Christian principle wears the appearance of being altogether directed outwards, and leaving its proper sphere.

Christian freedom is perverted to its very opposite, both in a religious and secular respect; on the one hand to the severest bondage, on the other to the most immoral excess—a barbarous intensity of every passion. The first half of the sixteenth century marks the beginning of the third period. Secularity appears now as gaining a consciousness of its intrinsic worth; it becomes aware that it possesses a value of its own in the morality, rectitude, probity, and activity of man. The consciousness of independent validity is aroused through the restoration of Christian freedom.

The Christian principle has now passed through the terrible

discipline of culture, and it first attains truth and reality through the Reformation. This third period extends to our own times. The principle of free spirit is here made the banner of the world, and from this principle are evolved the universal axioms of reason. Formal thought—the understanding—had been already developed, but thought received its true material first with the Reformation. From that Epoch thought began to gain a culture properly its own; principles were derived from it which were to be the norm for the constitution of the state. Political life was now to be consciously regulated by reason. Customary morality, traditional usage, lost their validity; the various claims insisted upon must prove their legitimacy as based on rational principles.

These epochs may be compared with the earlier empires. In the German eon, as the realm of totality, we see the earlier epochs resumed. Charlemagne's time may be compared with the Persian Empire; it is the period of substantive unity, this unity having its foundation in the inner man, the heart, and both in the spiritual and the secular still abiding in its simplicity. To the Greek world and its merely ideal unity the time preceding Charles V answers, where real unity no longer exists, because all phases of particularity have become fixed in privileges and peculiar rights. As, in the interior of the realms themselves, the different estates of the realm, with their several claims, are isolated, so do the various states in their foreign aspects occupy a merely external relation one to another. A diplomatic policy arises which, in the interest of a European balance of power, unites them with and against each other. It is the time in which the world becomes clear and manifest to all (discovery of America).

So, too, does consciousness gain clearness in the super-sensuous world, and respecting it. Substantial objective religion brings itself to sensuous clearness in the sensuous element (Christian art), and also becomes clear to itself in the element of inmost truth. We may compare this time with that of Pericles. The introversion of spirit begins (Socrates—Luther), though Pericles is wanting in this epoch. Charles V possesses enormous possibilities in point of outward appliances, and appears absolute in his power; but the inner spirit of Pericles, and therefore the absolute means of establishing a free sovereignty, is not in him. This is the epoch when spirit becomes clear to itself in separations occurring in the realm of reality; now the distinct elements of the German world manifest their essential nature.

The third epoch may be compared to the Roman world. The authority of national aim is acknowledged, and privileges melt away before the common object of the state.

Modern Times

Spirit at last perceives that nature—the world—must be an embodiment of reason. An interest in the contemplation and comprehension of the present world became universal. Thus experimental science became the science of the world; for experimental science involves, on the one hand, the observation of phenomena; on the other hand, also the discovery of the law, the essential being, the hidden force, that causes those phenomena—thus reducing the data supplied by observation to their simple principles. Intellectual consciousness was first extricated by Descartes from that sophistry of thought which unsettles everything. As it was the purely German nations among whom the principle of spirit first manifested itself, so it was by the Romanic nations that the abstract idea was first comprehended.

Experimental science, therefore, very soon made its way among them, in common with the Protestant English, but especially among the Italians. It seemed to men as if God had but just created the moon and stars, plants and animals; as if the laws of the universe were now established for the first time; for only then did they feel a real interest in the universe when they recognized their own reason in the reason that pervades it. The human eye became clear, perception quick, thought active and interpretative. The discovery of the laws of nature enabled men to contend against the monstrous superstition of the time, as also against all notions of mighty alien powers which magic alone could conquer.

The independent authority of subjectivity was maintained against belief founded on authority, and the laws of nature were recognized as the only bond connecting phenomena with phenomena. Man is at home in nature, and that alone passes for truth in which he finds himself at home; he is free through the acquaintance he has gained with nature.

Nor was thought less vigorously directed to the spiritual side. Right and social morality came to be looked upon as having their foundation in the actual present will of man, whereas formerly it was referred only to the command of God enjoined *ab extra*, written in the Old or New Testament, or appearing in the form of particular right, as opposed to that based on general principles, in old parchments as *privilegia*, or in international compacts. Luther had secured to mankind spiritual freedom, and the reconciliation of the objective and the subjective in the concrete. He had triumphantly established the position that man's eternal destiny must be wrought out in himself. But the import of that which is to take place in him—what truth is to become vital to him—was taken for granted by Luther, as something already given, something revealed by religion. Now the principle was set up that this import must be capable of actual investigation, and that to this basis of inward demonstration every dogma must be referred.

This is the point which consciousness has attained, and these are the principal phases of that form in which the principle of freedom has realized itself, for the history of the world is nothing but the development of the idea of freedom. But objective freedom—the laws of "real" freedom—demands the subjugation of the mere contingent will, for this is in its nature formal. If the objective is in itself rational, human insight and conviction must correspond with the reason which it embodies, and then we have the other essential element—subjective freedom—also realized. We have confined ourselves to the consideration of that progress of the idea which has led to this consummation. Philosophy concerns itself only with the glory of the idea mirroring itself in the history of the world, and with the development which the idea has passed through in realizing itself—*i.e.*, the idea of freedom, whose reality is the consciousness of freedom and nothing short of it.

That the history of the world, with all the changing scenes which its annals present, is this true process of development and the realization of spirit—this is the true *Theodikaia*, the justification of God in history. The spirit of man may be reconciled with the course of universal history only by perception of this truth—that all which has happened, all that happens daily, is not only not without God, but is essentially His work.

Arthur Schopenhauer

(1788–1860)

From

THE WORLD AS WILL AND IDEA

The World as Idea

"The world is my idea," is a truth valid for every living creature, though only man can consciously contemplate it. In doing so he attains philosophical wisdom. No truth is more absolutely certain than that all that exists for knowledge, and therefore this whole world, is only object in relation to subject, perception of a perceiver, in a word, idea. The world is idea.

This truth is by no means new; it lay by implication in the reflections of Descartes; but Berkeley first distinctly enunciated it; while Kant erred by ignoring it. So ancient is it that it was the fundamental principle of the Indian Vedanta, as Sir William Jones points out. In one aspect the world is idea; in the other aspect, the world is will.

That which knows all things and is known by none is the subject; and for this subject all exists. But the world as idea consists of two essential and inseparable halves. One half is the object, whose form consists of time and space, and through these of multiplicity; but the other half is the subject, lying not in space and time, for it subsists whole and undivided in every reflecting being. Thus any single individual endowed with the faculty of perception of the object, constitutes the whole world of idea as completely as the millions in existence; but let this single individual vanish, and the whole world as idea would disappear. Each of these halves possesses meaning and existence only in and through the other, appearing with and vanishing with it. Where the object begins the subject ends. One of Kant's great merits is that he discovered that the essential and universal forms of all objects—space, time, causality—lie *a priori* in our consciousness, for they may be discovered and fully known from a consideration of the subject, without any knowledge of the object.

Ideas of perception are distinct from abstract ideas. The former comprehend the whole world of experience; the latter are concepts, and are possessed by man alone amongst all creatures on earth; and the capacity for these, distinguishing him from the lower animals, is called reason.

Time and space can each be mentally presented separately from matter, but matter cannot be thought of apart from time and space. The combination of time and space in connection with matter constitutes action, that is, causation. The law of causation arises from change, that is from the fact that at the same part of space there is now one thing and then another, and this succession must be the result of some law of causality, seeing that there must be a determined part of space and a determined part of space for the change. Causality thus combines space with time.

Much vain controversy has arisen concerning the reality of the external universe, owing to the fallacious notion that because perception arises through the knowledge of causality, the relation of subject and object is that of cause and effect. For this relation only subsists between objects, that is between the immediate object and objects known indirectly. The object always presupposes the subject, and so there can be between those two no relation of reason and consequent. Therefore the controversy between realistic dogmatism and doctrinal skepticism is foolish. The former seeks to separate object and idea as cause and effect, whereas these two are really one; the latter supposes that in the idea we have only the effect, never the cause, and never know the real being, but merely its action. The correction of both these fallacies is the same, that object and idea are identical.

One of the most pressing of questions is, how certainty is to be reached, how judgments are to be established, and wherein knowledge and science consist. Reason is feminine in nature; it can only give after it has received. Of itself it possesses only the empty forms of its operation. Knowledge is the result of reason, so that we cannot accurately say that the lower animals know anything, but only that they apprehend through the faculty of perception.

The greatest value of knowledge is that it can be communicated and retained. This makes it inestimably important for practice. Rational or abstract knowledge is that knowledge which is peculiar to the reason as distinguished from the understanding. The use of reason is that it substitutes abstract concepts for ideas of perception, and adopts them as the guide of action.

The many-sided view of life which man, as distinguished from the lower animals, possesses through reason, makes him stand to them as the captain, equipped with chart, compass and quadrant, and with a knowledge of navigation of the ocean, stands to the ignorant sailors under his command.

Man lives two lives. Besides his life in the concrete is his life in the abstract. In the former he struggles, suffers, and dies as do the mere animal creatures. But in the abstract he quietly reflects on the plan of the universe as does a captain of a ship on the chart. He becomes in this abstract life of calm reasoning a deliberate observer of those elements which previously moved and agitated his emotions. Withdrawing into this serene contemplation he is like an actor who has played a part on the stage and then withdraws and as one of the audience quietly looks on at other actors energetically performing.

The result of this double life is that human serenity which furnishes so vivid a contrast to the lack of reason in the brutes. Reason has won to a wonderful extent the mastery over the animal nature. The climacteric stage of the mere exercise of reason is displayed in Stoicism, an ethical system which aims primarily not at virtue but at happiness, although this theory inculcates that happiness can be attained only through "ataraxia" (inward quietness or peace of mind), while this can only be gained by virtue. In other words, Zeno, the founder of the Stoic theory, sought to lift man up above the reach of pain and misery. But this use of pure reason involves a painful paradox, seeing that for an ultimate way of escape Stoicism is constrained to prescribe suicide. When compared with the Stoic, how different appear the holy conquerors of the world in Christianity, that sublime form of life which presents to us a picture wherein we see blended perfect virtue and supreme suffering.

The World as Will

We are compelled to further inquiry, because we cannot be satisfied with knowing that we have ideas, and that these are associated with certain laws, the general expression of which is the principle of sufficient reason. We wish to know the significance of our ideas. We ask whether this world is nothing more than a mere idea, not worthy of our notice if it is to pass by us like an empty dream or an airy vision, or whether it is something more substantial.

We can surely never arrive at the nature of things from without. No matter how assiduous our researches may be, we can never reach anything beyond images and names. We resemble a man going round a castle seeking vainly for an entrance and sometimes sketching the facades. And yet this is the method followed by all philosophers before me.

The truth about man is that he is not a pure knowing subject, not a winged cherub without a material body, contemplating the world from without. For he is himself rooted in that world. That is to say, he finds himself in the world as an *individual* whose knowledge, which is the essential basis of the whole world as idea, is yet ever communicated through the medium of the body, whose sensations are the starting point of the understanding of that world. His body is for him an idea like every other idea, an object among objects. He only knows its actions as he knows the changes in all other objects, and but for one aid to his understanding of himself he would find this idea and object as strange and incomprehensible as all others. That aid is *will*, which alone furnishes the key to the riddle of himself, solves the problem of his own existence, reveals to him the inner structure and significance of his being, his action, and his movements.

The body is the immediate object of will; it may be called the *objectivity of will*. Every true act of will is also instantly a visible act of the body, and every impression on the body is also at once an impression on the will. When it is opposed to the will it is called pain, and when consonant with the will it is called pleasure. The essential identity of body and will is shown by the fact that every violent movement of the will, that is to say, every emotion, directly agitates the body and interferes with its vital functions. So we may legitimately say, My body is the objectivity of my will.

It is simply owing to this special relation to one body that the knowing subject is an individual. Our knowing, being bound to individuality, necessitates that each of us can only be one, and yet each of us can know all. Hence arises the need for philosophy. The double knowledge which each of us possesses of his own body is the key to the nature of every phenomenon in the world. Nothing is either known to us or thinkable by us except will and idea. If we examine the reality of the body and its actions, we discover nothing beyond the fact that it is an idea, except the will. With this double discovery reality is exhausted.

We can ascribe no other kind of reality to the material world. If we maintain that it is something more than merely our idea, we must say that in its inmost nature it is that which we discover in ourselves as will. But the acts of will have always a ground or reason outside themselves in motives, which, however, never determine more than how we shall act at any given time or place under any given conditions or circumstances. The will must have some manifestation, and the body is that manifestation. By the movements of the body the will becomes visible, and thus the body may be said to be the *objectification of the will*. The perfect adaptation of the human and animal body to the human and animal will resembles, though it far exceeds, the correspondence between an instrument and its maker.

The World as Idea. Second Aspect

We have looked at the world as idea, object for a subject, and next at the world as will. All students of Plato know that the different grades of objectification of will which are manifested in countless individuals, and exist as their unrealized types or as the eternal forms of things, are the Platonic Ideas. Thus these various grades are related to individual things as their eternal forms or prototypes.

Thus the world in which we live is in its whole nature through and through *will*, and at the same time through and through *idea*. This idea always presupposes a form, object and subject. If we take away this form and ask what then remains, the answer must be that this can be nothing but *will*, which, properly speaking, is the *thing in itself.* Every human being discovers that he himself is this will, and that the world exists only for him does so in relation to his consciousness. Thus each human being is himself in a double aspect the whole world, the microcosm. And that which he realizes as his own real being exhausts the being of the whole world, the macrocosm. So, like man, the world is through and through *will,* and through and through *idea.*

Plato would say that an animal has no true being, but merely an apparent being, a constant becoming. The only true being is the Idea which embodies itself in that animal. That is to say, the Idea of the animal alone has true being, and is the object of real knowledge. Kant, with his theory of "the thing-in-itself" as the only reality, would say that the animal is only a phenomenon in time, space, and causality, which are conditions of our perception, not the thing-in-itself. So the individual as we see it at this particular moment will pass away, without any possibility of our knowing the thing-in-itself, for the knowledge of that is beyond our faculties, and would require another kind of knowledge than that which is possible for us through our understanding.

Thus do these two greatest philosophers of the West differ. The thing-in-itself must, according to Kant, be free from all forms associated with knowing. On the contrary, the Platonic idea is necessarily object, something known and thus different from the thing-in-itself, which cannot be apprehended. Yet Kant and Plato tend to agree, because the thing-in-itself is, after all, that which lays aside all the subordinate forms of phenomena, and has retained the first and most universal form, that of the idea in general, the form of being object for a subject. Plato attributes actual being only to the Ideas, and concedes only an illusive, dream-like existence to things in space and time, the real world for the individual.

The World as Will. Second Aspect

The last and most serious part of our consideration relates to human action and is of universal importance. Human nature tends to relate everything else to action. The world as idea is the perfect mirror of the will, in which it recognizes itself in graduating scales of distinctness and completeness. The highest degree of this consciousness is man, whose nature only completely expresses itself in the whole connected series of his actions.

Will is the thing-in-itself, the essence of the world. Life is only the mirror of the will. Life accompanies the will as the shadow the body. If will exists, so will life. So long as we are actuated by the will to live, we need have no fear of ceasing to live, even in the presence of death. True, we see the individual born and passing away; but the individual is merely phenomenal. Neither the will, nor the subject of cognition, is at all affected by birth or death.

It is not the individual, but only the species, that Nature cares for. She provides for the species with boundless prodigality through the incalculable profusion of seed and the great strength of fructification. She is ever ready to let the individual fall when it had served its end of perpetuating the species. Thus does Nature artlessly express the great truth that only the Ideas, not the individuals, have actual reality and are complete objectivity of the will.

Man is Nature himself, but Nature is only the objectified will to live. So the man who has comprehended this point of view may well console himself when contemplating death for himself or his friends, by turning his eyes to the immortal life of Nature, which he himself is. And thus we see that birth and death both really belong to life and that they take part in that constant mutation of matter which is consistent with the permanence of the species, notwithstanding the transitoriness of the individual.

The Will as Related to Time

Above all, we must not forget that the form of the phenomenon of the will, the form of life in reality, is really only the present, not the future nor the past. No man ever lived in the past, no man will live in the future. The present is the sole form of life in sure possession. The present exists always, together with its content, and both are fixed like the rainbow on the waterfall.

Now all object is the will so far as it has become idea, and the subject is the necessary correlative of the object. But real objects are in the present only. So nothing but conceptions and fancies are included in the past, while the present is the essential form of the phenomenon of the will, and inseparable from it. The present alone is perpetual and immovable. The fountain and support of it is the will to live, or the thing-in-itself, which we are.

Life is certain to the will, and the present is certain to life. Time is like a perpetually revolving globe. The hemisphere which is sinking is like the past, that which is rising is like the future, while the indivisible point at the top is like the actionless present. Or, time is like a running river and the present is a rock on which it breaks but which it cannot remove with itself. Therefore we are not concerned to investigate the past antecedent to life, nor to speculate on the future subsequent to death. We should simply seek to know the present, that being the sole form in which the will manifests itself. Therefore, if we are satisfied with life as it is, we may confidently regard it as endless and banish the fear of death as illusive. Our spirit is of a totally indestructible nature, and its energy endures from eternity to eternity. It is like the sun, which seems to set only to our earthly eyes, but which, in reality, never sets, but shines on unceasingly.

The problem of the freedom of the will is solved by the considerations which have been thus outlined. Since the will is not phenomenon, is not idea or object, but thing-in-itself, is not determined as a consequent through any reason, and knows no necessity, therefore it is *free*. But the person is never free, although he is the phenomenon of a free will, for this indisputable reason, that he is already the determined phenomenon of the free volition of this will, and is constrained to embody the direction of that volition in a multiplicity of actions.

Repentance never results from a change of will, for this is impossible, but from a change of knowledge. The essential in what I have willed I must continue to will, for I am identical with this will which lies outside time and change. Therefore I cannot repent of what I have willed, though I can repent of what I have done; because, constrained by false notions, I was led to do what did not accord with my will. Repentance is simply the discovery of this fuller and more correct knowledge.

Ralph Waldo Emerson

(1803–1882)

Self-Reliance

"Ne te quaesiveris extra."
Man is his own star; and the soul that can
Render an honest and a perfect man,
Commands all light, all influence, all fate;
Nothing to him falls early or too late.
Our acts our angels are, or good or ill,
Our fatal shadows that walk by us still.
—Epilogue to Beaumont and Fletcher's
Honest Man's Fortune

Cast the bantling on the rocks,
Suckle him with the she-wolf's teat,
Wintered with the hawk and fox,
Power and speed be hands and feet.

I read the other day some verses written by an eminent painter which were original and not conventional. The soul always hears an admonition in such lines, let the subject be what it may. The sentiment they instill is of more value than any thought they may contain. To believe your own thought, to believe that what is true for you in your private heart is true for all men—that is genius. Speak your latent conviction, and it shall be the universal sense; for the inmost in due time becomes the outmost, and our first thought is rendered back to us by the trumpets of the Last Judgment. Familiar as the voice of the mind is to each, the highest merit we ascribe to Moses, Plato and Milton is that they set at naught books and traditions, and spoke not what men, but what *they* thought. A man should learn to detect and watch that gleam of light which flashes across his mind from within, more than the luster of the firmament of bards and sages. Yet he dismisses without notice his thought, because it is his. In every work of genius we recognize our own rejected thoughts; they come back to us with a certain alienated majesty. Great works of art have no more affecting lesson for us than this. They teach us to abide by our spontaneous impression with good-humored inflexibility then most when the whole cry of voices is on the other side. Else tomorrow a stranger will say with masterly good sense precisely what we have thought and felt all the time, and we shall be forced to take with shame our own opinion from another.

There is a time in every man's education when he arrives at the conviction that envy is ignorance; that imitation is suicide; that he must take himself for better for worse as his portion; that though the wide universe is full of good, no kernel of nourishing corn can come to him but through his toil bestowed on that plot of ground which is given to him to till. The power which resides in him is new in nature, and none but he knows what that is which he can do, nor does he know until he has tried. Not for nothing one face, one character, one fact, makes much impression on him, and another none. This sculpture in the memory is not without pre-established harmony. The eye was placed where one ray should fall, that it might testify of that particular ray. We but half express ourselves, and are ashamed of that divine idea which each of us represents. It may be safely trusted as proportionate and of good issues, so it be faithfully imparted, but God will not have his work made manifest by cowards. A man is relieved and gay when he has put his heart into his work and done his best; but what he has said or done otherwise shall give him no peace. It is a deliverance which does not deliver. In the attempt his genius deserts him; no muse befriends; no invention, no hope.

Trust thyself: every heart vibrates to that iron string. Accept the place the divine providence has found for you, the society of your contemporaries, the connection of events. Great men have always done so, and confided themselves childlike to the genius of their age, betraying their perception that the absolutely trustworthy was seated at their heart, working through their hands, predominating in all their being. And we are now men, and must accept in the highest mind the same transcendent destiny; and not minors and invalids in a protected corner, not cowards fleeing before a revolution, but guides, redeemers and benefactors, obeying the Almighty effort and advancing on Chaos and the Dark.

What pretty oracles nature yields us on this text in the face and behavior of children, babes, and even brutes! That divided and rebel mind, that distrust of a sentiment because our arithmetic has computed the strength and means opposed to our purpose, these have not. Their mind being whole, their eye is as yet unconquered; and when we look in their faces we are disconcerted. Infancy conforms to nobody; all conform to it; so that one babe commonly makes four or five out of the adults who prattle and play to it. So God has armed youth and puberty and manhood no less with its own piquancy and charm, and made it enviable and gracious and its claims not to be put by, if it will stand by itself. Do not think the youth has no force, because he cannot speak to you and me. Hark! in the next room his voice is sufficiently clear and emphatic. It seems he knows how to speak to his contemporaries. Bashful or bold then, he will know how to make us seniors very unnecessary.

The nonchalance of boys who are sure of a dinner, and would disdain as much as a lord to do or say ought to conciliate one, is the healthy attitude of human nature. A boy is in the parlor what the pit is in the playhouse; independent, irresponsible, looking out from his corner on such people and facts as pass by, he tries and sentences them on their merits, in the swift, summary way of boys, as good, bad, interesting, silly, eloquent, troublesome. He cumbers himself never about consequences, about interests; he gives an independent, genuine verdict. You must court him; he does not court you. But the man is as it were clapped into jail by his Consciousness. As soon as he has once acted or spoken with *éclat* he is a committed person, watched by the sympathy or the hatred of hundreds, whose affections must now enter into his account. There is no Lethe for this. Ah, that he could pass again into his neutrality! Who can thus avoid all pledges and, having observed, observe again from the same unaffected, unbiased, unbribable, unaffrighted innocence— must always be formidable. He would utter opinions on all passing affairs, which being seen to be not private but necessary, would sink like darts into the ear of men and put them in fear.

These are the voices which we hear in solitude, but they grow faint and inaudible as we enter into the world. Society everywhere is in conspiracy against the manhood of every one of its members. Society is a joint-stock company, in which the members agree, for the better securing of his bread to each shareholder, to surrender the liberty and culture of the eater. The virtue in most request is conformity. Self-reliance is its aversion. It loves not realities and creators, but names and customs.

Whoso would be a man, must be a nonconformist. He who would gather immortal palms must not be hindered by the name of goodness, but must explore if it be goodness. Nothing is at last sacred but the integrity of your own mind. Absolve you to yourself, and you shall have the suffrage of the world. I remember an answer which when quite young I was prompted to make to a valued adviser who was wont to importune me with the dear old doctrines of the church. On my saying, "What have I to do with the sacredness of traditions, if I live wholly from within?" my friend suggested—"But these impulses may be from below, not from above." I replied, "They do not seem to me to be such; but if I am the Devil's child, I will live then from the Devil." No law can be sacred to me but that of my nature. Good and bad are but names very readily transferable to that or this; the only right is what is after my constitution; the only wrong what is against it. A man is to carry himself in the presence of all opposition as if every thing were titular and ephemeral but he. I am ashamed to think how easily we capitulate to badges and names, to large societies and dead institutions. Every decent and well-spoken individual affects and sways me more than is right. I ought to go upright and vital, and speak the rude truth in all ways. If malice and vanity wear the coat of philanthropy, shall that pass? If an angry bigot assumes this bountiful cause of Abolition, and comes to me with his last news from Barbados, why should I not say to him, "Go love thy infant; love thy wood-chopper; be good-natured and modest; have that grace; and never varnish your hard, uncharitable ambition with this incredible tenderness for black folk a thousand miles off. Thy love afar is spite at home." Rough and graceless would be such greeting, but truth is handsomer than the affectation of love. Your goodness must have some edge to it—else it is none. The doctrine of hatred must be preached, as the counteraction of the doctrine of love, when that pules and whines. I shun father and mother and wife and brother when my genius calls me. I would write on the lintels of the doorpost, *Whim.* I hope it is somewhat better than whim at last, but we cannot spend the day in explanation. Expect me not to show cause why I seek or why I exclude company. Then again, do not tell me, as a good man did today, of my obligation to put all poor men in good situations. Are they *my* poor? I tell thee, thou foolish philanthropist, that I grudge the dollar, the dime, the cent I give to such men as do not belong to me and to whom I do not belong. There is a class of persons to whom by all spiritual affinity I am bought and sold; for them I will go to prison if need be; but your miscellaneous popular charities; the education at college of fools; the building of meeting-houses to the vain end to which many now stand; alms to sots, and the thousand-fold Relief Societies; though I confess with shame I sometimes succumb and give the dollar, it is a wicked dollar, which by and by I shall have the manhood to withhold.

Virtues are, in the popular estimate, rather the exception than the rule. There is the man *and* his virtues. Men do what is called a good action, as some piece of courage or charity, much as they would pay a fine in expiation of daily nonappearance on parade. Their works are done as an apology or extenuation of their living in the world—as invalids and the insane pay a high board. Their virtues are penances. I do not wish to expiate, but to live. My life is for itself and not for a spectacle. I much prefer that it should be of a lower strain, so it be genuine and equal, than that it should be glittering and unsteady. I wish it to be sound and sweet, and not to need diet and bleeding. I ask primary evidence that you are a man, and refuse this appeal from the man to his actions. I know that for myself it makes no difference whether I do or forbear those actions which are reckoned excellent. I cannot consent to pay for a privilege where I have intrinsic right. Few and mean as my gifts may be, I actually am, and do not need for my own assurance or the assurance of my fellows any secondary testimony.

What I must do is all that concerns me, not what the people think. This rule, equally arduous in actual and in intellectual life, may serve for the whole distinction between greatness and meanness. It is the harder because you will always find those who think they know what is your duty better than you know it. It is easy in the world to live after the world's opinion; it is easy in solitude to live after our own; but the great man is he who in the midst of the crowd keeps with perfect sweetness the independence of solitude.

The objection to conforming to usages that have become

dead to you is that it scatters your force. It loses your time and blurs the impression of your character. If you maintain a dead church, contribute to a dead Bible-society, vote with a great party either for the government or against it, spread your table like base housekeepers—under all these screens I have difficulty to detect the precise man you are: and of course so much force is withdrawn from your proper life. But do your work, and I shall know you. Do your work, and you shall reinforce yourself. A man must consider what a blind-man's-buff is this game of conformity. If I know your sect I anticipate your argument. I hear a preacher announce for his text and topic the expediency of one of the institutions of his church. Do I not know beforehand that not possibly can he say a new and spontaneous word? Do I not know that with all this ostentation of examining the grounds of the institution he will do no such thing? Do I not know that he is pledged to himself not to look but at one side, the permitted side, not as a man, but as a parish minister? He is a retained attorney, and these airs of the bench are the emptiest affectation. Well, most men have bound their eyes with one or another handkerchief, and attached themselves to some one of these communities of opinion. This conformity makes them not false in a few particulars, authors of a few lies, but false in all particulars. Their every truth is not quite true. Their two is not the real two, their four not the real four; so that every word they say chagrins us and we know not where to begin to set them right. Meantime nature is not slow to equip us in the prison-uniform of the party to which we adhere. We come to wear one cut of face and figure, and acquire by degrees the gentlest asinine expression. There is a mortifying experience in particular, which does not fail to wreak itself also in the general history; I mean "the foolish face of praise," the forced smile which we put on in company where we do not feel at ease, in answer to conversation which does not interest us. The muscles, not spontaneously moved but moved by a low usurping willfulness, grow tight about the outline of the face, with the most disagreeable sensation.

For nonconformity the world whips you with its displeasure. And therefore a man must know how to estimate a sour face. The bystanders look askance on him in the public street or in the friend's parlor. If this aversion had its origin in contempt and resistance like his own he might well go home with a sad countenance; but the sour faces of the multitude, like their sweet faces, have no deep cause, but are put on and off as the wind blows and a newspaper directs. Yet is the discontent of the multitude more formidable than that of the senate and the college. It is easy enough for a firm man who knows the world to brook the rage of the cultivated classes. Their rage is decorous and prudent, for they are timid, as being very vulnerable themselves. But when to their feminine rage the indignation of the people is added, when the ignorant and the poor are aroused, when the unintelligent brute force that lies at the bottom of society is made to growl and mow, it needs the habit of magnanimity and religion to treat it godlike as a trifle of no concernment.

The other terror that scares us from self-trust is our consistency; a reverence for our past act or word because the eyes of others have no other data for computing our orbit than our past acts, and we are loath to disappoint them.

But why should you keep your head over your shoulder? Why drag about this corpse of your memory, lest you contradict somewhat you have stated in this or that public place? Suppose you should contradict yourself; what then? It seems to be a rule of wisdom never to rely on your memory alone, scarcely even in acts of pure memory, but to bring the past for judgment into the thousand-eyed present, and live ever in a new day. In your metaphysics you have denied personality to the Deity, yet when the devout motions of the soul come, yield to them heart and life, though they should clothe God with shape and color. Leave your theory, as Joseph his coat in the hand of the harlot, and flee.

A foolish consistency is the hobgoblin of little minds, adored by little statesmen and philosophers and divines. With consistency a great soul has simply nothing to do. He may as well concern himself with his shadow on the wall. Speak what you think now in hard words and tomorrow speak what tomorrow thinks in hard words again, though it contradict every thing you said today.—"Ah, so you shall be sure to be misunderstood."— Is it so bad then to be misunderstood? Pythagoras was misunderstood, and Socrates, and Jesus, and Luther, and Copernicus, and Galileo, and Newton, and every pure and wise spirit that ever took flesh. To be great is to be misunderstood.

I suppose no man can violate his nature. All the sallies of his will are rounded in by the law of his being, as the inequalities of Andes and Himmaleh are insignificant in the curve of the sphere. Nor does it matter how you gauge and try him. A character is like an acrostic or Alexandrian stanza; read it forward, backward, or across, it still spells the same thing. In this pleasing contrite wood-life which God allows me, let me regard day by day my honest thought without prospect or retrospect, and, I cannot doubt, it will be found symmetrical, though I mean it not and see it not. My book should smell of pines and resound with the hum of insects. The swallow over my window should interweave that thread or straw he carries in his bill into my web also. We pass for what we are. Character teaches above our wills. Men imagine that they communicate their virtue or vice only by overt actions, and do not see that virtue or vice emit a breath every moment.

There will be an agreement in whatever variety of actions so they be each honest and natural in their hour. For of one will, the actions will be harmonious, however unlike they seem. These varieties are lost sight of at a little distance, at a little height of thought. One tendency unites them all. The voyage of the best ship is a zigzag line of a hundred tacks. See the line from a sufficient distance, and it straightens itself to the average tendency. Your genuine action will explain itself and will explain your other genuine actions. Your conformity explains nothing. Act singly, and what you have already done singly will justify you now. Greatness appeals to the future. If I can be firm enough today to do right and scorn eyes, I must have done so much right before as to defend me now. Be it how it will, do right now. Always scorn appearances and you always may. The force of character is cumulative. All the foregone days of virtue work their health into this. What makes the majesty of the heroes of the senate and the field, which so fills the imagination? The consciousness of a train of great days and victories behind. They shed a united light on the advancing actor. He is attended as by a visible escort of angels. That is it which throws thunder into Chatham's voice, and dignity into Washington's port, and America into Adams's eye. Honor is venerable to us because it is no ephemera. It is always ancient virtue. We worship it today because it is not of today. We love it and pay it homage because it is not a trap for our love and homage, but is self-dependent, self-derived, and therefore of an old immaculate pedigree, even if shown in a young person.

I hope in these days we have heard the last of conformity and consistency. Let the words be gazetted and ridiculous henceforward. Instead of the gong for dinner, let us hear a whistle from the Spartan life. Let us never bow and apologize more. A great man is coming to eat at my house. I do not wish to please him; I wish that he should wish to please me I will stand here for humanity, and though I would make it kind, I would make it true. Let us affront and reprimand the smooth mediocrity and squalid contentment of the times, and hurl in the face of custom and trade and office, the fact which is the upshot of all history, that there is a great responsible Thinker and Actor working wherever a man works; that a true man belongs to no other time or place, but is the center of things. Where he is, there is nature. He measures you and all men and all events. Ordinarily, everybody in society reminds us of somewhat else, or of some other person. Character, reality, reminds you of nothing else; it takes place of the whole creation. The man must be so much that he must make all circumstances indifferent. Every true man is a cause, a country, and an age; requires infinite spaces and numbers and time fully to accomplish his design; and posterity seem to follow his steps as a train of clients. A man Caesar is born, and for ages after we have a Roman Empire. Christ is born, and millions of minds so grow and cleave to his genius that he is confounded with virtue and the possible of man. An institution is the lengthened shadow of one man; as, Monachism, of the Hermit Antony; the Reformation, of Luther; Quakerism, of Fox; Methodism, of Wesley; Abolition, of Clarkson. Scipio, Milton called "the height of Rome"; and all history resolves itself very easily into the biography of a few stout and earnest persons.

Let a man then know his worth, and keep things under his feet. Let him not peep or steal, or skulk up and down with the air of a charity-boy, a bastard, or an interloper in the world which exists for him. But the man in the street, finding no worth in himself which corresponds to the force which built a tower or sculptured a marble god, feels poor when he looks on these. To him a palace, a statue, or a costly book have an alien and forbidding air, much like a gay equipage, and seem to say like that, "Who are you, Sir?" Yet they all are his, suitors for his notice, petitioners to his faculties that they will come out and take possession. The picture waits for my verdict; it is not to command me, but I am to settle its claims to praise. That popular fable of the sot who was picked up dead-drunk in the street, carried to the duke's house, washed and dressed and laid in the duke's bed, and, on his waking, treated with all obsequious ceremony like the duke, and assured that he had been insane, owes its popularity to the fact that it symbolizes so well the state of man, who is in the world a sort of sot, but now and then wakes up, exercises his reason and finds himself a true prince.

Our reading is mendicant and sycophantic. In history our imagination plays us false. Kingdom and lordship, power and estate, are a gaudier vocabulary than private John and Edward in a small house and common day's work; but the things of life are the same to both; the sum total of both is the same. Why all this deference to Alfred and Scanderbeg and Gustavus? Suppose they were virtuous; did they wear out virtue? As great a stake depends on your private act today as followed their public and renowned steps. When private men shall act with original views, the luster will be transferred from the actions of kings to those of gentlemen.

The world has been instructed by its kings, who have so magnetized the eyes of nations. It has been taught by this colossal symbol the mutual reverence that is due from man to man. The joyful loyalty with which men have everywhere suffered the king, the noble, or the great proprietor to walk among them by a law of his own, make his own scale of men and things and reverse theirs, pay for benefits not with money but with honor, and represent the law in his person, was the hieroglyphic by which they obscurely signified their consciousness of their own right and comeliness, the right of every man.

The magnetism which all original action exerts is explained when we inquire the reason of self-trust. Who is the Trustee? What is the aboriginal Self, on which a universal reliance may be grounded? What is the nature and power of that science-baffling star, without parallax, without calculable elements, which shoots a ray of beauty even into trivial end impure actions, if the least mark of independence appear? The inquiry leads us to that source, at once the essence of genius, of virtue, and of life, which we call Spontaneity or Instinct. We denote this primary wisdom as Intuition, whilst all later teachings are tuitions. In that deep force, the last fact behind which analysis cannot go, all things find their common origin. For the sense of being which in calm hours rises, we know not how, in the soul, is not diverse from things, from space, from light, from time, from man, but one with them and proceeds obviously from the same source whence their life and being also proceed. We first share the life by which things exist and afterwards see them as appearances in nature and forget that we have shared their cause. Here is the fountain of action and of thought. Here are the lungs of that inspiration which giveth man wisdom and which cannot be denied without impiety and atheism. We lie in the lap of immense intelligence, which makes us receivers of its truth and organs of its activity. When we discern justice, when we discern truth, we do nothing of ourselves, but allow a passage to its beams. If we ask whence this comes, if we seek to pry into the soul that causes, all philosophy is at fault. Its presence or its absence is all we can affirm. Every man discriminates between the voluntary acts of his mind and his involuntary perceptions, and knows that to his involuntary perceptions a perfect faith is due. He may err in the expression of them, but he knows that these things are so, like day and night, not to be disputed. My willful actions and acquisitions are but roving; the idlest reverie, the faintest native emotion, command my curiosity and respect. Thoughtless people contradict as readily the statement of perceptions as of opinions, or rather much more readily; for they do not distinguish between perception and notion. They fancy that I choose to see this or that thing. But perception is not whimsical, but fatal. If I see a trait, my children will see it after me, and in course of time all mankind—although it may chance that no one has seen it before me. For my perception of it is as much a fact as the sun.

The relations of the soul to the divine spirit are so pure that it is profane to seek to interpose helps. It must be that when God speaketh he should communicate, not one thing, but all things; should fill the world with his voice; should scatter forth light, nature, time, souls, from the center of the present thought; and new date and new create the whole. Whenever a mind is simple and receives a divine wisdom, old things pass away—means, teachers, texts, temples fall; it lives now, and absorbs past and future into the present hour. All things are made sacred by relation to it—one as much as another. All things are dissolved to their center by their cause, and in the universal miracle petty and particular miracles disappear. If therefore a man claims to know and speak of God and carries you backward to the phraseology of some old moldered nation in another country, in another world, believe him not. Is the acorn better than the oak which is its fullness and completion? Is the parent better than the child into whom he has cast his ripened being? Whence then this worship of the past? The centuries are conspirators against the sanity and authority of the soul. Time and space are but physiological colors which the eye makes, but the soul is light: where it is, is day; where it was, is night; and history is an impertinence and an injury if it be any thing more than a cheerful apologue or parable of my being and becoming.

Man is timid and apologetic; he is no longer upright; he dares not say "I think," "I am," but quotes some saint or sage. He is ashamed before the blade of grass or the blowing rose. These roses under my window make no reference to former roses or to better ones; they are for what they are; they exist with God today. There is no time to them. There is simply the rose; it is perfect in every moment of its existence. Before a leaf-bud has burst, its whole life acts; in the full-blown flower there is no more; in the leafless root there is no less. Its nature is satisfied and it satisfies nature in all moments alike. But man postpones or remembers; he does not live in the present, but with reverted eye laments the past, or, heedless of the riches that surround him, stands on tiptoe to foresee the future. He cannot be happy and strong until he too lives with nature in the present, above time.

This should be plain enough. Yet see what strong intellects dare not yet hear God himself unless he speak the phraseology of I knew not what David, or Jeremiah, or Paul. We shall not always set so great a price on a few texts, on a few lives. We are like children who repeat by rote the sentences of grandames and tutors, and, as they grow older, of the men of talents and character they chance to see—painfully recollecting the exact words they spoke; afterwards, when they come into the point of view which those had who uttered these sayings, they under-stand them and are willing to let the words go; for at any time they can use words as good when occasion comes. If we live truly, we shall see truly. It is as easy for the strong man to be strong, as it is for the weak to be weak. When we have new perception, we shall gladly disburden the memory of its hoarded treasures as old rubbish. When a man lives with God, his voice shall be as sweet as the murmur of the brook and the rustle of the corn.

And now at last the highest truth on this subject remains unsaid; probably cannot be said; for all that we say is the far-off remembering of the intuition. That thought by what I can now nearest approach to say it, is this. When good is near you, when you have life in yourself, it is not by any known or accustomed way; you shall not discern the footprints of any other; you shall not see the face of man; you shall not hear any name; the way, the thought, the good, shall be wholly strange and new. It shall exclude example and experience. You take the way from man, not to man. All persons that ever existed are its forgotten ministers. Fear and hope are alike beneath it. There is somewhat low even in hope. In the hour of vision there is nothing that can be called gratitude, nor properly joy. The soul raised over passion beholds identity and eternal causation, perceives the self-existence of Truth and Right, and calms itself with knowing that all things go well. Vast spaces of nature, the Atlantic Ocean, the South Sea; long intervals of time, years, centuries, are of no account. This which I think and feel underlay every former state of life and circumstances, as it does underlie my present, and what is called life and what is called death.

Life only avails, not the having lived. Power ceases in the instant of repose; it resides in the moment of transition from a past to a new state, in the shooting of the gulf, in the darting to an aim. This one fact the world hates; that the soul *becomes*; for that forever degrades the past, turns all riches to poverty, all reputation to a shame, confounds the saint with the rogue, shoves Jesus and Judas equally aside. Why then do we prate of self-reliance? Inasmuch as the soul is present there will be power not confident but agent. To talk of reliance is a poor external way of speaking. Speak rather of that which relies because it works and is. Who has more obedience than I masters me, though he should not raise his finger. Round him I must revolve by the gravitation of spirits. We fancy it rhetoric when we speak of eminent virtue. We do not yet see that virtue is Height, and that a man or a company of men, plastic and permeable to principles, by the law of nature must overpower and ride all cities, nations, kings, rich men, poets, who are not.

This is the ultimate fact which we so quickly reach on this as on every topic, the resolution of all into the ever-blessed ONE. Self-existence is the attribute of the Supreme Cause, and it constitutes the measure of good by the degree in which it enters into all lower forms. All things real are so by so much virtue as they contain. Commerce, husbandry, hunting, whaling, war, eloquence, personal weight, are somewhat, and engage my respect as examples of its presence and impure action. I see the same law working in nature for conservation and growth. Power is, in nature, the essential measure of right. Nature suffers nothing to remain in her kingdoms which cannot help itself. The genesis and maturation of a planet, its poise and orbit, the bended tree recovering itself from the strong wind, the vital resources of every animal and vegetable, are demonstrations of the self-sufficing and therefore self-relying soul.

Thus all concentrates: let us not rove; let us sit at home with the cause. Let us stun and astonish the intruding rabble of men and books and institutions by a simple declaration of the divine fact. Bid the invaders take the shoes from off their feet, for God is here within. Let our simplicity judge them, and our docility to our own law demonstrate the poverty of nature and fortune beside our native riches.

But now we are a mob. Man does not stand in awe of man, nor is his genius admonished to stay at home, to put itself in communication with the internal ocean, but it goes abroad to beg a cup of water of the urns of other men. We must go alone. I like the silent church before the service begins, better than any preaching. How far off, how cool, how chaste the persons look, begirt each one with a precinct or sanctuary! So let us always sit. Why should we assume the faults of our friend, or wife, or father, or child, because they sit around our hearth, or are said to have the same blood? All men have my blood and I all men's. Not for that will I adopt their petulance or folly, even to the extent of being ashamed of it. But your isolation must not be mechanical, but spiritual, that is, must be elevation. At times the whole world seems to be in conspiracy to importune you with emphatic trifles. Friend, client, child, sickness, fear, want, charity, all knock at once at thy closet door and say— "Come out unto us." But keep thy state; come not into their confusion. The power men possess to annoy me I give them by a weak curiosity. No man can come near me but through my act. "What we love that we have, but by desire we bereave ourselves of the love."

If we cannot at once rise to the sanctities of obedience and faith, let us at least resist our temptations; let us enter into the state of war and wake Thor and Woden, courage and constancy, in our Saxon breasts. This is to be done in our smooth times by speaking the truth. Check this lying hospitality and lying affection. Live no longer to the expectation of these deceived and deceiving people with whom we converse. Say to them, "O father, O mother, O wife, O brother, O friend, I have lived with you after appearances hitherto. Henceforward I am the truth's. Be it known unto you that henceforward I obey no law less than the eternal law. I will have no covenants but proximities. I shall endeavor to nourish my parents, to support my family, to be the chaste husband of one wife—but these relations I must fill after a new and unprecedented way. I appeal from your customs. I must be myself. I cannot break myself any longer for you, or you. If you can love me for what I am, we shall be the happier. If you cannot, I will still seek to deserve that you should. I will not hide my tastes or aversions. I will so trust that what is deep is holy, that I will do strongly before the sun and moon whatever inly rejoices me and the heart appoints. If you are noble, I will love you; if you are not, I will not hurt you and myself by hypocritical attentions. If you are true, but not in the same truth with me, cleave to your companions; I will seek my own. I do this not selfishly but humbly and truly. It is alike your interest, and mine, and all men's, however long we have dwelt in lies, to live in truth. Does this sound harsh today? You will soon love what is dictated by your nature as well as mine, and if we follow the truth it will bring us out safe at last."—But so may you give these friends pain. Yes, but I cannot sell my liberty and my power, to save their sensibility. Besides, all persons have their moments of reason, when they look out into the region of absolute truth; then will they justify me and do the same thing.

The populace think that your rejection of popular standards is a rejection of all standard, and mere antinomianism; and the bold sensualist will use the name of philosophy to gild his crimes. But the law of consciousness abides. There are two confessionals, in one or the other of which we must be shriven. You may fulfill your round of duties by clearing yourself in the *direct*, or in the *reflex* way. Consider whether you have satisfied your relations to father, mother, cousin, neighbor, town, cat and dog—whether any of these can upbraid you. But I may also neglect this reflex standard and absolve me to myself. I have my own stern claims and perfect circle. It denies the name of duty to many offices that are called duties. But if I can discharge its debts it enables me to dispense with the popular code. If any one imagines that this law is lax, let him keep its commandment one day.

And truly it demands something godlike in him who has cast off the common motives of humanity and has ventured to trust himself for a taskmaster. High be his heart, faithful his will, clear his sight, that he may in good earnest be doctrine, society, law, to himself, that a simple purpose may be to him as strong as iron necessity is to others!

If any man consider the present aspects of what is called by distinction *society*, he will see the need of these ethics. The sinew and heart of man seem to be drawn out, and we are become timorous, desponding whimperers. We are afraid of truth, afraid of fortune, afraid of death, and afraid of each other. Our age yields no great and perfect persons. We want men and women who shall renovate life and our social state, but we see that most natures are insolvent, cannot satisfy their own wants, have an ambition out of all proportion to their practical force and do lean and beg day and night continually. Our housekeeping is mendicant, our arts, our occupations, our marriages, our religion we have not chosen, but society has chosen for us. We are parlor soldiers. We shun the rugged battle of fate, where strength is born.

If our young men miscarry in their first enterprises they lose all heart. If the young merchant fails, men say he is *ruined*. If the finest genius studies at one of our colleges and is not installed in an office within one year afterwards in the cities or suburbs of Boston or New York, it seems to his friends and to himself that he is right is being disheartened and in complaining the rest of his life. A sturdy lad from New Hampshire or Vermont, who in turn tries all the professions, who *teams it, forms it, peddles,* keeps a school, preaches, edits a newspaper, goes to Congress, buys a township, and so forth, in successive years, and always like a cat falls on his feet, is worth a hundred of these city dolls. He walks abreast with his days and feels no shame in not "studying a profession," for he does not postpone his life, but lives already. He has not one chance, but a hundred chances. Let a Stoic open the resources of man and tell men they are not leaning willows, but can and must detach themselves; that with the exercise of self-trust, new powers shall appear; that a man is the word made flesh, born to shed healing to the nations; that he should be ashamed of our compassion, and that the moment he acts from himself, tossing the laws, the books, idolatries and customs out of the window, we pity him no more but thank and revere him; and that teacher shall restore the life of man to splendor and make his name dear to all history.

It is easy to see that a greater self-reliance must work a revolution in all the offices and relations of men; in their religion; in their education; in their pursuits; their modes of living; their association: in their property; in their speculative views.

1. In what prayers do men allow themselves! That which they call a holy office is not so much as brave and manly. Prayer looks abroad and asks for some foreign addition to come through some foreign virtue, and loses itself in endless mazes of natural and supernatural, and mediatorial and miraculous. Prayer that craves a particular commodity, anything less than all good, is vicious. Prayer is the contemplation of the facts of life from the highest point of view. It is the soliloquy of a beholding and jubilant soul. It is the spirit of God pronouncing his works good. But prayer as a means to effect a private end is meanness and theft. It supposes dualism and not unity in

nature and consciousness. As soon as the man is at one with God, he will not beg. He will then see prayer in all action. The prayer of the farmer kneeling in his field to weed it, the prayer of the rower kneeling with the stroke of his oar, are true prayers heard throughout nature, though for cheap ends. Caratach, in Fletcher's "Bonduca," when admonished to inquire the mind of the god Audate, replies—

> His hidden meaning lies in our endeavors;
> Our valors are our best gods.

Another sort of false prayers are our regrets. Discontent is the want of self-reliance: it is infirmity of will. Regret calamities if you can thereby help the sufferer; if not, attend your own work and already the evil begins to be repaired. Our sympathy is just as base. We come to them who weep foolishly and sit down and cry for company, instead of imparting to them truth and health in rough electric shocks, putting them once more in communication with their own reason. The secret of fortune is joy in our hands. Welcome evermore to gods and men is the self-helping man. For him all doors are flung wide; him all tongues greet, all honors crown, all eyes follow with desire. Our love goes out to him and embraces him because he did not need it. We solicitously and apologetically caress and celebrate him because he held on his way and scorned our disapprobation. The gods love him because men hated him. "To the persevering mortal," said Zoroaster, "the blessed Immortals are swift."

As men's prayers are a disease of the will, so are their creeds a disease of the intellect. They say with those foolish Israelites, "Let not God speak to us, lest we die. Speak thou, speak any man with us, and we will obey." Everywhere I am hindered of meeting God in my brother, because he has shut his own temple doors and recites fables merely of his brother's, or his brother's brother's God. Every new mind is a new classification. If it prove a mind of uncommon activity and power, a Locke, a Lavoisier, a Hutton, a Bentham, a Fourier, it imposes its classification on other men, and lo! a new system. In proportion to the depth of the thought, and so to the number of the objects it touches and brings within reach of the pupil, is his complacency. But chiefly is this apparent in creeds and churches, which are also classifications of some powerful mind acting on the elemental thought of duty and man's relation to the Highest. Such is Calvinism, Quakerism, Swedenborgism. The pupil takes the same delight in subordinating every thing to the new terminology as a girl who has just learned botany in seeing a new earth and new seasons thereby. It will happen for a time that the pupil will find his intellectual power has grown by the study of his master's mind. But in all unbalanced minds the classification is idolized, passes for the end and not for a speedily exhaustible means, so that the walls of the system blend to their eye in the remote horizon with the walls of the universe; the luminaries of heaven seem to them hung on the arch their master built. They cannot imagine how you aliens have any right to see—how you can see; "It must be somehow that you stole the light from us." They do not yet perceive that light, unsystematic, indomitable, will break into any cabin, even into theirs. Let them chirp awhile and call it their own. If they are honest and do well, presently their neat new pinfold will be too strait and low, will crack, will lean, will rot and vanish, and the immortal light, all young and joyful, million-orbed, million-colored, will beam over the universe as on the first morning.

2. It is for want of self-culture that the superstition of Traveling, whose idols are Italy, England, Egypt, retains its fascination for all educated Americans. They who made England, Italy, or Greece venerable in the imagination, did so by sticking fast where they were, like an axis of the earth. In manly hours we feel that duty is our place. The soul is no traveler; the wise man stays at home, and when his necessities, his duties, on any occasion call him from his house, or into foreign lands, he is at home still and shall make men sensible by the expression of his countenance that he goes, the missionary of wisdom and virtue, and visits cities and men like a sovereign and not like an interloper or a valet.

I have no churlish objection to the circumnavigation of the globe for the purposes of art, of study, and benevolence, so that the man is first domesticated, or does not go abroad with the hope of finding somewhat greater than he knows. He who travels to be amused, or to get somewhat which he does not carry, travels away from himself, and grows old even in youth among old things. In Thebes, in Palmyra, his will and mind have become old and dilapidated as they. He carries ruins to ruins.

Traveling is a fool's paradise. Our first journeys discover to us the indifference of places. At home I dream that at Naples, at Rome, I can be intoxicated with beauty and lose my sadness. I pack my trunk, embrace my friends, embark on the sea and at last wake up in Naples, and there beside me is the stern fact, the sad self, unrelenting, identical, that I fled from. I seek the Vatican and the palaces. I affect to be intoxicated with sights and suggestions, but I am not intoxicated. My giant goes with me wherever I go.

3. But the rage of traveling is a symptom of a deeper unsoundness affecting the whole intellectual action. The intellect is vagabond, and our system of education fosters restlessness. Our minds travel when our bodies are forced to stay at home. We imitate; and what is imitation but the traveling of the mind? Our houses are built with foreign taste; our shelves are garnished with foreign ornaments; our opinions, our tastes, our faculties, lean, and follow the Past and the Distant. The soul created the arts wherever they have flourished. It was in his own mind that the artist sought his model. It was an application of his own thought to the thing to be done and the conditions to be observed. And why need we copy the Doric or the Gothic model? Beauty, convenience, grandeur of thought and quaint expression are as near to us as to any, and if the American artist will study with hope and love the precise thing to be done by him, considering the climate, the soil, the length of the day, the wants of the people, the habit and form of the government, he will create a house in which all these will find themselves fitted, and taste and sentiment will be satisfied also.

Insist on yourself; never imitate. Your own gift you can present every moment with the cumulative force of a whole life's cultivation; but of the adopted talent of another you have only an extemporaneous half possession. That which each can do best, none but his Maker can teach him. No man yet knows what it is, nor can, till that person has exhibited it. Where is the master who could have taught Shakespeare? Where is the master who could have instructed Franklin, or Washington, or Bacon, or Newton? Every great man is a unique. The

Scipionism of Scipio is precisely that part he could not borrow. Shakespeare will never be made by the study of Shakespeare. Do that which is assigned you, and you cannot hope too much or dare too much. There is at this moment for you an utterance brave and grand as that of the colossal chisel of Phidias, or trowel of the Egyptians, or the pen of Moses or Dante, but different from all these. Not possibly will the soul, all rich, all eloquent, with thousand-cloven tongue, deign to repeat itself; but if you can hear what these patriarchs say, surely you can reply to them in the same pitch of voice; for the ear and the tongue are two organs of one nature. Abide in the simple and noble regions of thy life, obey thy heart, and thou shalt reproduce the Foreworld again.

4. As our Religion, our Education, our Art look abroad, so does our spirit of society. All men plume themselves on the improvement of society, and no man improves.

Society never advances. It recedes as fast on one side as it gains on the other. It undergoes continual changes; it is barbarous, it is civilized, it is Christianized, it is rich, it is scientific; but this change is not amelioration. For everything that is given something is taken. Society acquires new arts and loses old instincts. What a contrast between the well-clad, reading, writing, thinking American, with a watch, a pencil and a bill of exchange in his pocket, and the naked New Zealander, whose property is a club, a spear, a mat and an undivided twentieth of a shed to sleep under! But compare the health of the two men and you shall see that the white man has lost his aboriginal strength. If the traveler tell us truly, strike the savage with a broad-axe and in a day or two the flesh shall unite and heal as if you struck the blow into soft pitch, and the same blow shall send the white to his grave.

The civilized man has built a coach, but has lost the use of his feet. He is supported on crutches, but lacks so much support of muscle. He has a fine Geneva watch, but he fails of the skill to tell the hour by the sun. A Greenwich nautical almanac he has, and so being sure of the information when he wants it, the man in the street does not know a star in the sky. The solstice he does not observe; the equinox he knows as little; and the whole bright calendar of the year is without a dial in his mind. His notebooks impair his memory; his libraries overload his wit; the insurance-office increases the number of accidents; and it may be a question whether machinery does not encumber; whether we have not lost by refinement some energy, by a Christianity, entrenched in establishments and forms, some vigor of wild virtue. For every Stoic was a Stoic; but in Christendom where is the Christian?

There is no more deviation in the moral standard than in the standard of height or bulk. No greater men are now than ever were. A singular equality may be observed between the great men of the first and of the last ages; nor can all the science, art, religion, and philosophy of the nineteenth century avail to educate greater men than Plutarch's heroes, three or four and twenty centuries ago. Not in time is the race progressive. Phocion, Socrates, Anaxagoras, Diogenes, are great men, but they leave no class. He who is really of their class will not be called by their name, but will be his own man, and in his turn the founder of a sect. The arts and inventions of each period are only its costume and do not invigorate men. The harm of the improved machinery may compensate its good. Hudson and Behring accomplished so much in their fishing-boats as to astonish Parry and Franklin, whose equipment exhausted the resources of science and art. Galileo, with an opera-glass, discovered a more splendid series of celestial phenomena than anyone since. Columbus found the New World in an undecked boat. It is curious to see the periodical disuse and perishing of means and machinery which were introduced with loud laudation a few years or centuries before. The great genius returns to essential man. We reckoned the improvements of the art of war among the triumphs of science, and yet Napoleon conquered Europe by the bivouac, which consisted of falling back on naked valor and disencumbering it of all aids. The Emperor held it impossible to make a perfect army, says Las Cases, "without abolishing our arms, magazines, commissaries and carriages, until, in imitation of the Roman custom, the soldier should receive his supply of corn, grind it in his hand-mill and bake his bread himself."

Society is a wave. The wave moves onward, but the water of which it is composed does not. The same particle does not rise from the valley to the ridge. Its unity is only phenomenal. The persons who make up a nation today, next year die, and their experience dies with them.

And so the reliance on Property, including the reliance on

governments which protect it, is the want of self-reliance. Men have looked away from themselves and at things so long that they have come to esteem the religious, learned and civil institutions as guards of property, and they deprecate assaults on these, because they feel them to be assaults on property. They measure their esteem of each other by what each has, and not by what each is. But a cultivated man becomes ashamed of his property, out of new respect for his nature. Especially he hates what he has if he see that it is accidental—came to him by inheritance, or gift, or crime; then he feels that it is not having; it does not belong to him, has no root in him and merely lies there because no revolution or no robber takes it away. But that which a man is, does always by necessity acquire; and what the man acquires, is living property, which does not wait the beck of rulers, or mobs, or revolutions, or fire, or storm, or bankruptcies, but perpetually renews itself wherever the man breathes. "Thy lot or portion of life," said the Caliph Ali, "is seeking after thee; therefore be at rest from seeking after it." Our dependence on these foreign goods leads us to our slavish respect for numbers. The political parties meet in numerous conventions; the greater the concourse and with each new uproar of announcement—The delegation from Essex! The Democrats from New Hampshire! The Whigs of Maine!—the young patriot feels himself stronger than before by a new thousand of eyes and arms. In like manner the reformers summon conventions and vote and resolve in multitude. Not so, O friends! will the God deign to enter and inhabit you, but by a method precisely the reverse. It is only as a man puts off all foreign support and stands alone that I see him to be strong and to prevail. He is weaker by every recruit to his banner. Is not a man better than a town? Ask nothing of men, and, in the endless mutation, thou only firm column must presently appear the upholder of all that surrounds thee. He who knows that power is inborn, that he is weak because he has looked for good out of him and elsewhere, and, so perceiving, throws himself unhesitatingly on his thought, instantly rights himself, stands in the erect position, commands his limbs, works miracles; just as a man who stands on his feet is stronger than a man who stands on his head.

So use all that is called Fortune. Most men gamble with her, and gain all, and lose all, as her wheel rolls. But do thou leave as unlawful these winnings, and deal with Cause and Effect, the chancellors of God. In the Will work and acquire, and thou hast chained the wheel of Chance, and shall sit hereafter out of fear from her rotations. A political victory, a rise of rents, the recovery of your sick or the return of your absent friend, or some other favorable event raises your spirits, and you think good days are preparing for you. Do not believe it. Nothing can bring you peace but yourself. Nothing can bring you peace but the triumph of principles.

John Stuart Mill

(1806–1873)

From

PRINCIPLES OF POLITICAL ECONOMY

The Production of Wealth

In every department of human affairs, practice long precedes science. The conception, accordingly, of political economy as a branch of science is extremely modern; but the subject with which its inquiries are conversant—wealth—has, in all ages, constituted one of the chief practical interests of mankind. Everyone has a notion, sufficiently correct for common purposes, of what is meant by "wealth." Money, being the instrument of an important public and private purpose, is rightly regarded as wealth; but everything else which serves any human purpose, and which nature does not supply gratuitously, is wealth also. Wealth may be defined as all useful or agreeable things which possess exchangeable value.

The production of wealth—the extraction of the instruments of human subsistence and enjoyment from the materials of the globe—is evidently not an arbitrary thing. It has its necessary conditions.

The requisites of production are two—labor and appropriate natural objects. Labor is either bodily or mental. Of the other requisite it is to be remarked that the objects supplied by nature are, except in a few unimportant cases, only instrumental to human wants after having undergone some transformations by human exertion.

Nature does more, however, than supply materials; she also supplies powers. Of natural powers, some are practically unlimited, others limited in quantity, and much of the economy of society depends on the limited quantity in which some of the most important natural agents exist, and more particularly land. As soon as there is not so much of a natural agent to be had as would be used if it could be obtained for the asking, the ownership or use of it acquires an exchangeable value. Where there is more land wanted for cultivation than a place possesses of a certain quality and advantages of situation, land of that quality and situation may be sold for a price, or let for an annual rent.

Labor employed on external nature in modes subservient to production is employed either directly, or indirectly, in previous or concomitant operations designed to facilitate, perhaps essential to the possibilities of, the actual production. One of the modes in which labor is employed indirectly requires particular notice, namely, when it is employed in producing subsistence to maintain the laborers while they are engaged in the production. This previous employment of labor is an indispensable condition to every productive operation. In order to raise any product there are needed labor, tools, and materials, and food to feed the laborers. But the tools and materials can be remunerated only from the product when obtained. The food, on the contrary, is intrinsically useful, and the labor expended in producing it, and recompensed by it, needs not to be remunerated over again from the produce of the subsequent labor which it has fed.

The claim to remuneration founded on the possession of food is remuneration for abstinence, not for labor. If a person has a store of food, he has it in his power to consume it himself in idleness. If, instead, he gives it to productive laborers to support them during their work, he can claim a remuneration from the produce. He will, in fact, expect his advance of food to come back to him with an increase, called, in the language of business, a profit.

Thus, there is necessary to productive operations, besides labor and natural agents, a stock, previously accumulated, of the products of labor. This accumulated stock is termed capital. Capital is frequently supposed to be synonymous with money, but money can afford no assistance to production. To do this it must be exchanged for other things capable of contributing to production. What capital does for production is to afford the shelter, tools, and materials which the work requires, and to feed and otherwise maintain the laborers during the process. Whatever things are destined for this use are capital. That industry is limited by capital is self-evident. There can be no more industry than is supplied with materials to work up and food to eat. Nevertheless, it is often forgotten that the people of a country are maintained and have their wants supplied, not by the produce of present labor, but of past, and it long continued to be believed that laws and governments, without creating capital, could create industry.

All capital is the result of saving. Somebody must have produced it, and forborne to consume it, or it is the result of an excess of production over consumption. Although saved, and the result of saving, it is nevertheless consumed—exchanged partly for tools which are worn out by use, partly for materials destroyed in the using, and by consumption of the ultimate product; and, finally, paid in wages to productive laborers who consume it for their daily wants. The greater part, in value, of the wealth now existing in England has been produced by human hands within the last twelve months. A very small proportion, indeed, was in existence ten years ago. The land subsists, and is almost the only thing that subsists. Capital is kept in existence, not by preservation, but by perpetual reproduction.

The Distribution of Wealth

The laws and conditions of the production of wealth partake of the character of physical truths. There is nothing optional or arbitrary about them. It is not so with the distribution of wealth. That is a matter of human institution solely.

Among the different modes of distributing the produce of land and labor which have been adopted, attention is first claimed by the primary institution on which the economical arrangements of society have always rested—private property.

The institution of property consists in the recognition, in each person, of a right to the exclusive disposal of the fruits of their own labor and abstinence, and implies the right of the possessor of the fruits of previous labor to what has been produced by others by the cooperation between present labor and those fruits of past labor—that is, the freedom of acquiring by contract.

We now proceed to the hypothesis of a threefold division of the produce, among laborers, landlords, and capitalists, beginning with the subject of wages.

Wages depend mainly upon the demand and supply of labor, or, roughly, on the proportion between population and capital. It is a common saying that wages are high when trade is good. Capital which was lying idle is brought into complete efficiency, and wages, in the particular occupation concerned, rise. But this is but a temporary fluctuation, and nothing can permanently alter *general* wages except an increase or diminution of capital itself compared with the quantity of labor offering itself to be hired.

Again, high prices can only raise wages if the producers and dealers, receding more, are induced to add to their capital or, at least, to their purchases of labor. But high prices of this sort, if they benefit one class of laborers, can only do so at the expense of others, since all other people, by paying those high prices, have their purchasing power reduced by an equal degree.

Another common opinion, which is only partially true, is that wages vary with the price of food, rising when it rises and falling when it falls. In times of scarcity, people generally compete more violently for employment, and lower the labor market against themselves. But dearness or cheapness of food, when of a permanent character, may affect wages. If food grows permanently dearer without a rise of wages, a greater number of children will prematurely die, and thus wages will ultimately be higher; but only because the number of people will be smaller than if food had remained cheap. Certain rare circumstances excepted, high wages imply restraints on population.

As the wages of the laborer are the remuneration of labor, so the profits of the capitalist are properly the remuneration of abstinence. They are what he gains by forbearing to consume his capital for his own uses and allowing it to be consumed by productive laborers for their uses. Of these gains, however, a part only is properly an equivalent for the use of the capital itself; namely, so much as a solvent person would be willing to pay for the loan of it. This, as everybody knows, is called interest. What a person expects to gain who superintends the employment of his own capital is always more than this. The rate of profit greatly exceeds the rate of interest. The surplus is partly compensation for risk and partly remuneration for the devotion of his time and labor. Thus, the three parts into which profit may be regarded as resolving itself, may be described, respectively, as interest, insurance, and wages of superintendence.

The requisites of production being labor, capital, and natural agents, the only person besides the laborer and the capitalist whose consent is necessary to production is he who possesses exclusive power over some natural agent. The land is the principal natural agent capable of being so appropriated, and the consideration paid for its use is called rent.

It is at once evident that rent is the effect of a monopoly. If all the land of the country belonged to one person he could fix the rent at his pleasure. The whole people would be dependent on his will for the necessaries of life. But even when monopolized—in the sense of being limited in quantity—land will command a price only if it exists in less quantity than the demand, and no land ever pays rent unless, in point of fertility and situation, it belongs to those superior kinds which exist in less quantity than the demand.

Any land yields just so much more than the ordinary profits of stock as it yields more than what is returned by the worst land in cultivation. The surplus is what is paid as rent to the landlord. The standard of rent, therefore, is the excess of the produce of any land beyond what would be returned to the same capital if employed on the worst land in cultivation, or, generally, in the least advantageous circumstances.

Of Exchange and Value

Of the two great departments of political economy, the production of wealth and its distribution, value has to do with the latter alone. The conditions and laws of production would be unaltered if the arrangements of society did not depend on, or admit of, exchange.

Value always means in political economy value in exchange, the command which its possession gives over purchasable commodities in general; whereas, by the price of a thing is understood its value in money.

That a thing may have value in exchange two conditions are necessary. It must be of some use—that is, it must conduce to some purpose; and secondly, there must be some difficulty in its attainment. This difficulty is of three kinds. It may consist in an absolute limitation of supply, as in the case of wines which can be grown only in peculiar circumstances of soil, climate, and exposure; in the labor and expense requisite to produce the commodity; or, thirdly, the limitation of the quantity which can be produced at a given cost, to which class agricultural produce belongs, increased production beyond a certain limit entailing increased cost.

When the production of a commodity is the effect of labor and expenditure, there is a minimum value, which is the essential condition of its permanent production, and must be sufficient to repay the cost of production, and, besides, the ordinary expectation of profit. This may be called the necessary value. When the commodity can be made in indefinite quantity, this *necessary* value is also the maximum which the producers can expect. If it is such that it brings a rate of profit higher than is customary, capital rushes in to share in this extra gain, and, by increasing the supply, reduces the value. Accordingly, by the operation of supply and demand the values of things are made to conform in the long run to the cost of production.

The introduction of money does not interfere with the operation of any of the laws of value. Things which by barter would exchange for one another will, if sold for money, sell for an equal amount of it, and so will exchange for one another, still through the process of exchanging them will consist of two operations instead of one. Money is a commodity, and its value is determined like that of other commodities, temporarily by demand and supply and permanently by cost of production.

Credit, as a substitute for money, is but a transfer of capital from hand to hand, generally from persons unable to employ it to hands more competent to employ it efficiently in production. Credit is not a productive power in itself, though without it the productive powers already existing could not be brought into complete employment.

In international trade we find that the law that permanent value is proportioned to cost of production does not hold good between commodities produced in distant places as it does in those produced in adjacent places.

Between distant places, and especially between different countries, profits may continue different, because persons do not usually remove themselves or their capital to a distant place without a very strong motive. If capital removed to remote parts of the world as readily, and for as small an inducement, as it moves to another quarter of the same town, profits would be equivalent all over the world, and all things would be produced in the places where the same labor and capital would produce them in greatest quantity and of best quality. A tendency may even now be observed towards such a state of things; capital is becoming more and more cosmopolitan.

It is not a difference in the *absolute* cost of production which determines the interchange between distant places, but a difference in the *comparative* cost. We may often by trading with foreigners obtain their commodities at a smaller expense of labor and capital than they cost to the foreigners themselves. The bargain is advantageous to the foreigner because the commodity which he receives in exchange, though it has cost us less, would probably have cost him more.

The value of a commodity brought from a distant place does not depend on the cost of production in the place from whence it comes, but on the cost of its acquisition in that place; which in the case of an imported article means the cost of production of the thing which is exported to pay for it. In other words, the values of foreign commodities depend on the terms of international exchange, which, in turn, depend on supply and demand.

It may be established that when two countries trade together in two commodities the exchange value of these commodities relatively to each other will adjust itself to the inclinations and circumstances of the consumers on both sides in such manner that the quantities required by each country of the article which it imports from its neighbor shall be exactly sufficient to pay for one another, a law which holds of any greater number of commodities. International values depend also on the means of production available in each country for the supply of foreign markets, but the practical result is little affected thereby.

On the Influence of Government

One of the most disputed questions in political science and in practical statesmanship relates to the proper limits of the functions and agency of governments. It may be agreed that they fall into two classes: functions which are either inseparable from the idea of government or are exercised habitually by all governments; and those respecting which it has been considered questionable whether governments should exercise them or not. The former may be termed the *necessary,* the latter the *optional,* functions of government.

It may readily be shown that the admitted functions of government embrace a much wider field than can easily be included within the ring-fence of any restrictive definition, and that it is hardly possible to find any ground of justification common to them all, except the comprehensive one of general expediency; nor to limit the interference of government by any universal rule, save the simple and vague one that it should never be admitted but when the case of expediency is strong.

A most important consideration in viewing the economical effects arising from performance of necessary government functions is the means adopted by government to raise the revenue which is the condition of their existence.

The qualities desirable in a system of taxation have been embodied by Adam Smith in four maxims or principles, which may be said to have become classical:

(1) The subjects of every state ought to contribute to the support of the government as nearly as possible in proportion to their respective abilities; that is, in proportion to the revenue which they respectively enjoy under the protection of the state.

(2) The tax which each individual has to pay ought to be certain, and not arbitrary. A great degree of inequality is not nearly so great an evil as a small degree of uncertainty.

(3) Every tax ought to be levied at the time or in the manner in which it is most likely to be convenient for the contributor to pay it. Taxes upon such consumable goods as are articles of luxury are all finally paid by the consumer, and generally in a manner that is very convenient to him.

(4) Every tax ought to be so contrived as to take out and keep out of the pockets of the people as little as possible over and above what it brings into the public treasury.

Taxes on commodities may be considered in the following way. Suppose that a commodity is capable of being made by two different processes. It is the interest of the community that of the two methods producers should adopt that which produces the best article at the lowest price. Suppose, however, that a tax is laid on one of the processes, and no tax at all, or one of lesser amount, on the other. If the tax falls, as it is, of course, intended to do, upon the process which the producers would have adopted, it creates an artificial motive for preferring the untaxed process though the inferior of the two. If, therefore, it has any effect at all it causes the commodity to be produced of worse quality, or at a greater expense of labor; it causes so much of the labor of the community to be wasted, and the capital employed in supporting and remunerating the labor to be expended as uselessly as if it were spent in hiring men to dig holes and fill them up again. The loss falls on the consumers, though the capital of the country is also eventually diminished by the diminution of their means of saving, and in some degree of their inducements to save.

Taxes on foreign trade are of two kinds: taxes on imports and on exports. On the first aspect of the matter it would seem that both these taxes are paid by the consumers of the commodity. The true state of the case, however, is much more complicated.

By taxing exports we may draw into our coffers, at the expense of foreigners, not only the whole tax, but more than the tax; in other cases we shall gain exactly the tax; in others less than the tax. In this last case, a part of the tax is borne by ourselves, possibly the whole, even more than the whole.

If the imposition of the tax does not diminish the demand it will leave the trade exactly as it was before. We shall import as much and export as much; the whole of the tax will be paid out of our own pockets.

But the imposition of a tax almost always diminishes the demand more or less. It may therefore be laid down as a principle that a tax on imported commodities, when it really operates as a tax, and not as a prohibition, either total or partial, almost always falls in part upon the foreigners who consume our goods. It is not, however, on the person from whom we buy, but on those who buy from us that a portion of our custom duties spontaneously falls. It is the foreign consumer of our exported commodities who is obliged to pay a higher price for them because we maintain revenue duties on foreign goods.

. . . .

We now reach the consideration of the grounds and limits of the principle of *laissez-faire,* or non-interference by government.

Whatever theory we adopt respecting the foundation of the social union there is a circle round every human being which no government ought to be permitted to overstep; there is a part of the life of every person of years of discretion within which the individuality of that person ought to reign uncontrolled either by any other individual or by the public collectively. Scarcely any degree of utility short of absolute necessity will justify prohibitory regulation, unless it can also be made to recommend itself to the general conscience.

A general objection to government agency is that every increase of the functions devolving on the government is an increase of its power both in the form of authority and, still more, in the indirect form of influence. Though a better organization of governments would greatly diminish the force of the objection to the mere multiplication of their duties, it would still remain true that in all the advanced communities the great majority of things are worse done by the intervention of government than the individuals most interested in the matter would do them if left to themselves.

Letting alone, in short, should be the practice; every departure from it, unless required by some great good, is a certain evil.

Charles Darwin

(1809–1882)

From

THE ORIGIN OF SPECIES

Recapitulation and Conclusion

As this whole volume [*The Origin of Species*] is one long argument, it may be convenient to the reader to have the leading facts and inferences briefly recapitulated.

That many and serious objections may be advanced against the theory of descent with modification through variation and natural selection, I do not deny. I have endeavored to give them their full force. Nothing at first can appear more difficult to believe than that the more complex organs and instincts have been perfected, not by means superior to, though analogous with, human reason, but by the accumulation of innumerable slight variations, each good for the individual possessor. Nevertheless, this difficulty, though appearing to our imagination insuperably great, cannot be considered real if we admit the following propositions, namely, that all parts of the organization and instincts offer, at least, individual differences—that there is a struggle for existence leading to the preservation of profitable deviations of structure or instinct—and, lastly, that gradations in the state of perfection of each organ may have existed, each good of its kind. The truth of these propositions cannot, I think, be disputed.

It is, no doubt, extremely difficult even to conjecture by what gradations many structures have been perfected, more especially amongst broken and failing groups of organic beings, which have suffered much extinction, but we see so many strange gradations in nature, that we ought to be extremely cautious in saying that any organ or instinct, or any whole structure, could not have arrived at its present state by many graduated steps. There are, it must be admitted, cases of special difficulty opposed to the theory of natural selection; and one of the most curious of these is the existence in the same community of two or three defined castes of workers or sterile female ants, but I have attempted to show how these difficulties can be mastered.

With respect to the almost universal sterility of species when first crossed, which forms so remarkable a contrast with the almost universal fertility of varieties when crossed, I must refer the reader to the recapitulation of the facts given at the end of the ninth chapter, which seem to me conclusively to show that this sterility is no more a special endowment than is the incapacity of two distinct kinds of trees to be grafted together; but that it is incidental on differences confined to the reproductive systems of the intercrossed species. We see the truth of this conclusion in the vast difference in the results of crossing the same two species reciprocally—that is, when one species is first used as the father and then as the mother. Analogy from the consideration of dimorphic and trimorphic plants clearly leads to the same conclusion, for when the forms are illegitimately united, they yield few or no seed, and their offspring are more or less sterile; and these forms belong to the same undoubted species, and differ from each other in no respect except in their reproductive organs and functions.

Although the fertility of varieties when intercrossed and of their mongrel offspring has been asserted by so many authors to be universal, this cannot be considered as quite correct after the facts given on the high authority of Gärtner and Kölreuter. Most of the varieties which have been experimented on have been produced under domestication; and as domestication (I do not mean mere confinement) almost certainly tends to eliminate that sterility which, judging from analogy, would have affected the parent-species if intercrossed, we ought not to expect that domestication would likewise induce sterility in their modified descendants when crossed. This elimination of sterility apparently follows from the same cause which allows our domestic animals to breed freely under diversified circumstances; and this again apparently follows from their having been gradually accustomed to frequent changes in their conditions of life.

A double and parallel series of facts seems to throw much light on the sterility of species, when first crossed, and of their hybrid offspring. On the one side, there is good reason to believe that slight changes in the conditions of life give vigor and fertility to all organic beings. We know also that a cross between the distinct individuals of the same variety, and between distinct varieties, increases the number of their offspring, and certainly gives to them increased size and vigor. This is chiefly owing to the forms which are crossed having been exposed to somewhat different conditions of life; for I have ascertained by a laborious series of experiments that if all the individuals of the same variety be subjected during several generations to the same conditions, the good derived from crossing is often much diminished or wholly disappears. This is one side of the case. On the other side, we know that species which have long been exposed to nearly uniform conditions, when they are subjected under confinement to new and greatly changed conditions, either perish, or if they survive, are rendered sterile, though retaining perfect health. This does not occur, or only in a very slight degree, with our domesticated productions, which have long been exposed to fluctuating conditions. Hence when we find that hybrids produced by a cross between two distinct species are few in number, owing to their perishing soon after conception or at a very early age, or if surviving that they are rendered more or less sterile, it seems highly probable that this result is due to their having been in fact subjected to a great change in their conditions of life, from being compounded of two distinct organizations. He who will explain in a definite manner why, for instance, an elephant or a fox will not breed under confinement in its native country, whilst the domestic pig or dog will breed freely under the most diversified conditions, will at the same time be able to give a definite answer to the question why two distinct species, when crossed, as well as their hybrid offspring, are generally rendered more or less sterile, whilst two domesticated varieties when crossed and their mongrel offspring are perfectly fertile.

Turning to geographical distribution, the difficulties encountered on the theory of descent with modification are serious enough. All the individuals of the same species, and all the species of the same genus, or even higher group, are descended from common parents; and therefore, in however distant and isolated parts of the world they may now be found, they must in the course of successive generations have traveled from some one point to all the others. We are often wholly unable even to conjecture how this could have been effected. Yet, as we have reason to believe that some species have retained the same specific form for very long periods of time, immensely long as measured by years, too much stress ought not to be laid on the occasional wide diffusion of the same species; for during very long periods there will always have been a good chance for wide migration by many means. A broken or interrupted range may often be accounted for by the extinction of the species in the intermediate regions. It cannot be denied that we are as yet very ignorant as to the full extent of the various climatal and geographical changes which have affected the earth during modern periods; and such changes will often have facilitated migration. As an example, I have attempted to show how potent has been the influence of the Glacial period on the distribution of the same and of allied species throughout the world. We are as yet profoundly ignorant of the many occasional means of transport. With respect to distinct species of the same genus inhabiting distant and isolated regions, as the process of modification has necessarily been slow, all the means of migration will have been possible during a very long period; and consequently the difficulty of the wide diffusion of the species of the same genus is in some degree lessened.

As according to the theory of natural selection an interminable number of intermediate forms must have existed, linking together all the species in each group by gradations as fine as are our existing varieties, it may be asked: Why do we not see these linking forms all around us? Why are not all organic beings blended together in an inextricable chaos? With respect to existing forms, we should remember that we have no right to expect (excepting in rare cases) to discover *directly* connecting links between them, but only between each and some extinct and supplanted form. Even on a wide area, which has during a long period remained continuous, and of which the climatic and other conditions of life change insensibly in proceeding from a district occupied by one species into another district occupied by a closely allied species, we have no just right to expect often to find intermediate varieties in the intermediate zones. For we have reason to believe that only a few species of a genus ever undergo change; the other species becoming utterly extinct and leaving no modified progeny. Of the species which do change, only a few within the same country change at the same time; and all modifications are slowly effected. I have also shown that the intermediate varieties which probably at first existed in the intermediate zones, would be liable to be supplanted by the allied forms on either hand; for the latter, from existing in greater numbers, would generally be modified and improved at a quicker rate than the intermediate varieties, which existed in lesser numbers; so that the intermediate varieties would, in the long run, be supplanted and exterminated.

On this doctrine of the extermination of an infinitude of connecting links, between the living and extinct inhabitants of the world, and at each successive period between the extinct and still older species, why is not every geological formation charged with such links? Why does not every collection of fossil remains afford plain evidence of the gradation and mutation of the forms of life? Although geological research has undoubtedly revealed the former existence of many links, bringing numerous forms of life much closer together, it does not yield the infinitely many fine gradations between past and present species required on the theory; and this is the most obvious of the many objections which may be urged against it. Why, again, do whole groups of allied species appear, though this appearance is often false, to have come in suddenly on the successive geological stages? Although we now know that organic beings appeared on this globe, at a period incalculably remote, long before the lowest bed of the Cambrian system was deposited, why do we not find beneath this system great piles of strata stored with the remains of the progenitors of the Cambrian fossils? For on the theory, such strata must somewhere have been deposited at these ancient and utterly unknown epochs of the world's history.

I can answer these questions and objections only on the supposition that the geological record is far more imperfect than most geologists believe. The number of specimens in all our museums is absolutely as nothing compared with the countless generations of countless species which have certainly existed. The parent-form of any two or more species would not be in all its characters directly intermediate between its modified offspring, any more than the rock-pigeon is directly intermediate in crop and tail between its descendants, the pouter and fantail pigeons. We should not be able to recognize a species as the parent of another and modified species, if we were to examine the two ever so closely, unless we possessed most of the intermediate links; and owing to the imperfection of the geological record, we have no just right to expect to find so many links. If two or three, or even more linking forms were discovered, they would simply be ranked by many naturalists as so many new species, more especially if found in different geological sub-stages, let their differences be ever so slight. Numerous existing doubtful forms could be named which are probably varieties; but who will pretend that in future ages so many fossil links will be discovered, that naturalists will be able to decide whether or not these doubtful forms ought to be called varieties? Only a small portion of the world has been geologically explored. Only organic beings of certain classes can be preserved in a fossil condition, at least in any great number. Many species when once formed never undergo any further change but become extinct without leaving modified descendants; and the periods, during which species have undergone modification, though long as measured by years, have probably been short in comparison with the periods during which they retain the same form. It is the dominant and widely ranging species which vary most frequently and vary most, and varieties are often at first local—both causes rendering the discovery of intermediate links in any one formation less likely. Local varieties will not spread into other and distant regions until they are considerably modified and improved; and when they have spread, and are discovered in a geological formation, they appear as if suddenly created there; and will be simply classed as new species. Most formations have been intermittent in their accumulation; and their duration has probably been shorter than the average duration of specific forms. Successive formations are in most cases separated from each other by blank intervals of time of great length; for fossiliferous formations thick enough to resist future degradations can as a general rule be accumulated only where much sediment is deposited on the subsiding bed of the sea. During the alternate periods of elevation and of stationary level the record will generally be blank. During these latter periods there will probably be more variability in the forms of life; during periods of subsidence, more extinction.

With respect to the absence of strata rich in fossils beneath the Cambrian formation, I can recur only to the hypothesis given in the tenth chapter; namely, that though our continents and oceans have endured for an enormous period in nearly their present relative positions, we have no reason to assume that this has always been the case; consequently formations much older than any now known may lie buried beneath the great oceans. With respect to the lapse of time not having been sufficient since our planet was consolidated for the assumed amount of organic change, and this objection, as urged by Sir William Thompson, is probably one of the gravest as yet advanced, I can only say, firstly, that we do not know at what rate species change as measured by years, and secondly, that many philosophers are not as yet willing to admit that we know enough of the constitution of the universe and of the interior of our globe to speculate with safety on its past duration.

That the geological record is imperfect all will admit; but that it is imperfect to the degree required by our theory, few will be inclined to admit. If we look to long enough intervals of time, geology plainly declares that species have all changed; and they have changed in the manner required by the theory, for they have changed slowly and in a graduated manner. We clearly see this in the fossil remains from consecutive formations invariably being much more closely related to each other, than are the fossils from widely separated formations.

Such is the sum of the several chief objections and difficulties which may be justly urged against the theory; and I have now briefly recapitulated the answers and explanations which, as far as I can see, may be given. I have felt these difficulties far too heavily during many years to doubt their weight. But it deserves especial notice that the more important objections relate to questions on which we are confessedly ignorant; nor do we know how ignorant we are. We do not know all the possible transitional gradations between the simplest and the most perfect organs; it cannot be pretended that we know all the varied means of Distribution during the long lapse of years, or that we know how imperfect is the Geological Record. Serious as these several objections are, in my judgment they are by no means sufficient to overthrow the theory of descent with subsequent modification.

Now let us turn to the other side of the argument. Under domestication we see much variability, caused, or at least excited, by changed conditions of life; but often in so obscure a manner, that we are tempted to consider the variations as spontaneous. Variability is governed by many complex laws— by correlated growth, compensation, the increased use and disuse of parts, and the definite action of the surrounding conditions. There is much difficulty in ascertaining how largely our domestic productions have been modified; but we may safely infer that the amount has been large, and that modifications can be inherited for long periods. As long as the conditions of life remain the same, we have reason to believe that a modification, which has already been inherited for many generations, may continue to be inherited for an almost infinite number of generations. On the other hand, we have evidence that variability when it has once come into play, does not cease under domestication for a very long period; nor do we know that it ever ceases, for new varieties are still occasionally produced by our oldest domesticated productions.

Variability is not actually caused by man; he only unintentionally exposes organic beings to new conditions of life, and then nature acts on the organization and causes it to vary. But man can and does select the variations given to him by nature, and thus accumulates them in any desired manner. He thus adapts animals and plants for his own benefit or pleasure. He may do this methodically, or he may do it unconsciously by preserving the individuals most useful or pleasing to him without any intention of altering the breed. It is certain that he can largely influence the character of a breed by selecting, in each successive generation, individual differences so slight as to be inappreciable except by an educated eye. This unconscious process of selection has been the great agency in the formation of the most distinct and useful domestic breeds. That many breeds produced by man have to a large extent the character of natural species, is shown by the inextricable doubts whether many of them are varieties or aboriginally distinct species.

There is no reason why the principles which have acted so

efficiently under domestication should not have acted under nature. In the survival of favored individuals and races, during the constantly-recurrent Struggle for Existence, we see a powerful and ever-acting form of Selection. The struggle for existence inevitably follows from the high geometrical ratio of increase which is common to all organic beings. This high rate of increase is proved by calculation—by the rapid increase of many animals and plants during a succession of peculiar seasons, and when naturalized in new countries. More individuals are born than can possibly survive. A grain in the balance may determine which individuals shall live and which shall die— which variety or species shall increase in number, and which shall decrease, or finally become extinct. As the individuals of the same species come in all respects into the closest competition with each other, the struggle will generally be most severe between them; it will be almost equally severe between the varieties of the same species, and next in severity between the species of the same genus. On the other hand the struggle will often be severe between beings remote in the scale of nature. The slightest advantage in certain individuals, at any age or during any season, over those with which they come into competition, or better adaptation in however slight a degree to the surrounding physical conditions, will, in the long run, turn the balance.

With animals having separated sexes, there will be in most cases a struggle between the males for the possession of the females. The most vigorous males, or those which have most successfully struggled with their conditions of life, will generally leave most progeny. But success will often depend on the males having special weapons, or means of defense, or charms; and a slight advantage will lead to victory.

As geology plainly proclaims that each land has undergone great physical changes, we might have expected to find that organic beings have varied under nature, in the same way as they have varied under domestication. And if there has been any variability under nature, it would be an unaccountable fact if natural selection had not come into play. It has often been asserted, but the assertion is incapable of proof, that the amount of variation under nature is a strictly limited quantity. Man, though acting on external characters alone and often capriciously, can produce within a short period a great result by adding up mere individual differences in his domestic productions; and every one admits that species present individual differences. But, besides such differences, all naturalists admit that natural varieties exist, which are considered sufficiently distinct to be worthy of record in systematic works. No one has drawn any clear distinction between individual differences and slight varieties; or between more plainly marked varieties and sub-species, and species. On separate continents, and on different parts of the same continent when divided by barriers of any kind, and on outlying islands, what a multitude of forms exist, which some experienced naturalists rank as varieties, others as geographical races or sub-species, and others as distinct, though closely allied species!

If then, animals and plants do vary, let it be ever so slightly or slowly, why should not variations or individual differences, which are in any way beneficial, be preserved and accumulated through natural selection, or the survival of the fittest? If man can by patience select variations useful to him, why, under changing and complex conditions of life, should not variations useful to nature's living products often arise, and be preserved or selected? What limit can be put to this power, acting during long ages and rigidly scrutinizing the whole constitution, structure, and habits of each creature—favoring the good and rejecting the bad? I can see no limit to this power, in slowly and beautifully adapting each form to the most complex relations of life. The theory of natural selection, even if we look no farther than this, seems to be in the highest degree probable. I have already recapitulated, as fairly as I could, the opposed difficulties and objections: now let us turn to the special facts and arguments in favor of the theory.

On the view that species are only strongly marked and permanent varieties, and that each species first existed as a variety, we can see why it is that no line of demarcation can be drawn between species, commonly supposed to have been produced by special acts of creation, and varieties which are acknowledged to have been produced by secondary laws. On this same view we can understand how it is that in a region where many species of a genus have been produced, and where they now flourish, these same species should present many varieties; for where the manufactory of species has been active, we might expect, as a general rule, to find it still in action; and this is the case if varieties be incipient species. Moreover, the species of the larger genera, which afford the greater number of varieties or incipient species, retain to a certain degree the character of varieties; for they differ from each other by a less amount of difference than do the species of smaller genera. The closely allied species also of the larger genera apparently have restricted ranges, and in their affinities they are clustered in little groups round other species—in both respects resembling varieties. These are strange relations on the view that each species was independently created, but are intelligible if each existed first as a variety.

As each species tends by its geometrical rate of reproduction to increase inordinately in number; and as the modified descendants of each species will be enabled to increase by as much as they become more diversified in habits and structure, so as to be able to seize on many and widely different places in the economy of nature, there will be a constant tendency in natural selection to preserve the most divergent offspring of any one species. Hence, during a long-continued course of modification, the slight differences characteristic of varieties of the same species, tend to be augmented into the greater differences characteristic of the species of the same genus. New and improved varieties will inevitably supplant and exterminate the older, less improved, and intermediate varieties; and thus species are rendered to a large extent defined and distinct objects. Dominant species belonging to the larger groups within each class tend to give birth to new and dominant forms; so that each large group tends to become still larger, and at the same time more divergent in character. But as all groups cannot thus go on increasing in size, for the world would not hold them, the more dominant groups beat the less dominant. This tendency in the large groups to go on increasing in size and diverging in character, together with the inevitable contingency of much extinction, explains the arrangement of all the forms of life in groups subordinate to groups, all within a few great classes, which has prevailed throughout all time. This grand fact of the grouping of all organic beings under what is called the Natural System, is utterly inexplicable on the theory of creation.

As natural selection acts solely by accumulating slight, successive, favorable variations, it can produce no great or sudden modifications; it can act only by short and slow steps. Hence, the canon of "Natura non facit saltum," which every fresh addition to our knowledge tends to confirm, is on this theory intelligible. We can see why throughout nature the same general end is gained by an almost infinite diversity of means, for every peculiarity when once acquired is long inherited, and structures already modified in many different ways have to be adapted for the same general purpose. We can, in short, see why nature is prodigal in variety, though niggard in innovation. But why this should be a law of nature if each species has been independently created no man can explain.

Many other facts are, as it seems to me, explicable on this theory. How strange it is that a bird, under the form of a woodpecker, should prey on insects on the ground; that upland geese which rarely or never swim, should possess webbed feet; that a thrush-like bird should dive and feed on subaquatic insects; and that a petrel should have the habits and structure fitting it for the life of an awk! and so in endless other cases. But on the view of each species constantly trying to increase in number, with natural selection always ready to adapt the slowly varying descendants of each to any unoccupied or ill-occupied place in nature, these facts cease to be strange, or might even have been anticipated.

We can to a certain extent understand how it is that there is so much beauty throughout nature; for this may be largely attributed to the agency of selection. That beauty, according to our sense of it, is not universal, must be admitted by everyone who will look at some venomous snakes, at some fishes and at certain hideous bats with a distorted resemblance to the human face. Sexual selection has given the most brilliant colors, elegant patterns, and other ornaments to the males, and sometimes to both sexes of many birds, butterflies, and other animals. With birds it has often rendered the voice of the male musical to the female, as well as to our ears. Flowers and fruit have been rendered conspicuous by brilliant colors in contrast with the green foliage, in order that the flowers may be readily seen, visited and fertilized by insects, and the seeds disseminated by birds. How it comes that certain colors, sounds, and forms should give pleasure to man and the lower animals—that is, how the sense of beauty in its simplest form was first acquired—we do not know any more than how certain odorous and flavors were first rendered agreeable.

As natural selection acts by competition, it adapts and improves the inhabitants of each country only in relation to their co-inhabitants; so that we need feel no surprise at the species of any one country, although on the ordinary view supposed to have been created and specially adapted for that country, being beaten and supplanted by the naturalized productions from another land. Nor ought we to marvel if all the contrivances in nature be not, as far as we can judge, absolutely perfect, as in the case even of the human eye; or if some of them be abhorrent to our ideas of fitness. We need not marvel at the sting of the bee, when used against an enemy, causing the bee's own death; at drones being produced in such great numbers for one single act, and being then slaughtered by their sterile sisters; at the astonishing waste of pollen by our fir-trees; at the instinctive hatred of the queen-bee for her own fertile daughters; at the ichneumonidae feeding within the living bodies of caterpillars; or at other such cases. The wonder indeed is, on the theory of natural selection, that more cases of the want of absolute perfection have not been detected.

The complex and little known laws governing the production of varieties are the same, as far as we can judge, with the laws which have governed the production of distinct species. In both cases physical conditions seem to have produced some direct and definite effect, but how much we cannot say. Thus, when varieties enter any new station, they occasionally assume some of the characters proper to the species of that station. With both varieties and species, use and disuse seem to have produced a considerable effect; for it is impossible to resist this conclusion when we look, for instance, at the loggerheaded duck, which has wings incapable of flight, in nearly the same condition as in the domestic duck; or when we look at the burrowing tucu-tucu, which is occasionally blind, and then at certain moles, which are habitually blind and have their eyes covered with skin; or when we look at the blind animals inhabiting the dark caves of America and Europe. With varieties and species, correlated variation seems to have played an important part, so that when one part has been modified other parts have been necessarily modified. With both varieties and species, reversions to long-lost characters occasionally occur. How inexplicable on the theory of creation is the occasional appearance of stripes on the shoulders and legs of the several species of the horse-genus and of their hybrids! How simply is this fact explained if we believe that these species are all descended from a striped progenitor, in the same manner as the several domestic breeds of the pigeon are descended from the blue and barred rock-pigeon!

On the ordinary view of each species having been independently created, why should specific characters, or those by which the species of the same genus differ from each other, be more variable than generic characters in which they all agree? Why, for instance, should the color of a flower be more likely to vary in any one species of a genus, if the other species possess differently colored flowers, than if all possessed the same colored flowers? If species are only well-marked varieties, of which the characters have become in a high degree permanent, we can understand this fact; for they have already varied since they branched off from a common progenitor in certain characters, by which they have come to be specifically distinct from each other; therefore these same characters would be more likely again to vary than the generic characters which have been inherited without change for an immense period. It is inexplicable on the theory of creation why a part developed in a very unusual manner in one species alone of a genus, and therefore, as we may naturally infer, of great importance to that species, should be eminently liable to variation; but, on our view, this part has undergone, since the several species branched off from a common progenitor, an unusual amount of variability and modification, and therefore we might expect the part generally to be still variable. But a part may be developed in the most unusual manner, like the wing of a bat, and yet not be more variable than any other structure, if the part be common to many subordinate forms, that is, if it has been inherited for a very long period; for in this case, it will have been rendered constant by long-continued natural selection.

Glancing at instincts, marvelous as some are, they offer no greater difficulty than do corporeal structures on the theory of the natural selection of successive slight, but profitable modifications. We can thus understand why nature moves by graduated steps in endowing different animals of the same class with their several instincts. I have attempted to show how much light the principle of gradation throws on the admirable architectural powers of the hive-bee. Habit no doubt often comes into play in modifying instincts; but it certainly is not indispensable, as we see in the case of neuter insects, which leave no progeny to inherit the effects of long-continued habit. On the view of all the species of the same genus having descended from a common parent, and having inherited much in common, we can understand how it is that allied species, when placed under widely different conditions of life, yet follow nearly the same instincts; why the thrushes of tropical and temperate South America, for instance, line their nests with mud like our British species. On the view of instincts having been slowly acquired through natural selection, we need not marvel at some instincts being not perfect and liable to mistakes, and at many instincts causing other animals to suffer.

If species be only well-marked and permanent varieties, we can at once see why their crossed offspring should follow the same complex laws in their degrees and kinds of resemblance to their parents—in being absorbed into each other by successive crosses, and in other such points—as do the crossed offspring of acknowledged varieties. This similarity would be a strange fact, if species had been independently created and varieties had been produced through secondary laws.

If we admit that the geological record is imperfect to an extreme degree, then the facts, which the record does give, strongly support the theory of descent with modification. New species have come on the stage slowly and at successive intervals; and the amount of change, after equal intervals of time, is widely different in different groups. The extinction of species and of whole groups of species which has played so conspicuous a part in the history of the organic world, almost inevitably follows from the principle of natural selection; for old forms are supplanted by new and improved forms. Neither single species nor groups of species reappear when the chain of ordinary generation is once broken. The gradual diffusion of dominant forms, with the slow modification of their descendants, causes the forms of life, after long intervals of time, to appear as if they had changed simultaneously throughout the world. The fact of the fossil remains of each formation being in some degree intermediate in character between the fossils in the formations above and below, is simply explained by their intermediate position in the chain of descent. The grand fact that all extinct beings can be classed with all recent beings, naturally follows from the living and the extinct being the offspring of common parents. As species have generally diverged in character during their long course of descent and modification, we can understand why it is that the more ancient forms, or early progenitors of each group, so often occupy a position in some degree intermediate between existing groups. Recent forms are generally looked upon as being, on the whole, higher in the scale of organization than ancient forms; and they must be higher, in so far as the later and more improved forms have conquered the older and less improved forms in the struggle for life; they have also generally had their organs more specialized for different functions. This fact is perfectly compatible with numerous beings still retaining simple and but little improved structures, fitted for simple conditions of life; it is likewise compatible with some forms having retrograded in organization, by having become at each stage of descent better fitted for new and degraded habits of life. Lastly, the wonderful law of the long endurance of allied forms on the same continent—of marsupials in Australia, of edentata in America, and other such cases—is intelligible, for within the same country the existing and the extinct will be closely allied by descent.

Looking to geographical distribution, if we admit that there has been during the long course of ages much migration from one part of the world to another, owing to former climatal and geographical changes and to the many occasional and unknown means of dispersal, then we can understand, on the theory of descent with modification, most of the great leading facts in Distribution. We can see why there should be so striking a parallelism in the distribution of organic beings throughout space, and in their geological succession throughout time; for in both cases the beings have been connected by the bond of ordinary generation, and the means of modification have been the same. We see the full meaning of the wonderful fact, which has struck every traveler, namely, that on the same continent, under the most diverse conditions, under heat and cold, on mountain and lowland, on deserts and marshes, most of the inhabitants within each great class are plainly related; for they are the descendants of the same progenitors and early colonists. On this same principle of former migration, combined in most cases with modification, we can understand, by the aid of the Glacial period, the identity of some few plants, and the close alliance of many others, on the most distant mountains, and in the northern and southern temperate zones; and likewise the close alliance of some of the inhabitants of the sea in the northern and southern temperate latitudes, though separated by the whole intertropical ocean. Although two countries may present physical conditions as closely similar as the same species ever require, we need feel no surprise at their inhabitants being widely different, if they have been for a long period completely sundered from each other; for as the relation of organism to organism is the most important of all relations, and as the two countries will have received colonists at various periods and in different proportions, from some other country or from each other, the course of modification in the two areas will inevitably have been different.

On this view of migration, with subsequent modification, we see why oceanic islands are inhabited by only few species, but of these, why many are peculiar or endemic forms. We clearly see why species belonging to those groups of animals which cannot cross wide spaces of the ocean, as frogs and terrestrial mammals, do not inhabit oceanic islands; and why, on the other hand, new and peculiar species of bats, animals which can traverse the ocean, are found on islands far distant from any continent. Such cases as the presence of peculiar species of bats on oceanic islands and the absence of all other terrestrial mammals, are facts utterly inexplicable on the theory of independent acts of creation.

The existence of closely allied or representative species in any two areas, implies, on the theory of descent with modification, that the same parent-forms formerly inhabited both areas; and we almost invariably find that wherever many closely allied species inhabit two areas, some identical species are still common to both. Wherever many closely allied yet distinct species occur, doubtful forms and varieties belonging to the same groups likewise occur. It is a rule of high generality that the inhabitants of each area are related to the inhabitants of the nearest source whence immigrants might have been derived. We see this in the striking relation of nearly all plants and animals of the Galapagos archipelago, of Juan Fernandez, and of the other American islands, to the plants and animals of the neighboring American mainland; and of those of the Cape de Verde archipelago, and of the other African islands to the African mainland. It must be admitted that these facts receive no explanation on the theory of creation.

The fact, as we have seen, that all past and present organic beings can be arranged within a few great classes, in groups subordinate to groups, and with the extinct groups often falling in between the recent groups, is intelligible on the theory of natural selection with its contingencies of extinction and divergence of character. On these same principles we see how it is, that the mutual affinities of the forms within each class are so complex and circuitous. We see why certain characters are far more serviceable than others for classification;—why adaptive characters, though of paramount importance to the beings, are of hardly any importance in classification; why characters derived from rudimentary parts, though of no service to the beings, are often of high classificatory value; and why embryological characters are often the most valuable of all. The real affinities of all organic beings, in contradistinction to their adaptive resemblances, are due to inheritance or community of descent. The Natural System is a genealogical arrangement, with the acquired grades of difference, marked by the terms, varieties, species, genera, families, etc.; and we have to discover the lines of descent by the most permanent characters whatever they may be and of however slight vital importance.

The similar framework of bones in the hand of a man, wing of a bat, fin of the porpoise, and leg of the horse—the same number of vertebrae forming the neck of the giraffe and of the elephant—and innumerable other such facts, at once explain themselves on the theory of descent with slow and slight successive modifications. The similarity of pattern in the wing and in the leg of a bat, though used for such different purpose—in the jaws and legs of a crab—in the petals, stamens, and pistils

of a flower, is likewise, to a large extent, intelligible on the view
of the gradual modification of parts or organs, which were aboriginally alike in an early progenitor in each of these classes.
On the principle of successive variations not always superven-
ing at an early age, and being inherited at a corresponding not
early period of life, we clearly see why the embryos of mammals, birds, reptiles, and fishes should be so closely similar,
and so unlike the adult forms. We may cease marveling at the
embryo of an air-breathing mammal or bird having branchial
slits and arteries running in loops, like those of a fish which has
to breathe the air dissolved in water by the aid of well-developed branchiae.

Disuse, aided sometimes by natural selection, will often
have reduced organs when rendered useless under changed
habits or conditions of life; and we can understand on this view
the meaning of rudimentary organs. But disuse and selection
will generally act on each creature, when it has come to maturity and has to play its full part in the struggle for existence,
and will thus have little power on an organ during early life;
hence the organ will not be reduced or rendered rudimentary at
this early age. The calf, for instance, has inherited teeth, which
never cut through the gums of the upper jaw, from an early
progenitor having well-developed teeth; and we may believe,
that the teeth in the mature animal were formerly reduced by
disuse, owing to the tongue and palate, or lips, having become
excellently fitted through natural selection to browse without
their aid; whereas in the calf, the teeth have been left unaffected, and on the principle of inheritance at corresponding
ages have been inherited from a remote period to the present
day. On the view of each organism with all its separate parts
having been specially created, how utterly inexplicable is it
that organs bearing the plain stamp of inutility, such as the
teeth in the embryonic calf or the shriveled wings under the
soldered wing-covers of many beetles, should so frequently
occur. Nature may be said to have taken pains to reveal her
scheme of modification, by means of rudimentary organs, of
embryological and homologous structures, but we are too blind
to understand her meaning.

I have now recapitulated the facts and considerations which
have thoroughly convinced me that species have been modified,

during a long course of descent. This has been effected chiefly through the natural selection of numerous successive, slight, favorable variations; aided in an important manner by the inherited effects of the use and disuse of parts; and in an unimportant manner, that is in relation to adaptive structures, whether past or present, by the direct action of external conditions, and by variations which seem to us in our ignorance to arise spontaneously. It appears that I formerly underrated the frequency and value of these latter forms of variation, as leading to permanent modifications of structure independently of natural selection. But as my conclusions have lately been much misrepresented, and it has been stated that I attribute the modification of species exclusively to natural selection, I may be permitted to remark that in the first edition of this work, and subsequently, I placed in a most conspicuous position—namely, at the close of the Introduction—the following words: "I am convinced that natural selection has been the main but not the exclusive means of modification." This has been of no avail. Great is the power of steady misrepresentation; but the history of science shows that fortunately this power does not long endure.

It can hardly be supposed that a false theory would explain, in so satisfactory a manner as does the theory of natural selection, the several large classes of facts above specified. It has recently been objected that this is an unsafe method of arguing; but it is a method used in judging of the common events of life, and has often been used by the greatest natural philosophers. The undulatory theory of light has thus been arrived at; and the belief in the revolution of the earth on its own axis was until lately supported by hardly any direct evidence. It is no valid objection that science as yet throws no light on the far higher problem of the essence or origin of life. Who can explain what is the essence of the attraction of gravity? No one now objects to following out the results consequent on this unknown element of attraction; notwithstanding that Leibnitz formerly accused Newton of introducing "occult qualities and miracles into philosophy."

I see no good reason why the views given in this volume should shock the religious feelings of anyone. It is satisfactory, as showing how transient such impressions are, to remember that the greatest discovery ever made by man, namely, the law of the attraction of gravity, was also attacked by Leibnitz, "as subversive of natural, and inferentially of revealed, religion." A celebrated author and divine has written to me that "he has gradually learnt to see that it is just as noble a conception of the Deity to believe that He created a few original forms capable of self-development into other and needful forms, as to believe that He required a fresh act of creation to supply the voids caused by the action of His laws."

Why, it may be asked, until recently did nearly all the most eminent living naturalists and geologists disbelieve in the mutability of species? It cannot be asserted that organic beings in a state of nature are subject to no variation; it cannot be proved that the amount of variation in the course of long ages is a limited quality; no clear distinction has been, or can be, drawn between species and well-marked varieties. It cannot be maintained that species when intercrossed are invariably sterile, and varieties invariably fertile; or that sterility is a special endowment and sign of creation. The belief that species were immutable productions was almost unavoidable as long as the history of the world was thought to be of short duration; and now that we have acquired some idea of the lapse of time, we are too apt to assume, without proof, that the geological record is so perfect that it would have afforded us plain evidence of the mutation of species, if they had undergone mutation.

But the chief cause of our natural unwillingness to admit that one species has given birth to clear and distinct species, is that we are always slow in admitting great changes of which we do not see the steps. The difficulty is the same as that felt by so many geologists, when Lyell first insisted that long lines of inland cliffs had been formed, and great valleys excavated, by the agencies which we see still at work. The mind cannot possibly grasp the full meaning of the term of even a million years; it cannot add up and perceive the full effects of many slight variations, accumulated during an almost infinite number of generations.

Although I am fully convinced of the truth of the views given in this volume under the form of an abstract, I by no means expect to convince experienced naturalists whose minds are stocked with a multitude of facts all viewed, during a long course of years, from a point of view directly opposite to mine. It is so easy to hide our ignorance under such expressions as the "plan of creation," "unity of design," etc., and to think that we give an explanation when we only restate a fact. Anyone whose disposition leads him to attach more weight to unexplained difficulties than to the explanation of a certain number of facts will certainly reject the theory. A few naturalists, endowed with much flexibility of mind, and who have already begun to doubt the immutability of species, may be influenced by this volume; but I look with confidence to the future—to young and rising naturalists, who will be able to view both sides of the question with impartiality. Whoever is led to believe that species are mutable will do good service by conscientiously expressing his conviction; for thus only can the load of prejudice by which this subject is overwhelmed be removed.

Several eminent naturalists have of late published their belief that a multitude of reputed species in each genus are not real species; but that other species are real, that is, have been independently created. This seems to me a strange conclusion to arrive at. They admit that a multitude of forms, which till lately they themselves thought were special creations, and which are still thus looked at by the majority of naturalists, and which consequently have all the external characteristic features of true species—they admit that these have been produced by variation, but they refuse to extend the same view to other and slightly different forms. Nevertheless they do not pretend that they can define, or even conjecture, which are the created forms of life, and which are those produced by secondary laws. They admit variation as a *vera causa* in one case, they arbitrarily reject it in another, without assigning any distinction in the two cases. The day will come when this will be given as a curious illustration of the blindness of preconceived opinion. These authors seem no more startled at a miraculous act of creation than at an ordinary birth. But do they really believe that at innumerable periods in the earth's history certain elemental atoms have been commanded suddenly to flash into living tissues? Do they believe that at each supposed act of creation one individual or many were produced? Were all the infinitely numerous kinds of animals and plants created as eggs or seed, or as full grown? and in the case of mammals, were they created bearing the false marks of nourishment from the mother's womb? Undoubtedly some of these same questions cannot be answered by those who believe in the appearance or creation of only a few forms of life, or of some one form alone. It has been maintained by several authors that it is as easy to believe in the creation of a million beings as of one; but Maupertuis' philosophical axiom "of least action" leads the mind more willingly to admit the smaller number; and certainly we ought not to believe that innumerable beings within each great class have been created with plain, but deceptive, marks of descent from a single parent.

As a record of a former state of things, I have retained in the foregoing paragraphs, and elsewhere, several sentences which imply that naturalists believe in the separate creation of each species; and I have been much censured for having thus expressed myself. But undoubtedly this was the general belief when the first edition of the present work appeared. I formerly spoke to very many naturalists on the subject of evolution, and never once met with any sympathetic agreement. It is probable that some did then believe in evolution, but they were either silent, or expressed themselves so ambiguously that it was not easy to understand their meaning. Now things are wholly changed, and almost every naturalist admits the great principle of evolution. There are, however, some who still think that species have suddenly given birth, through quite unexplained means, to new and totally different forms: but, as I have attempted to show, weighty evidence can be opposed to the admission of great and abrupt modifications. Under a scientific point of view, and as leading to further investigation, but little advantage is gained by believing that new forms are suddenly developed in an inexplicable manner from old and widely different forms, over the old belief in the creation of species from the dust of the earth.

It may be asked how far I extend the doctrine of the modification of species. The question is difficult to answer, because the more distinct the forms are which we consider, by so much the arguments in favor of community of descent become fewer in number and less in force. But some arguments of the greatest weight extend very far. All the members of whole classes are connected together by a chain of affinities, and all can be classed on the same principle, in groups subordinate to groups. Fossil remains sometimes tend to fill up very wide intervals between existing orders.

Organs in a rudimentary condition plainly show that an early progenitor had the organ in a fully developed condition; and this in some cases implies an enormous amount of modification in the descendants. Throughout whole classes various structures are formed on the same pattern, and at a very early age the embryos closely resemble each other. Therefore I cannot doubt that the theory of descent with modification embraces all the members of the same great class or kingdom. I believe that animals are descended from at most only four or five progenitors, and plants from an equal or lesser number.

Analogy would lead me one step farther, namely, to the belief that all animals and plants are descended from some one prototype. But analogy may be a deceitful guide. Nevertheless all living things have much in common, in their chemical composition, their cellular structure, their laws of growth, and their liability to injurious influences. We see this even in so trifling a fact as that the same poison often similarly affects plants and animals; or that the poison secreted by the gall-fly produces monstrous growths on the wild rose or oak-tree. With all organic beings excepting perhaps some of the very lowest, sexual production seems to be essentially similar. With all, as far as is at present known the germinal vesicle is the same; so that all organisms start from a common origin. If we look even to the two main divisions—namely, to the animal and vegetable kingdoms—certain low forms are so far intermediate in character that naturalists have disputed to which kingdom they should be referred. As Professor Asa Gray has remarked, "the spores and other reproductive bodies of many of the lower algae may claim to have first a characteristically animal, and then an unequivocally vegetable existence." Therefore, on the principle of natural selection with divergence of character, it does not seem incredible that, from such low and intermediate form, both animals and plants may have been developed; and, if we admit this, we must likewise admit that all the organic beings which have ever lived on this earth may be descended from some one primordial form. But this inference is chiefly grounded on analogy and it is immaterial whether or not it be accepted. No doubt it is possible, as Mr. G. H. Lewes has urged, that at the first commencement of life many different forms were evolved; but if so we may conclude that only a very few have left modified descendants. For, as I have recently remarked in regard to the members of each great kingdom, such as the Vertebrata Articulata etc., we have distinct evidence in their embryological homologous and rudimentary structures that within each kingdom all the members are descended from a single progenitor.

When the views advanced by me in this volume, and by Mr. Wallace, or when analogous views on the origin of species are generally admitted, we can dimly foresee that there will be a considerable revolution in natural history. Systematists will be able to pursue their labors as at present; but they will not be incessantly haunted by the shadowy doubt whether this or that form be a true species. This, I feel sure and I speak after experience, will be no slight relief. The endless disputes whether or not some fifty species of British brambles are good species will cease. Systematists will have only to decide (not that this will be easy) whether any form be sufficiently constant and distinct from other forms, to be capable of definition; and if definable, whether the differences be sufficiently important to deserve a specific name. This latter point will become a far more essential consideration than it is at present; for differences, however slight, between any two forms if not blended by intermediate gradations, are looked at by most naturalists as sufficient to raise both forms to the rank of species.

Hereafter we shall be compelled to acknowledge that the only distinction between species and well-marked varieties is, that the latter are known, or believed, to be connected at the present day by intermediate gradations, whereas species were formerly thus connected. Hence, without rejecting the consideration of the present existence of intermediate gradations between any two forms we shall be led to weigh more carefully and to value higher the actual amount of difference between them. It is quite possible that forms now generally acknowledged to be merely varieties may hereafter be thought worthy of specific names; and in this case scientific and common language will come into accordance. In short, we shall have to treat species in the same manner as those naturalists treat genera, who admit that genera are merely artificial combinations made for convenience. This may not be a cheering prospect; but we shall at least be free from the vain search for the undiscovered and undiscoverable essence of the term species.

The other and more general departments of natural history will rise greatly in interest. The terms used by naturalists, of affinity, relationship, community of type, paternity, morphology, adaptive characters, rudimentary and aborted organs, etc., will cease to be metaphorical, and will have a plain signification. When we no longer look at an organic being as a savage looks at a ship, as something wholly beyond his comprehension; when we regard every production of nature as one which has had a long history; when we contemplate every complex structure and instinct as the summing up of many contrivances, each useful to the possessor, in the same way as any great mechanical invention is the summing up of the labor, the experience, the reason, and even the blunders of numerous workmen; when we thus view each organic being, how far more interesting—I speak from experience—does the study of natural history become!

A grand and almost untrodden field of inquiry will be opened, on the causes and laws of variation, on correlation, on the effects of use and disuse, on the direct action of external conditions, and so forth. The study of domestic productions will rise immensely in value. A new variety raised by man will be a more important and interesting subject for study than one more species added to the infinitude of already recorded species. Our classifications will come to be, as far as they can be so made, genealogies; and will then truly give what may be called the plan of creation. The rules for classifying will no doubt become simpler when we have a definite object in view. We possess no pedigrees or armorial bearings; and we have to discover and trace the many diverging lines of descent in our natural genealogies, by characters of any kind which have long been inherited. Rudimentary organs will speak infallibly with respect to the nature of long-lost structures. Species and groups of species which are called aberrant, and which may fancifully be called living fossils, will aid us in forming a picture of the ancient forms of life. Embryology will often reveal to us the structure, in some degree obscured, of the prototype of each great class.

When we feel assured that all the individuals of the same species, and all the closely allied species of most genera, have within a not very remote period descended from one parent, and have migrated from some one birthplace; and when we better know the many means of migration, then, by the light which geology now throws, and will continue to throw, on former changes of climate and of the level of the land, we shall surely be enabled to trace in an admirable manner the former migrations of the inhabitants of the whole world. Even at present, by comparing the differences between the inhabitants of the sea on the opposite sides of a continent, and the nature of the various inhabitants on that continent, in relation to their apparent means of immigration, some light can be thrown on ancient geography.

The noble science of Geology loses glory from the extreme imperfection of the record. The crust of the earth with its imbedded remains must not be looked at as a well-filled museum, but as a poor collection made at hazard and at rare intervals. The accumulation of each great fossiliferous formation will be recognized as having depended on an unusual concurrence of favorable circumstances, and the blank intervals between the successive stages as having been of vast duration. But we shall be able to gauge with some security the duration of these intervals by a comparison of the preceding and succeeding organic forms. We must be cautious in attempting to correlate as strictly contemporaneous two formations, which do not include many identical species, by the general succession of the forms of life. As species are produced and exterminated by slowly acting and still existing causes, and not by miraculous acts of creation; and as the most important of all causes of organic change is one which is almost independent of altered and perhaps suddenly altered physical conditions, namely, the mutual relation of organism to organism—the improvement of one organism entailing the improvement or the extermination of others; it follows, that the amount of organic change in the fossils of consecutive formations probably serves as a fair measure of the relative though not actual lapse of time. A number of species, however, keeping in a body might remain for a long period unchanged, whilst within the same period several of these species by migrating into new countries and coming into competition with foreign associates, might become modified; so that we must not overrate the accuracy of organic change as a measure of time.

In the future I see open fields for far more important researches. Psychology will be securely based on the foundation already well laid by Mr. Herbert Spencer, that of the necessary acquirement of each mental power and capacity by gradation. Much light will be thrown on the origin of man and his history.

Authors of the highest eminence seem to be fully satisfied with the view that each species has been independently created. To my mind it accords better with what we know of the laws impressed on matter by the Creator, that the production and extinction of the past and present inhabitants of the world should have been due to secondary causes, like those determining the birth and death of the individual. When I view all beings not as special creations, but as the lineal descendants of some few beings which lived long before the first bed of the Cambrian system was deposited, they seem to me to become ennobled. Judging from the past, we may safely infer that not one living species will transmit its unaltered likeness to a distant futurity. And of the species now living very few will transmit progeny of any kind to a far distant futurity; for the manner in which all organic beings are grouped, shows that the greater number of species in each genus, and all the species in many genera, have left no descendants, but have become utterly extinct. We can so far take a prophetic glance into futurity as to foretell that it will be the common and widely-spread species, belonging to the larger and dominant groups within each class, which will ultimately prevail and procreate new and dominant species. As all the living forms of life are the lineal descendants of those which lived long before the Cambrian epoch, we may feel certain that the ordinary succession by generation has never once been broken, and that no cataclysm has desolated the whole world. Hence we may look with some confidence to a secure future of great length. And as natural selection works solely by and for the good of each being, all corporeal and mental endowments will tend to progress towards perfection.

It is interesting to contemplate a tangled bank, clothed with many plants of many kinds, with birds singing on the bushes, with various insects flitting about, and with worms crawling through the damp earth, and to reflect that these elaborately constructed forms, so different from each other, and dependent upon each other in so complex a manner, have all been produced by laws acting around us. These laws, taken in the largest sense, being Growth with Reproduction; Inheritance which is almost implied by reproduction; Variability from the indirect and direct action of the conditions of life, and from use and disuse; a Ratio of Increase so high as to lead to a Struggle for Life, and as a consequence to Natural Selection, entailing Divergence of Character and the Extinction of less-improved forms. Thus, from the war of nature, from famine and death, the most exalted object which we are capable of conceiving, namely, the production of the higher animals, directly follows. There is grandeur in this view of life, with its several powers, having been originally breathed by the Creator into a few forms or into one; and that, whilst this planet has gone cycling on according to the fixed law of gravity, from so simple a beginning endless forms most beautiful and most wonderful have been, and are being evolved.

Henry David Thoreau
(1817–1862)

From

CIVIL DISOBEDIENCE

I heartily accept the motto—"That government is best which governs least," and I should like to see it acted up to more rapidly and systematically. Carried out, it finally amounts to this, which also I believe—"That government is best which governs not at all"; and when men are prepared for it, that will be the kind of government which they will have. Government is at best but an expedient; but most governments are usually, and all governments are sometimes, inexpedient. The objections which have been brought against a standing army, and they are many and weighty, and deserve to prevail may also at last be brought against a standing government. The standing army is only an arm of the standing government. The government itself, which is only the mode which the people have chosen to execute their will, is equally liable to be abused and perverted before the people can act through it. Witness the present Mexican War, the work of comparatively a few individuals using the standing government as their tool; for, in the outset, the people would not have consented to this measure

This American government—what is it but a tradition, though a recent one, endeavoring to transmit itself unimpaired to posterity, but each instant losing some of its integrity? It has not the vitality and force of a single living man; for a single man can bend it to his will. It is a sort of wooden gun to the people themselves. But it is not the less necessary for this; for the people must have some complicated machinery or other, and hear its din, to satisfy that idea of government which they have. Governments show thus how successfully men can be imposed on, even impose on themselves, for their own advantage. It is excellent, we must all allow. Yet this government never of itself furthered any enterprise, but by the alacrity with which it got out of its way. *It* does not keep the country free. *It* does not settle the West. *It* does not educate. The character inherent in the American people has done all that has been accomplished; and it would have done somewhat more, if the government had not sometimes got in its way. For government is an expedient by which men would fain succeed in letting one another alone; and, as has been said, when it is most expedient, the governed are most let alone by it. Trade and commerce, if they were not made of India-rubber, would never manage to bounce over the obstacles which legislators are continually putting in their way; and, if one were to judge these men wholly by the effects of their actions and not partly by their intentions, they would deserve to be classed and punished with those mischievous persons who put obstructions on the railroads.

But, to speak practically and as a citizen, unlike those who call themselves no-government men, I ask for, not at once no government, but *at once* a better government. Let every man make known what kind of government would command his respect, and that will be one step toward obtaining it.

After all, the practical reason why, when the power is once in the hands of the people, a majority are permitted, and for a long period continue, to rule is not because they are most likely to be in the right, nor because this seems fairest to the minority, but because they are physically the strongest. But a government in which the majority rule in all cases cannot be based on justice, even as far as men understand it. Can there not be a government in which majorities do not virtually decide right and wrong, but conscience?—in which majorities decide only those questions to which the rule of expediency is applicable? Must the citizen ever for a moment, or in the least degree, resign his conscience to the legislator? Why has every man a conscience, then? I think that we should be men first, and subjects afterward. It is not desirable to cultivate a respect for the law, so much as for the right. The only obligation which I have a right to assume is to do at any time what I think right. It is truly enough said, that a corporation has no conscience; but a corporation of conscientious men is a corporation *with* a conscience. Law never made men a whit more just; and, by means of their respect for it, even the well-disposed are daily made the agents of injustice. A common and natural result of an undue respect for law is, that you may see a file of soldiers, colonel, captain, corporal, privates, powder-monkeys, and all, marching in admirable order over hill and dale to the wars, against their wills, ay, against their common sense and consciences, which makes it very steep marching indeed, and produces a palpitation of the heart. They have no doubt that it is a damnable business in which they are concerned; they are all peaceably inclined. Now, what are they? Men at all? Or small movable forts and magazines, at the service of some unscrupulous man in power? . . .

How does it become a man to behave toward this American government today? I answer, that he cannot without disgrace be associated with it. I cannot for an instant recognize that political organization as *my* government which is the *slave's* government also.

All men recognize the right of revolution; that is, the right to refuse allegiance to, and to resist, the government, when its tyranny or its inefficiency are great and unendurable. But almost all say that such is not the case now. But such was the case, they think, in the Revolution of '75. If one were to tell me that this was a bad government because it taxed certain foreign commodities brought to its ports, it is most probable that I should not make an ado about it, for I can do without them. All machines have their friction; and possibly this does enough good to counterbalance the evil. At any rate, it is a great evil to make a stir about it. But when the friction comes to have its machine, and oppression and robbery are organized, I say, let us not have such a machine any longer. In other words; when a sixth of the population of a nation which has undertaken to be the refuge of liberty are slaves, and a whole country is unjustly overrun and conquered by a foreign army, and subjected to military law, I think that it is not too soon for honest men to rebel and revolutionize. What makes this duty the more urgent is the fact that the country so overrun is not our own, but ours is the invading army. . . .

All voting is a sort of gaming, like checkers or backgammon, with a slight moral tinge to it, a playing with right and wrong, with moral questions; and betting naturally accompanies it. The character of the voters is not staked. I cast my vote, perchance, as I think right; but I am not vitally concerned that that right should prevail. I am willing to leave it to the majority. Its obligation, therefore, never exceeds that of expediency. Even voting *for the right* is *doing* nothing for it. It is only expressing to men feebly your desire that it should prevail. A wise man will not leave the right to the mercy of chance, nor wish it to prevail through the power of the majority. There is but little virtue in the action of masses of men. When the majority shall at length vote for the abolition of slavery, it will be because they are indifferent to slavery, or because there is but little slavery left to be abolished by their vote. *They* will then be the only slaves. Only *his* vote can hasten the abolition of slavery who asserts his own freedom by his vote. . . .

It is not a man's duty, as a matter of course, to devote himself to the eradication of any, even the most enormous wrong; he may still properly have other concerns to engage him; but it is his duty, at least, to wash his hands of it, and, if he gives it no thought longer, not to give it practically his support. If I devote myself to other pursuits and contemplations, I must first see, at least, that I do not pursue them sitting upon another man's shoulders. I must get off him first, that he may pursue his contemplations too. See what gross inconsistency is tolerated. I have heard some of my townsmen say, "I should like to have them order me out to help put down an insurrection of the slaves, or to march to Mexico—see if I would go"; and yet these very men have each, directly by their allegiance, and so indirectly, at least, by their money, furnished a substitute. The soldier is applauded who refuses to serve in an unjust war by those who do not refuse to sustain the unjust government which makes the war; is applauded by those whose own act and authority he disregards and sets at naught; as if the state were penitent to that degree that it hired one to scourge it while it sinned, but not to that degree that it left off sinning for a moment. Thus, under the name of Order and Civil Government, we are all made at last to pay homage to and support our own meanness. After the first blush of sin comes its indifference; and from immoral it becomes, as it were, *un*moral, and not quite unnecessary to that life which we have made.

The broadest and most prevalent error requires the most disinterested virtue to sustain it. The slight reproach to which the virtue of patriotism is commonly liable, the noble are most likely to incur. Those who, while they disapprove of the character and measures of a government, yield to it their allegiance and support are undoubtedly its most conscientious supporters, and so frequently the most serious obstacles to reform. Some are petitioning the state to dissolve the Union, to disregard the requisitions of the President. Why do they not dissolve it themselves—the union between themselves and the state—and refuse to pay their quota into its treasury? Do not they stand in the same relation to the state that the state does to the Union? And have not the same reasons prevented the state from resisting the Union which have prevented them from resisting the state?

How can a man be satisfied to entertain an opinion merely, and enjoy *it?* Is there any enjoyment in it, if his opinion is that he is aggrieved? If you are cheated out of a single dollar by your neighbor, you do not rest satisfied with knowing that you are cheated, or with saying that you are cheated, or even with petitioning him to pay you your due; but you take effectual steps at once to obtain the full amount, and see that you are never cheated again. Action from principle, the perception add the performance of right, changes things and relations; it is essentially revolutionary, and does not consist wholly with anything which was. It not only divides states and churches, it divides families; ay, it divides the *individual,* separating the diabolical in him from the divine.

Unjust laws exist: shall we be content to obey them, or shall we endeavor to amend them, and obey them until we have succeeded, or shall we transgress them at once? Men generally, under such a government as this, think that they ought to wait until they have persuaded the majority to alter them. They think that, if they should resist, the remedy would be worse than the evil. But it is the fault of the government itself that the remedy *is* worse than the evil. *It* makes it worse. Why is it not more apt to anticipate and provide for reform? Why does it not cherish its wise minority? Why does it cry and resist before it is hurt? Why does it not encourage its citizens to be on the alert to point out its faults, and *do* better than it would have them? Why does it always crucify Christ, and excommunicate Copernicus and Luther, and pronounce Washington and Franklin rebels? . . .

As for adopting the ways which the state has provided for

remedying the evil, I know not of such ways. They take too much time, and a man's life will be gone. I have other affairs to attend to. I came into this world, not chiefly to make this a good place to live in, but to live in it, be it good or bad. A man has not everything to do, but something; and because he cannot do *everything*, it is not necessary that he should do *something* wrong. It is not my business to be petitioning the Governor or the Legislature any more than it is theirs to petition me; and if they should not hear my petition, what should I do then? But in this case the state has provided no way: its very Constitution is the evil. This may seem to be harsh and stubborn and unconciliatory; but it is to treat with the utmost kindness and consideration the only spirit that can appreciate or deserves it. So is all change for the better, like birth and death, which convulse the body.

I do not hesitate to say, that those who call themselves Abolitionists should at once effectually withdraw their support, both in person and property, from the government of Massachusetts and not wait till they constitute a majority of one, before they suffer the right to prevail through them. I think that it is enough if they have God on their side, without waiting for that other one. Moreover, any man more right than his neighbors constitutes a majority of one already.

I meet this American government, or its representative, the state government, directly, and face to face, once a year—no more—in the person of its tax-gatherer; this is the only mode in which a man situated as I am necessarily meets it; and it then says distinctly, Recognize me; and the simplest, most effectual, and, in the present posture of affairs, the indispensablest mode of treating with it on this head, of expressing your little satisfaction with and love for it, is to deny it then. My civil neighbor, the tax-gatherer, is the very man I have to deal with—for it is, after all, with men and not with parchment that I quarrel—and he has voluntarily chosen to be an agent of the government. How shall he ever know well what he is and does as an officer of the government, or as a man, until he is obliged to consider whether he shall treat me, his neighbor, for whom he has respect, as a neighbor and well-disposed man, or as a maniac and disturber of the peace, and see if he can get over this obstruction to his neighborliness without a ruder and more impetuous thought or speech corresponding with his action. I know this well, that if one thousand, if one hundred, if ten men whom I could name— if ten *honest* men only—ay, if *one* HONEST man, in this State of Massachusetts, *ceasing to hold slaves,* were actually to withdraw from this copartnership, and be locked up in the county jail therefore, it would be the abolition of slavery in America. For it matters not how small the beginning may seem to be: what is once well done is done forever. But we love better to talk about it: that we say is our mission. Reform keeps many scores of newspapers in its service, but not one man. . . .

Under a government which imprisons any unjustly, the true place for a just man is also a prison. The proper place today, the only place which Massachusetts has provided for her freer and less desponding spirits, is in her prisons, to be put out and locked out of the State by her own act, as they have already put themselves out by their principles. It is there that the fugitive slave, and the Mexican prisoner on parole, and the Indian come to plead the wrongs of his race should find them; on that separate, but more free and honorable ground, where the State places those who are not *with* her, but *against* her—the only house in a slave State in which a free man can abide with honor. If any think that their influence would be lost there, and their voices no longer afflict the ear of the State, that they would not be as an enemy within its walls, they do not know by how much truth is stronger than error, nor how much more eloquently and effectively he can combat injustice who has experienced a little in his own person. Cast your whole vote, not a strip of paper merely, but your whole influence. A minority is powerless while it conforms to the majority; it is not even a minority then; but it is irresistible when it clogs by its whole weight. If the alternative is to keep all just men in prison, or give up war and slavery, the State will not hesitate which to choose. If a thousand men were not to pay their tax-bills this year, that would not be a violent and bloody measure, as it would be to pay them, and enable the State to commit violence and shed innocent blood. This is, in fact, the definition of a peaceable revolution, if any such is possible. If the tax-gatherer, or any other public officer, asks me, as one has done, "But what shall I do?" my answer is, "If you really wish to do anything, resign your office." When the subject has refused allegiance, and the officer has resigned his office, then the revolution is accomplished. But even suppose blood should flow. Is there not a sort of blood shed when the conscience is wounded? Through this wound a man's real manhood and immortality flow out, and he bleeds to an everlasting death. I see this blood flowing now. . . .

When I converse with the freest of my neighbors, I perceive that, whatever they may say about the magnitude and seriousness of the question, and their regard for the public tranquillity, the long and the short of the matter is, that they cannot spare the protection of the existing government, and they dread the consequences to their property and families of disobedience to it. For my own part, I should not like to think that I ever rely on the protection of the State. But, if I deny the authority of the State when it presents its tax-bill, it will soon take and waste all my property, and so harass me and my children without end. This is hard. This makes it impossible for a man to live honestly, and at the same time comfortably, in outward respects. It will not be worth the while to accumulate property; that would be sure to go again. You must hire or squat somewhere, and raise but a small crop, and eat that soon. You must live within yourself, and depend upon yourself always tucked up and ready for a start, and not have many affairs. A man may grow rich in Turkey even, if he will be in all respects a good subject of the Turkish government. Confucius said: "If a state is governed by the principles of reason, poverty and misery are subjects of shame; if a state is not governed by the principles of reason, riches and honors are the subjects of shame." No: until I want the protection of Massachusetts to be extended to me in some distant Southern port, where my liberty is endangered, or until I am bent solely on building up an estate at home by peaceful enterprise, I can afford to refuse allegiance to Massachusetts, and her right to my property and life. It costs me less in every sense to incur the penalty of disobedience to the State than it would to obey. I should feel as if I were worth less in that case.

Some years ago, the State met me on behalf of the Church, and commanded me to pay a certain sum toward the support of a clergyman whose preaching my father attended, but never I myself. "Pay," it said, "or be locked up in the jail." I declined to pay. But, unfortunately, another man saw fit to pay it. I did not see why the schoolmaster should be taxed to support the priest, and not the priest the schoolmaster; for I was not the State's schoolmaster, but I supported myself by voluntary subscription. I did not see why the lyceum should not present its tax-bill, and have the State to back its demand, as well as the Church. However, at the request of the select men, I condescended to make some such statement as this in writing:— "Know all men by these presents, that I, Henry Thoreau, do not wish to be regarded as a member of any incorporated society which I have not joined." This I gave to the town clerk; and he has it. The State, having thus learned that I did not wish to be regarded as a member of that church, has never made a like demand on me since; though it said that it must adhere to its original presumption that time. If I had known how to name them, I should then have signed off in detail from all the societies which I never signed on to; but I did not know where to find a complete list.

I have paid no poll-tax for six years. I was put into a jail once on this account, for one night; and, as I stood considering the walls of solid stone, two or three feet thick, the door of wood and iron, a foot thick, and the iron grating which strained the light, I could not help being struck with the foolishness of that institution which treated me as if I were mere flesh and blood and bones, to be locked up. I wondered that it should have concluded at length that this was the best use it could put me to, and had never thought to avail itself of my services in some way. I saw that, if there was a wall of stone between me and my townsmen, there was if a still more difficult one to climb or break through before they could get to be as free as I was. I did not for a moment feel confined, and the walls seemed a great waste of stone and mortar. I felt as if I alone of all my townsmen had paid my tax. They plainly did not know how to treat me, but behaved like persons who are underbred. In every threat and in every compliment there was a blunder; for they thought that my chief desire was to stand the other side of that stone wall. I could not but smile to see how industriously they locked the door on my meditations, which followed them out again without let or hindrance, and they were really all that was dangerous. As they could not reach me, they had resolved to punish my body; just as boys, if they cannot come at some person against whom they have a spite, will abuse his dog. I saw that the State was half-witted, that it was timid as a lone woman with her silver spoons, and that it did not know its friends from its foes, and I lost all my remaining respect for it, and pitied it.

Thus the State never intentionally confronts a man's sense, intellectual or moral, but only his body, his senses. It is not armed with superior wit or honesty, but with superior physical strength. I was not born to be forced. I will breathe after my own fashion. Let us see who is the strongest. What force has a multitude? They only can force me who obey a higher law than I. They force me to become like themselves. I do not hear of *men* being *forced* to live this way or that by masses of men. What sort of life were that to live? When I meet a government which says to me, "Your money or your life," why should I be in haste to give it my money? It may be in a great strait, and not know what to do: I cannot help that. It must help itself; do as I do. It is not worth the while to snivel about it. I am not responsible for the successful working of the machinery of society. I am not the son of the engineer. I perceive that, when an acorn and a chestnut fall side by side, the one does not remain inert to make way for the other, but both obey their own laws, and spring and grow and flourish as best they can, till one, perchance, overshadows and destroys the other. If a plant cannot live according to its nature, it dies; and so a man.

The night in prison was novel and interesting enough. The prisoners in their shirt-sleeves were enjoying a chat and the evening air in the doorway, when I entered. But the jailer said, "Come, boys, it is time to lock up"; and so they dispersed, and I heard the sound of their steps returning into the hollow apartments. My roommate was introduced to me by the jailer as "a first-rate fellow and a clever man." When the door was locked, he showed me where to hang my hat, and how he managed matters there. The rooms were whitewashed once a month; and this one, at least, was the whitest, most simply furnished, and probably the neatest apartment in the town. He naturally wanted to know where I came from, and what brought me there; and, when I had told him, I asked him in my turn how he came there, presuming him to be an honest man, of course; and, as the world goes, I believe he was. "Why," said he, "they accuse me of burning a barn; but I never did it." As near as I could discover, he had probably gone to bed in a barn when drunk, and smoked his pipe there; and so a barn was burnt. He had the reputation of being a clever man, had been there some three months waiting for his trial to come on, and would have to wait as much longer; but he was quite domesticated and contented, since he got his board for nothing, and thought that he was well treated.

He occupied one window, and I the other; and I saw that if one stayed there long, his principal business would be to look out the window. I had soon read all the tracts that were left there, and examined where former prisoners had broken out, and where a grate had been sawed off, and heard the history of the various occupants of that room; for I found that even here there was a history and a gossip which never circulated beyond the walls of the jail. Probably this is the only house in the town where verses are composed, which are afterward printed in a circular form, but not published. I was shown quite a long list of verses which were composed by some young men who had been detected in an attempt to escape, who avenged themselves by singing them.

I pumped my fellow-prisoner as dry as I could, for fear I should never see him again; but at length he showed me which was my bed, and left me to blow out the lamp.

It was like traveling into a far country, such as I had never expected to behold, to lie there for one night. It seemed to me that I never had heard the town-clock strike before, nor the evening sounds of the village; for we slept with the windows open, which were inside the grating. It was to see my native village in the light of the Middle Ages, and our Concord was turned into a Rhine stream, and visions of knights and castles passed before me. They were the voices of old burghers that I heard in the streets. I was an involuntary spectator and auditor of whatever was done and said in the kitchen of the adjacent village-inn—a wholly new and rare experience to me. It was a closer view of my native town. I was fairly inside of it. I never had seen its institutions before. This is one of its peculiar institutions; for it is a shire town. I began to comprehend what its inhabitants were about.

In the morning, our breakfasts were put through the hole in the door, in small oblong-square tin pans, made to fit, and holding a pint of chocolate, with brown bread, and an iron spoon.

When they called for the vessels again, I was green enough to return what bread I had left; but my comrade seized it, and said that I should lay that up for lunch or dinner. Soon after he was let out to work at haying in a neighboring field, whither he went every day, and would not be back till noon; so he bade me good-day, saying that he doubted if he should see me again.

When I came out of prison—for someone interfered, and paid that tax—I did not perceive that great changes had taken place on the common, such as he observed who went in a youth and emerged a tottering and gray-headed man; and yet a change had to my eyes come over the scene—the town, and State, and country—greater than any that mere time could effect. I saw yet more distinctly the State in which I lived. I saw to what extent the people among whom I lived could be trusted as good neighbors and friends; that their friendship was for summer weather only; that they did not greatly propose to do right; that they were a distinct race from me by their prejudices and superstitions. . . .

It was formerly the custom in our village, when a poor debtor came out of jail, for his acquaintances to salute him, looking through their fingers, which were crossed to represent the grating of a jail window, "How do ye do?" My neighbors did not thus salute me, but first looked at me, and then at one another, as if I had returned from a long journey. I was put into jail as I was going to the shoemaker's to get a shoe which was mended. When I was let out the next morning, I proceeded to finish my errand, and, having put on my mended shoe, joined a huckleberry party, who were impatient to put themselves under my conduct; and in half an hour—for the horse was soon tackled—was in the midst of a huckleberry field, on one of our highest hills, two miles off, and then the State was nowhere to be seen. . . .

I have never declined paying the highway tax, because I am as desirous of being a good neighbor as I am of being a bad subject; and as for supporting schools, I am doing my part to educate my fellow-countrymen now. It is for no particular item in the tax-bill that I refuse to pay it. I simply wish to refuse allegiance to the State, to withdraw and stand aloof from it effectually. I do not care to trace the course of my dollar, if I could, till it buys a man or a musket to shoot with—the dollar is innocent—but I am concerned to trace the effects of my allegiance. In fact, I quietly declare war with the State, after my fashion, though I will still make what use and get what advantage of her I can, as is usual in such cases.

If others pay the tax which is demanded of me, from a sympathy with the State, they do but what they have already done in their own case, or rather they abet injustice to a greater extent than the State requires. If they pay the tax from a mistaken interest in the individual taxed, to save his property, or prevent his going to jail, it is because they have not considered wisely how far they let their private feelings interfere with the public good.

This, then, is my position at present. But one cannot be too much on his guard in such a case, lest his action be biased by obstinacy or an undue regard for the opinions of men. Let him see that he does only what belongs to himself and to the hour. . . .

I do not wish to quarrel with any man or nation. I do not wish to split hairs, to make fine distinctions, or set myself up as better than my neighbors. I seek rather, I may say, even an excuse for conforming to the laws of the land. I am but too ready to conform to them. Indeed, I have reason to suspect myself on this head; and each year, as the tax-gatherer comes round, I find myself disposed to review the acts and position of the general and State governments, and the spirit of the people, to discover a pretext for conformity. . . .

No man with a genius for legislation has appeared in America. They are rare in the history of the world. There are orators, politicians, and eloquent men, by the thousand; but the speaker has not yet opened his mouth to speak who is capable of settling the much-vexed questions of the day. We love eloquence for its own sake, and not for any truth which it may utter, or any heroism it may inspire. Our legislators have not yet learned the comparative value of free trade and of freedom, of union, and of rectitude, to a nation. They have no genius or talent for comparatively humble questions of taxation and finance, commerce and manufactures and agriculture. If we were left solely to the wordy wit of legislators in Congress for our guidance, uncorrected by the seasonable experience and the effectual complaints of the people, America would not long retain her rank among the nations. For eighteen hundred years, though perchance I have no right to say it, the New Testament has been written; yet where is the legislator who has wisdom and practical talent enough to avail himself of the light which it sheds on the science of legislation?

The authority of government, even such as I am willing to submit to—for I will cheerfully obey those who know and can do better than I, and in many things even those who neither know nor can do so well—is still an impure one: to be strictly just, it must have the sanction and consent of the governed. It can have no pure right over my person and property but what I concede to it. The progress from an absolute to a limited monarchy, from a limited monarchy to a democracy, is a progress toward a true respect for the individual. Even the Chinese philosopher was wise enough to regard the individual as the basis of the empire. Is a democracy, such as we know it, the last improvement possible in government? Is it not possible to take a step further towards recognizing and organizing the rights of man? There will never be a really free and enlightened State until the State comes to recognize the individual as a higher and independent power, from which all its own power and authority are derived, and treats him accordingly. I please myself with imagining a State at last which can afford to be just to all men, and to treat the individual with respect as a neighbor; which even would not think it inconsistent with its own repose if a few were to live aloof from it, not meddling with it, nor embraced by it, who fulfilled all the duties of neighbors and fellowmen. A State which bore this kind of fruit, and suffered it to drop off as fast as it ripened, would prepare the way for a still more perfect and glorious State, which also I have imagined, but not yet anywhere seen.

Karl Marx

(1818–1883)

From

CAPITAL: A CRITICAL ANALYSIS

The Genesis of Capitalist Production

Money and commodities are not capital, any more than are the means of production and of subsistence. They need to be transformed into capital. This transformation can only take place under conditions that separate laborers from all property, and from the means by which they can realize the profits of their labor; that is to say, from the possession of their means of production. The process of this separation clears the way for the capitalist system.

The economic structure of capitalistic society has developed from the economic structure of feudal society. The dissolution of the latter set free the elements of the former. The immediate producer, the laborer, could only dispose of his own person after he had ceased to be attached as a serf to the soil. Then, to be able to sell his labor wherever he could find a market, he must further have escaped from the medieval guilds and their rules and regulations, as from so many fetters on labor. But these new freedmen, on the other hand, only thus made merchandise of their labor after they had been deprived of their own means of production, and of all the guarantees of existence furnished under the old feudalism And the history of this, their expropriation, is written in history in characters of blood and fire.

The industrial capitalists, the new potentates, had to displace not only the guild-masters of handicrafts, but also the feudal lords, who were in possession of the sources of wealth. But though the conquerors thus triumphed, they have risen by means as opprobrious as those by which, long before, the Roman freedman overcame his *patronus*. The servitude of the laborer was the starting point of the development which involved the rise of the laborer and the genesis of the capitalist.

The form of this servitude was changed by the transformation of feudal exploitation into capitalist exploitation.

The inauguration of the capitalist era dates from the sixteenth century. The process consisted in the tearing of masses of men from their means of subsistence, to be hurled as free proletarians on the labor market. The basis of the whole process is the expropriation of the peasant from the soil. The history of this expropriation, differing in various countries, has the classic form only in England.

The prelude of the revolution which founded the capitalist mode of production was played at the beginning of the sixteenth century by the breaking up of the bands of feudal retainers, who, as Sir James Steuart well says, "everywhere uselessly filled house and castle." The old nobility had been devoured by the great feudal wars; the new was a child of its time, for which money was the power of all powers. Transformation of arable land into sheepwalks was therefore its cry, and an expropriation of small peasants was initiated which threatened the ruin of the country. Thornton declares that the English working-class was precipitated without any transition from its golden into its iron age.

To the evictions a direct impulse had been given by the rapid increase of the Flemish wool manufacturers and the corresponding rise in the price of wool in England. At length such a deterioration ensued in the condition of the common people that Queen Elizabeth, on a journey through the land, exclaimed, "*Pauper ubique jacet,*" and in the forty-third year of her reign the nation was constrained to acknowledge the terrible pauperism that had arisen by the introduction of the poor-rate.

Even in the last decade of the seventeenth century, the yeomanry, or independent peasants, outnumbered the farmers, and they formed the main strength of Cromwell's army. About 1750 the yeomen had vanished, and not long afterwards was lost the common land of the agricultural laborer.

Communal property was an old institution which had lived on under the aegis of feudalism. Under the "glorious revolution" which brought William of Orange to England, the landlord and capitalist appropriators of surplus value inaugurated the new era by thefts of land on a colossal scale. Thus was formed the foundation of the princely domains of the English oligarchy. In the eighteenth century the law itself became the instrument of the theft of the people's land, and the transformation of communal land into private property had for its sequel the parliamentary form of robbery in shape of the Acts for the Enclosure of Commons.

Immense numbers of the agricultural population were by this transformation "set free" as proletarians for the manufacturing industry.

After the foregoing consideration of the forcible creation of a class of outlawed proletarians, converted into wage-laborers, the question remains—Whence came the capitalists originally? The capitalist farmer developed very gradually, first as a bailiff, somewhat corresponding to the old Roman *villicus;* then as a *métaver,* or semi-farmer, dividing stock and product with the landowner; next as the farmer proper, making his own capital increase by employing wage-laborers, and paying part of the profit to the landlord as rent. The agricultural revolution of the sixteenth century enriched the farmer in proportion as it impoverished the mass of the agricultural people. The continuous rise in the price of commodities swelled the money capital of the farmer automatically, and he grew rich at the expense both of landlord and laborer. It is thus not surprising that at the close of the sixteenth century England had a class of capitalist farmers who were wealthy, considering the conditions of the age.

The Genesis of the Industrial Capitalist

By degrees the agricultural population was transformed into material elements of variable capital. For the peasants were constrained, now that they had been expropriated and cast adrift, to purchase their value in the form of wages from their new masters, the industrial capitalists. So they were transformed into an element of constant capital.

Consider the case of Westphalian peasants who, in the time of Frederic II, were all spinners of flax, and were forcibly expropriated from the soil they had owned under feudal tenure. Some, however, remained and were converted into day-laborers for large farmers. At the same time arose large flax-spinning and weaving factories in which would work men who had been "set free" from the soil. The flax looks just the same as before, but a new social soul has entered its body, for it now forms a part of the constant capital of the master manufacturer.

The flax which was formerly produced by a number of families, who also spun it in retail fashion after growing it, is now concentrated in the establishment of a single capitalist, who employs others to spin and weave it for him. So the extra labor which formerly realized extra income to many peasant families now brings profit to a few capitalists. The spindles and the looms formerly scattered over the country are now crowded into great labor barracks. The machines and raw material are now transformed from means of independent livelihood for the peasant spinners and weavers into means for mastering them and extracting out of them badly-paid labor.

The genesis of the industrial capitalist did not proceed in such a gradual way as that of the farmer, for it was accelerated by the commercial demands of the new world-market created by the great discoveries of the end of the fifteenth century. The Middle Ages had handed down two distinct forms of capital— the usurer's capital and the merchant's capital. For a time the money capital formed by means of usury and commerce was prevented from conversion into industrial capital, in the country by feudalism, in the towns by the guilds. These hindrances vanished with the disappearance of feudal society and the expropriation and partial eviction of the rural population. The new manufactures were established at seaports, or at inland points beyond the control of the old municipalities and their guilds. Hence, in England arose an embittered struggle of the corporate towns against these new industrial nurseries.

The power of the state, concentrating and organizing the force of society, hastened the transition, shortening the process of transformation of the feudal mode of production into the capitalist mode.

The next development of the capitalist era was the rise of the stock exchange and the great banks. The latter were at first merely associations of private speculators, who, in exchange for privileges bestowed on them, advanced money to help the governments. The Bank of England, founded in 1684, began by lending money to the government at eight per cent. At the same time it was empowered by parliament to coin money out of the same capital, by lending it again to the public in the form of bank-notes.

By degrees the Bank of England became the eternal creditor of the nation, and so arose the national debt, together with an international credit system, which has often concealed one or other of the sources of primitive accumulation of this or that people. One of the main lines of international business is the lending out of enormous amounts of capital by one country to another. Much capital which today appears in America without any certificate of birth, was yesterday in England, the capitalized blood of her children.

Terrible cruelty characterized much of the development of industrial capitalism, both on the Continent and in England. The birth of modern industry is heralded by a great slaughter of the innocents. Like the royal navy, the factories were recruited by the press-gang. Cottages and workhouses were ransacked for poor children to recruit the factory staffs, and these were forced to work by turns during the greater part of the night. As Lancashire was thinly populated and great numbers of hands were suddenly wanted, thousands of little hapless creatures, whose nimble little fingers were especially wanted, were sent down to the north from the workhouses of London, Birmingham, and other towns. These apprentices were flogged, tortured, and fettered. The profits of manufacturers were enormous. At length Sir Robert Peel brought in his bill for the protection of children.

With the growth of capitalist production during the manufacturing period the public conscience of Europe had lost the last remnant of shame, and the nations cynically boasted of every infamy that reinforced capitalistic accumulation. Liverpool waxed fat on the slave trade. The child-slavery in the European manufactories needed for its pedestal the slavery, pure and simple, of the negroes imported into America. If money, according to Marie Augier, "comes into the world with a congenital bloodstain on one cheek," capital comes dripping from head to foot, from every pore, with blood and dirt.

Commodities, Exchange and Capital

A commodity is an object, external to ourselves, which by its properties in some way satisfies human wants. The utility of a thing constitutes its use-value. Use-values of commodities form the substance of all wealth, and also become the material repositories of exchange-value. The magnitude of the value of any article is determined by the labor-time socially necessary for its production. So the value of a commodity would remain constant if the labor-time required for its production also remained constant. But the latter varies with every variation in the productiveness of labor.

An article may have use-value, and yet be without value, if its utility is not due to labor, as in the case of air, or virgin soil, or natural meadows. If a thing be useless, so is the labor contained in it, for, as the labor does not count as such, it therefore creates no value. A coat is worth twice as much as ten yards of linen, because the linen contains only half as much labor as the coat. All labor is the expenditure of human labor-power in a special form and with a definite aim, and in this, its character of concrete useful labor, it produces use-values.

Everyone knows, if he knows nothing else, that commodities have a value form common to them all, and presenting a marked contrast with the varied bodily forms of their use-values. I mean their money form.

Every owner of a commodity wishes to part with it in exchange for other commodities, but only those whose use-value satisfies some want of his. To the owner of a commodity, every other commodity is, in regard to his own, a particular equivalent. Consequently his own commodity is the universal equivalent for all others. But, since this applies to every owner, there is, in fact, no commodity acting as a universal equivalent. It was soon seen that a particular commodity would not become the universal equivalent except by a social act. The social action, therefore, has set apart the particular commodity in which all values are represented, and the bodily form of this commodity has become the form of the socially recognized universal equivalent—money.

The first chief function of money is to supply commodities with the material for the expression of their values. It thus serves as a universal measure of value, and only by virtue of this function does gold, the commodity *par excellence,* become money. But money itself has no price. As the measure of value and the standard of price, money has two distinct functions to perform. It is the measure of value inasmuch as it is the socially recognized incarnation of human labor; it is the standard of price inasmuch as it is a fixed weight of metal. As the measure of value it serves to convert the values of all the various commodities into prices or imaginary quantities of gold. As the standard of price it measures those quantities of gold.

The word pound was the money-name given to an actual pound weight of silver. When, as a measure of value, gold superseded silver, the word pound became, as a money-name, differentiated from the same word as a weight-name. The prices, or quantities of gold, into which the values of commodities are ideally changed are now expressed in the names of coins, or in the legally valid names of the subdivisions of the gold standard. Hence, instead of saying, "A quarter of wheat is worth an ounce of gold," the English would say, "It is worth £3 17s. 10 1/2 d." In this fashion commodities express by their prices how much they are worth, and money serves as *money of account* whenever it is a question of fixing the value of an article in its money-form. When Anarcharsis was asked for what purpose the Greeks used money, he replied, "For reckoning."

Every laborer in adding new labor also adds new value. In what way? Evidently, only by laboring productively in a particular way: the spinner by his spinning, the weaver by his weaving, the smith by his forging. Each use-value disappears, only to reappear under a new form in some new use-value. By virtue of its general character, as being expenditure of human labor-power in the abstract, spinning adds a new value to the values of cotton and spindle. On the other hand, by virtue of its special character, as being a concrete, useful process, the same labor of spinning both transfers the values of the means of production to the product and preserves them in the product. Hence at one and the same time there is produced a twofold result.

By the simple addition of a certain quantity of labor, new value is added, and by the quality of this added labor the original values of the means of production are preserved in the product. That part of capital which is represented by means of production, by the raw material, auxiliary material, and the instruments of labor, does not, in the process of production, undergo any quantitative alteration of value. I therefore call it the constant part of capital, or, more briefly, *constant capital.*

On the other hand, that part of capital represented by labor-power does, in the process of production, undergo an alteration of value. It both reproduces the equivalent of its own value, and also produces an excess, a surplus value, which may itself vary.

This part of capital is continually being transformed from a constant into a variable magnitude. I therefore call it the variable part of capital, or, shortly, *variable capital.*

Accumulation of Capital

The first condition of the accumulation of capital is that the capitalist must have contrived to sell his commodities, and to re-convert the greater portion of the money thus received into capital. Whatever be the proportion of surplus-value which the industrial capitalist retains for himself or yields up to others, he is the one who, in the first instance, appropriates it.

The process of production incessantly converts material wealth into capital, into means of creating more wealth and means of enjoyment for the capitalist. On the other hand, the laborer, on quitting the process, is nothing more than he was when he began it. He is a source of wealth, but has not the slightest means of making wealth his own. The product of the laborer is incessantly converted not only into commodities, but into capital, into means of subsistence that buy the laborer, and into means of production that command the producers.

The capitalist as constantly produces labor-power; in short, he produces the laborer, but as a wage-laborer. This incessant reproduction, this perpetuation of the laborer, is the *sine qua non* of capitalist production.

From a social point of view, the working-class is just as much an appendage of capital as the ordinary instruments of labor. The appearance of independence is kept up by means of a constant change of employers, and by the legal fiction of a contract. In former times capital legislatively enforced its proprietary rights over the free laborer.

Capitalist production reproduces and perpetuates the condition for exploiting the laborer. The economical bondage of the laborer is both caused and hidden by the periodic sale of himself to changing masters. Capitalist production, under its aspect of a continuous connected process, produces not only commodities, not only surplus value, but it also produces and reproduces the capitalist relation; on the one side the capitalist, on the other the wage-laborer.

Capital presupposes wage-labor, and wage-labor presupposes capital. One is a necessary condition to the existence of the other. The two mutually call each other into existence. Does an operative in a cotton-factory produce nothing but cotton goods? No, he produces capital. He produces values that give fresh command over his labor, and that, by means of such command, create fresh values.

Every individual capital is a larger or smaller concentration of means of production, with a corresponding command over a larger or smaller labor-army. Every accumulation becomes the means of new accumulation. The growth of social capital is affected by the growth of many individual capitals.

With the accumulation of capital, therefore, the number of capitalists grows to a greater or less extent. Two points characterize this kind of concentration which grows directly out of, or rather is identical with, accumulation. First, the increasing concentration of the social means of production in the hands of individual capitalists is, other things remaining equal, limited by the degree of increase of social wealth. Secondly, the part of social capital domiciled in each particular sphere of production is divided among many capitalists who face one another as independent commodity-producers competing with each other.

Accumulation and the concentration accompanying it are, therefore, not only scattered, but the increase of each functioning capital is thwarted by the formation of new and the subdivision of old capitals. Accumulation, therefore, presents itself on the one hand as increasing concentration of the means of production and of the command over labor; on the other, as repulsion of many individual capitalists one from another.

William James

(1842–1910)

From

THE VARIETIES OF RELIGIOUS EXPERIENCE

Philosophy

The subject of Saintliness left us face to face with the question, Is the sense of divine presence a sense of anything objectively true? We turned first to mysticism for an answer, and found that although mysticism is entirely willing to corroborate religion, it is too private (and also too various) in its utterances to be able to claim a universal authority. But philosophy publishes results which claim to be universally valid if they are valid at all, so we now turn with our question to philosophy. Can philosophy stamp a warrant of veracity upon the religious man's sense of the divine?

I imagine that many of you at this point begin to indulge in guesses at the goal to which I am tending. I have undermined the authority of mysticism, you say, and the next thing I shall probably do is to seek to discredit that of philosophy. Religion, you expect to hear me conclude, is nothing but an affair of faith, based either on vague sentiment, or on that vivid sense of the reality of things unseen of which in my second lecture and in the lecture on Mysticism I gave so many examples. It is essentially private and individualistic; it always exceeds our powers of formulation; and although attempts to pour its contents into a philosophic mold will probably always go on, men being what they are, yet these attempts are always secondary processes which in no way add to the authority, or warrant the veracity, of the sentiments from which they derive their own stimulus and borrow whatever glow of conviction they may themselves possess. In short, you suspect that I am planning to defend feeling at the expense of reason, to rehabilitate the primitive and unreflective, and to dissuade you from the hope of any Theology worthy of the name.

To a certain extent I have to admit that you guess rightly. I do believe that feeling is the deeper source of religion, and that philosophic and theological formulas are secondary products, like translations of a text into another tongue. But all such statements are misleading from their brevity, and it will take the whole hour for me to explain to you exactly what I mean.

When I call theological formulas secondary products, I mean that in a world in which no religious feeling had ever existed, I doubt whether any philosophic theology could ever have been framed. I doubt if dispassionate intellectual contemplation of the universe, apart from inner unhappiness and need of deliverance on the one hand and mystical emotion on the other, would ever have resulted in religious philosophies such as we now possess. Men would have begun with animistic explanations of natural fact, and criticized these away into scientific ones, as they actually have done. In the science they would have left a certain amount of "psychical research," even as they now will probably have to re-admit a certain amount. But high-flying speculations like those of either dogmatic or idealistic theology, these they would have had no motive to venture on, feeling no need of commerce with such deities. These speculations must, it seems to me, be classed as over-beliefs, buildings out performed by the intellect into directions of which feeling originally supplied the hint.

But even if religious philosophy had to have its first hint supplied by feeling, may it not have dealt in a superior way with the matter which feeling suggested? Feeling is private and dumb, and unable to give an account of itself. It allows that its results are mysteries and enigmas, declines to justify them rationally, and on occasion is willing that they should even pass for paradoxical and absurd. Philosophy takes just the opposite attitude. Her aspiration is to reclaim from mystery and paradox whatever territory she touches. To find an escape from obscure and wayward personal persuasion to truth objectively valid for all thinking men has ever been the intellect's most cherished ideal. To redeem religion from unwholesome privacy, and to give public status and universal right of way to its deliverances, has been reason's task.

I believe that philosophy will always have opportunity to labor at this task. We are thinking beings, and we cannot exclude the intellect from participating in any of our functions. Even in soliloquizing with ourselves, we construe our feelings intellectually. Both our personal ideals and our religious and mystical experiences must be interpreted congruously with the kind of scenery which our thinking mind inhabits. The philosophic climate of our time inevitably forces its own clothing on us. Moreover, we must exchange our feelings with one another, and in doing so we have to speak, and to use general and abstract verbal formulas. Conceptions and constructions are thus a necessary part of our religion; and as moderator amid the clash of hypotheses, and mediator among the criticisms of one man's constructions by another, philosophy will always have much to do. It would be strange if I disputed this, when these very lectures which I am giving are (as you will see more clearly from now onwards) a laborious attempt to extract from the privacies of religious experience some general facts which can be defined in formulas upon which everybody may agree.

Religious experience, in other words, spontaneously and inevitably engenders myths, superstitions, dogmas, creeds, and metaphysical theologies, and criticisms of one set of these by the adherents of another. Of late, impartial classifications and comparisons have become possible, alongside of the denunciations and anathemas by which the commerce between creeds used exclusively to be carried on. We have the beginnings of a "Science of Religions," so-called; and if these lectures could ever be accounted a crumb-like contribution to such a science I should be made very happy.

But all these intellectual operations, whether they be constructive or comparative and critical, presuppose immediate experiences as their subject-matter. They are interpretative and inductive operations, operations after the fact, consequent upon religious feeling, not coordinate with it, not independent of what it ascertains.

The intellectualism in religion which I wish to discredit pretends to be something altogether different from this. It assumes to construct religious objects out of the resources of logical reason alone, or of logical reason drawing rigorous inference from non-subjective facts. It calls its conclusions dogmatic theology, or philosophy of the absolute, as the case may be; it does not call them science of religions. It reaches them in an *a priori* way, and warrants their veracity.

Warranted systems have ever been the idols of aspiring souls. All-inclusive, yet simple; noble, clean, luminous, stable, rigorous, true—what more ideal refuge could there be than such a system would offer to spirits vexed by the muddiness and accidentality of the world of sensible things? Accordingly, we find inculcated in the theological schools of today, almost as much as in those of the fore-time, a disdain for merely possible or probable truth, and of results that only private assurance can grasp. Scholastics and idealists both express this disdain. Principal John Caird, for example, writes as follows in his Introduction to the Philosophy of Religion:

"Religion must indeed be a thing of the heart; but in order to elevate it from the region of subjective caprice and wayward-ness, and to distinguish between that which is true and false in religion, we must appeal to an objective standard. That which enters the heart must first be discerned by the intelligence to be true. It must be seen as having in its own nature a right to dominate feeling, and as constituting the principle by which feeling must be judged. In estimating the religious character of individuals, nations, or races, the first question is, not how they feel, but what they think and believe—not whether their reli-gion is one which manifests itself in emotions, more or less vehement and enthusiastic, but what are the *conceptions* of God and divine things by which these emotions are called forth. Feeling is necessary in religion, but it is by the *content* or intel-ligent basis of a religion, and not by feeling, that its character and worth are to be determined."

Cardinal Newman, in his work, *The Idea of a University*, gives more emphatic expression still to this disdain for sentiment. Theology, he says, is a science in the strictest sense of the word. I will tell you, he says, what it is not—not "physical evi-dences" for God, not "natural religion," for these are but vague subjective interpretations:

"If," he continues, "the Supreme Being is powerful or skillful, just so far as the telescope shows power, or the microscope shows skill, if his moral law is to be ascertained simply by the physical processes of the animal frame, or his will gathered from the immediate issues of human affairs, if his Essence is just as high and deep and broad as the universe and no more; if this be the fact, then will I confess that there is no specific science about God, that theology is but a name, and a protest in its behalf an hypocrisy. Then, pious as it is to think of Him, while the pageant of experiment or abstract reasoning passes by, still such piety is nothing more than a poetry of thought, or an ornament of language, a certain view taken of Nature which one man has and another has not, which gifted minds strike out, which others see to be admirable and ingenious, and which all would be the better for adopting. It is but the theology of Nature, just as we talk of the *philosophy* or the *romance* of history, or the *poetry* of childhood, or the picturesque or the sentimental or the humorous, or any other abstract quality which the genius or the caprice of the individual, or the fashion of the day, or the consent of the world, recognizes in any set of objects which are subjected to its contemplation. I do not see much difference between avowing that there is no God, and implying that nothing definite can be known for certain about Him."

What I mean by Theology, continues Newman, is none of these things: "I simply mean the *Science of God,* or the truths we know about God, put into a system, just as we have a science of the stars and call it astronomy, or of the crust of the earth and call it geology."

In both these extracts we have the issue clearly set before us: Feeling valid only for the individual is pitted against reason valid universally. The test is a perfectly plain one of fact. Theology based on pure reason must in point of fact convince men universally. If it did not, wherein would its superiority consist? If it only formed sects and schools, even as sentiment and mysticism form them, how would it fulfill its program of freeing us from personal caprice and waywardness? This perfectly definite practical test of the pretensions of philosophy to found religion on universal reason simplifies my procedure today. I need not discredit philosophy by laborious criticism of its arguments. It would suffice if I show that as a matter of history it fails to prove its pretension to be "objectively" convincing. In fact, philosophy does so fail. It does not banish differences; it founds schools and sects just as feeling does. I believe, in fact, that the logical reason of man operates in this field of divinity exactly as it has always operated in love, or in patriotism, or in politics, or in any other of the wider affairs of life, in which our passions or our mystical intuitions fix our beliefs beforehand. It finds arguments for our conviction, for indeed it *has* to find them. It amplifies and defines our faith, and dignifies it and lends it words and plausibility. It hardly ever engenders it; it cannot now secure it.

Lend me your attention while I run through some of the points of the older systematic theology. You find them in both Protestant and Catholic manuals, best of all in the innumerable textbooks published since Pope Leo's Encyclical recommending the study of Saint Thomas. I glance first at the arguments by which dogmatic theology establishes God's existence, after that at those by which it establishes his nature.

The arguments for God's existence have stood for hundreds of years with the waves of unbelieving criticism breaking against them, never totally discrediting them in the ears of the faithful, but on the whole slowly and surely washing out the mortar from between their joints. If you have a God already whom you believe in, these arguments confirm you. If you are atheistic, they fail to set you right. The proofs are various. The "cosmological" one, so-called, reasons from the contingence of the world to a First Cause which must contain whatever perfections the world itself contains. The "argument from design" reasons, from the fact that Nature's laws are mathematical, and her parts benevolently adapted to each other, that this cause is both intellectual and benevolent. The "moral argument" is that the moral law presupposes a lawgiver. The "argument *ex consensu gentium*" is that the belief in God is so widespread as to be grounded in the rational nature of man, and should therefore carry authority with it.

As I just said, I will not discuss these arguments technically. The bare fact that all idealists since Kant have felt entitled either to scout or to neglect them shows that they are not solid enough to serve as religion's all-sufficient foundation. Absolutely impersonal reasons would be in duty bound to show more general convincingness. Causation is indeed too obscure a principle to bear the weight of the whole structure of theology. As for the argument from design, see how Darwinian ideas have revolutionized it. Conceived as we now conceive them, as so many fortunate escapes from almost limitless processes of destruction, the benevolent adaptations which we find in Nature suggest a deity very different from the one who figured in the earlier versions of the argument. The fact is that these arguments do but follow the combined suggestions of the facts and of our feeling. They prove nothing rigorously. They only corroborate our preexistent partialities.

If philosophy can do so little to establish God's existence, how stands it with her efforts to define his attributes? It is worth while to look at the attempts of systematic theology in this direction.

Since God is First Cause, this science of sciences says, he differs from all his creatures in possessing existence *a se*. From this "a-se-ity" on God's part, theology deduces by mere logic most of his other perfections. For instance, he must be both *necessary* and *absolute*, cannot not be, and cannot in any way be determined by anything else. This makes Him absolutely unlimited from without, and unlimited also from within; for limitation is non-being; and God is being itself. This unlimitedness makes God infinitely perfect. Moreover, God is *One*, and *Only*, for the infinitely perfect can admit no peer. He is *Spiritual*, for were He composed of physical parts, some other power would have to combine them into the total, and his aseity would thus be contradicted. He is therefore both simple and non-physical in nature. He is *simple metaphysically* also, that is to say, his nature and his existence cannot be distinct, as they are in finite substances which share their formal natures with one another, and are individual only in their material aspect. Since God is one and only, his *essentia* and his *esse* must be given at one stroke. This excludes from his being all those distinctions, so familiar in the world of finite things between potentiality and actuality, substance and accidents, being and activity, existence and attributes. We can talk, it is true, of God's powers, acts, and attributes, but these discriminations are only "virtual," and made from the human point of view. In God all these points of view fall into an absolute identity of being.

This absence of all potentiality in God obliges Him to be *immutable*. He is actuality, through and through. Were there anything potential about Him, He would either lose or gain by its actualization, and either loss or gain would contradict his perfection. He cannot, therefore, change. Furthermore, He is *immense, boundless;* for could He be outlined in space, He would be composite, and this would contradict his indivisibility. He is therefore *omnipresent,* indivisibly there, at every point of space. He is similarly wholly present at every point of time—in other words *eternal.* For if He began in time, He would need a prior cause, and that would contradict his aseity. If He ended, it would contradict his necessity. If He went through any succession, it would contradict his immutability.

He has *intelligence* and *will* and every other creature-perfection, for *we* have them, and *effectus nequit superare causam.* In Him, however, they are absolutely and eternally in act, and their *object,* since God can be bounded by naught that is external, can primarily be nothing else than God himself. He knows himself, then, in one eternal indivisible act, and wills himself with an infinite self-pleasure. Since He must of logical necessity thus love and will himself, He cannot be called "free" *ad intra,* with the freedom of contrarieties that characterizes finite creatures. *Ad extra,* however, or with respect to his creation, God is free. He cannot *need* to create, being perfect in being and in happiness already. He wills to create, then, by an absolute freedom.

Being thus a substance endowed with intellect and will and freedom, God is a *person*; and a *living* person also, for He is both object and subject of his own activity, and to be this distinguishes the living from the lifeless. He is thus absolutely *self-sufficient*: his *self-knowledge* and *self-love* are both of them infinite and adequate, and need no extraneous conditions to perfect them.

He is *omniscient,* for in knowing himself as Cause He knows all creature things and events by implication. His knowledge is *previsive,* for He is present to all time. Even our free acts are known beforehand to Him, for otherwise his wisdom would admit of successive moments of enrichment, and this would contradict his immutability. He is *omnipotent* for everything that does not involve logical contradiction. He can make *being*—in other words his power includes *creation*. If what He creates were made of his own substance, it would have to be infinite in essence, as that substance is; but it is finite; so it must be non-divine in substance. If it were made of a substance, an eternally existing matter, for example, which God found there to his hand, and to which He simply gave its form, that would contradict God's definition as First Cause, and make Him a mere mover of something caused already. The things he creates, then, He creates *ex nihilo*, and gives them absolute being as so many finite substances additional to himself. The forms which he imprints upon them have their prototypes in his ideas. But as in God there is no such thing as multiplicity, and as these ideas for us are manifold, we must distinguish the ideas as they are in God and the way in which our minds externally imitate them. We must attribute them to Him only in a *terminative* sense, as differing aspects, from the finite point of view, of his unique essence. God of course is holy, good, and just. He can do no evil, for He is positive being's fullness, and evil is negation. It is true that He has created physical evil in places, but only as a means of wider good, for *bonum totius praeeminet bonum partis*. Moral evil He cannot will, either as end or means, for that would contradict his holiness. By creating free beings He *permits* it only, neither his justice nor his goodness obliging Him to prevent the recipients of freedom from misusing the gift.

As regards God's purpose in creating, primarily it can only have been to exercise his absolute freedom by the manifestation to others of his glory. From this it follows that the others must be rational beings, capable in the first place of knowledge, love, and honor, and in the second place of happiness, for the knowledge and love of God is the mainspring of felicity. In so far forth one may say that God's secondary purpose in creating is *love*.

I will not weary you by pursuing these metaphysical determinations farther, into the mysteries of God's Trinity, for example. What I have given will serve as a specimen of the orthodox philosophical theology of both Catholics and Protestants. Newman, filled with enthusiasm at God's list of perfections, continues the passage which I began to quote to you by a couple of pages of a rhetoric so magnificent that I can hardly refrain from adding them, in spite of the inroad they would make upon our time. He first enumerates God's attributes sonorously, then celebrates his ownership of everything in earth and Heaven, and the dependence of all that happens upon his permissive will. He gives us scholastic philosophy "touched with emotion," and every philosophy should be touched with emotion to be rightly understood. Emotionally, then, dogmatic theology is worth something to minds of the type of Newman's. It will aid us to estimate what it is worth intellectually, if at this point I make a short digression.

What God hath joined together, let no man put asunder. The Continental schools of philosophy have too often overlooked the fact that man's thinking is organically connected with his conduct. It seems to me to be the chief glory of English and Scottish thinkers to have kept the organic connection in view. The guiding principle of British philosophy has in fact been that every difference must *make* a difference, every theoretical difference somewhere issue in a practical difference, and that the best method of discussing points of theory is to begin by ascertaining what practical difference would result from one alternative or the other being true. What is the particular truth in question *known as?* In what facts does it result? What is its cash-value in terms of particular experience? This is the characteristic English way of taking up a question. In this way, you remember, Locke takes up the question of personal identity. What you mean by it is just your chain of particular memories, says he. That is the only concretely verifiable part of its significance. All further ideas about it, such as the oneness or manyness of the spiritual substance on which it is based, are therefore void of intelligible meaning; and propositions touching such ideas may be indifferently affirmed or denied. So Berkeley with his "matter." The cash-value of matter is our physical sensations. That is what it is known as, all that we concretely verify of its conception. That, therefore, is the whole meaning of the term "matter"—any other pretended meaning is mere wind of words. Hume does the same thing with causation. It is known as habitual antecedence, and as tendency on our part to look

for something definite to come. Apart from this practical meaning it has no significance whatever, and books about it may be
committed to the flames, says Hume. Dugald Stewart and
Thomas Brown, James Mill, John Mill, and Professor Bain,
have followed more or less consistently the same method; and
Shadworth Hodgson has used the principle with full explicit-
ness. When all is said and done, it was English and Scotch
writers, and not Kant, who introduced "the critical method"
into philosophy, the one method fitted to make philosophy a
study worthy of serious men. For what seriousness can possibly
remain in debating philosophic propositions that will never
make an appreciable difference to us in action? And what
could it matter, if all propositions were practically indifferent,
which of them we should agree to call true or which false?

An American philosopher of eminent originality, Mr. Charles
Sanders Peirce, has rendered thought a service by disentangling
from the particulars of its application the principle by which
these men were instinctively guided, and by singling it out as
fundamental and giving to it a Greek name. He calls it the principle of *pragmatism,* and he defends it somewhat as follows:

Thought in movement has for its only conceivable motive the
attainment of belief, or thought at rest. Only when our thought
about a subject has found its rest in belief can our action on the
subject firmly and safely begin. Beliefs, in short, are rules for
action; and the whole function of thinking is but one step in the
production of active habits. If there were any part of a thought
that made no difference in the thought's practical consequences, then that part would be no proper element of the
thought's significance. To develop a thought's meaning we need
therefore only determine what conduct it is fitted to produce;
that conduct is for us its sole significance; and the tangible fact
at the root of all our thought-distinctions is that there is no one
of them so fine as to consist in anything but a possible difference of practice. To attain perfect clearness in our thoughts of
an object, we need then only consider what sensations, immediate or remote, we are conceivably to expect from it, and what
conduct we must prepare in case the object should be true. Our
conception of these practical consequences is for us the whole
of our conception of the object, so far as that conception has
positive significance at all.

This is the principle of Peirce, the principle of pragmatism. Such a principle will help us on this occasion to decide, among the various attributes set down in the scholastic inventory of God's perfections, whether some be not far less significant than others.

If, namely, we apply the principle of pragmatism to God's metaphysical attributes, strictly so called, as distinguished from his moral attributes, I think that, even were we forced by a coercive logic to believe them, we still should have to confess them to be destitute of all intelligible significance. Take God's aseity, for example; or his necessariness; his immateriality; his "simplicity" or superiority to the kind of inner variety and succession which we find in finite beings, his indivisibility, and lack of the inner distinctions of being and activity, substance and accident, potentiality and actuality, and the rest; his repudiation of inclusion in a genus; his actualized infinity; his "personality," apart from the moral qualities which it may comport; his relations to evil being permissive and not positive; his self-sufficiency, self-love, and absolute felicity in himself:—candidly speaking, how do such qualities as these make any definite connection with our life? And if they severally call for no distinctive adaptations of our conduct, what vital difference can it possibly make to a man's religion whether they be true or false?

For my own part, although I dislike to say ought that may grate upon tender associations, I must frankly confess that even though these attributes were faultlessly deduced, I cannot conceive of its being of the smallest consequence to us religiously that any one of them should be true. Pray, what specific act can I perform in order to adapt myself the better to God's simplicity? Or how does it assist me to plan my behavior, to know that his happiness is anyhow absolutely complete? In the middle of the century just past, Mayne Reid was the great writer of books of out-of-door adventure. He was forever extolling the hunters and field-observers of living animals' habits, and keeping up a fire of invective against the "closet-naturalists," as he called them, the collectors and classifiers, and handlers of skeletons and skins. When I was a boy, I used to think that a closet-naturalist must be the vilest type of wretch under the sun. But surely the systematic theologians are the closet-naturalists of the deity, even in Captain Mayne Reid's sense. What is their deduction of metaphysical attributes but a shuffling and matching of pedantic dictionary-adjectives, aloof from morals, aloof from human needs, something that might be worked out from the mere word "God" by one of those logical machines of wood and brass which recent ingenuity has contrived as well as by a man of flesh and blood. They have the trail of the serpent over them. One feels that in the theologians' hands, they are only a set of titles obtained by a mechanical manipulation of synonyms; verbality has stepped into the place of vision, professionalism into that of life. Instead of bread we have a stone; instead of a fish, a serpent. Did such a conglomeration of abstract terms give really the gist of our knowledge of the deity, schools of theology might indeed continue to flourish but religion, vital religion, would have taken its flight from this world. What keeps religion going is something else than abstract definitions and systems of concatenated adjectives, and something different from faculties of theology and their professors. All these things are after-effects, secondary accretions upon those phenomena of vital conversation with the unseen divine, of which I have shown you so many instances, renewing themselves *in secula saeculorum* in the lives of humble private men.

So much for the metaphysical attributes of God! From the point of view of practical religion, the metaphysical monster which they offer to our worship is an absolutely worthless invention of the scholarly mind.

What shall we now say of the attributes called moral? Pragmatically, they stand on an entirely different footing. They positively determine fear and hope and expectation, and are foundations for the saintly life. It needs but a glance at them to show how great is their significance.

God's holiness, for example: being holy, God can will nothing but the good. Being omnipotent, he can secure its triumph. Being omniscient, he can see us in the dark. Being just, he can punish us for what he sees. Being loving, he can pardon too. Being unalterable, we can count on him securely. These qualities enter into connection with our life, it is highly important that we should be informed concerning them. That God's purpose in creation should be the manifestation of his glory is also an attribute which has definite relations to our practical life. Among other things it has given a definite character to worship in all Christian countries. If dogmatic theology really does prove beyond dispute that a God with characters like these exists, she may well claim to give a solid basis to religious sentiment. But verily, how stands it with her arguments?

It stands with them as ill as with the arguments for his existence. Not only do post-Kantian idealists reject them root and branch, but it is a plain historic fact that they never have converted anyone who has found in the moral complexion of the world, as he experienced it, reasons for doubting that a good God can have framed it. To prove God's goodness by the scholastic argument that there is no non-being in his essence would sound to such a witness simply silly.

No! the book of Job went over this whole matter once for all and definitively. Ratiocination is a relatively superficial and unreal path to the deity: "I will lay mine hand upon my mouth; I have heard of Thee by the hearing of the ear, but now mine eye seeth Thee." An intellect perplexed and baffled, yet a trustful sense of presence—such is the situation of the man who is sincere with himself and with the facts, but who remains religious still.

We must therefore, I think, bid a definitive good-by to dogmatic theology. In all sincerity our faith must do without that warrant. Modern idealism, I repeat, has said good-by to this theology forever. Can modern idealism give faith a better warrant, or must she still rely on her poor self for witness?

The basis of modern idealism is Kant's doctrine of the Transcendental Ego of Apperception. By this formidable term Kant merely meant the fact that the consciousness "I think them" must (potentially or actually) accompany all our objects. Former skeptics had said as much, but the "I" in question had remained for them identified with the personal individual. Kant abstracted and depersonalized it, and made it the most universal of all his categories, although for Kant himself the Transcendental Ego had no theological implications.

It was reserved for his successors to convert Kant's notion of *Bewusstsein überhaupt,* or abstract consciousness, into an infinite concrete self-consciousness which is the soul of the world, and in which our sundry personal self-consciousnesses have their being. It would lead me into technicalities to show you even briefly how this transformation was in point of fact effected. Suffice it to say that in the Hegelian school, which today so deeply influences both British and American thinking, two principles have borne the brunt of the operation.

The first of these principles is that the old logic of identity never gives us more than a post-mortem dissection of *disjecta membra,* and that the fullness of life can be construed to thought only by recognizing that every object which our thought may propose to itself involves the notion of some other object which seems at first to negate the first one.

The second principle is that to be conscious of a negation is already virtually to be beyond it. The mere asking of a question or expression of a dissatisfaction proves that the answer or the satisfaction is already imminent; the finite, realized as such, is already the infinite *in posse.*

Applying these principles, we seem to get a propulsive force into our logic which the ordinary logic of a bare, stark self-identity in each thing never attains to. The objects of our thought now act within our thought, act as objects act when given in experience. They change and develop. They introduce something other than themselves along with them; and this other, at first only ideal or potential, presently proves itself also to be actual. It supersedes the thing at first supposed, and both verifies and corrects it, in developing the fullness of its meaning.

The program is excellent; the universe *is* a place where things are followed by other things that both correct and fulfill them; and a logic which gave us something like this movement of fact would express truth far better than the traditional school-logic, which never gets of its own accord from anything to anything else, and registers only predictions and subsumptions, or static resemblances and differences. Nothing could be more unlike the methods of dogmatic theology than those of these new logic. Let me quote in illustration some passages from the Scottish transcendentalist whom I have already named.

"How are we to conceive," Principal Caird writes, "of the reality in which all intelligence rests?" He replies: "Two things may without difficulty be proved, *viz.*, that this reality is an absolute Spirit, and conversely that it is only in communion with this absolute Spirit or Intelligence that the finite Spirit can realize itself. It is absolute; for the faintest movement of human intelligence would be arrested, if it did not presuppose the absolute reality of intelligence, of thought itself. Doubt or denial themselves presuppose and indirectly affirm it. When I pronounce anything to be true, I pronounce it, indeed, to be relative to thought, but not to be relative to my thought, or to the thought of any other individual mind. From the existence of all individual minds as such I can abstract; I can think them away. But that which I cannot think away is thought or self-consciousness itself, in its independence and absoluteness, or, in other words, an Absolute Thought or Self-Consciousness."

Here, you see, Principal Caird makes the transition which Kant did not make: he converts the omnipresence of consciousness in general as a condition of "truth" being anywhere possible, into an omnipresent universal consciousness, which he identifies with God in his concreteness. He next proceeds to use the principle that to acknowledge your limits is in essence to be beyond them; and makes the transition to the religious experience of individuals in the following words:

"If [Man] were only a creature of transient sensations and impulses, of an ever coming and going succession of intuitions, fancies, feelings, then nothing could ever have for him the character of objective truth or reality. But it is the prerogative of man's spiritual nature that he can yield himself up to a thought and will that are infinitely larger than his own. As a thinking, self-conscious being, indeed, he may be said, by his very nature, to live in the atmosphere of the Universal Life. As a thinking being, it is possible for me to suppress and quell in my consciousness every movement of self-assertion, every notion and opinion that is merely mine, every desire that belongs to me as this particular Self, and to become the pure medium of a thought that is universal—in one word, to live no more my own life, but let my consciousness be possessed and suffused by the Infinite and Eternal life of spirit. And yet it is just in this renunciation of self that I truly gain myself, or realize the highest possibilities of my own nature. For whilst in one sense we give up self to live the universal and absolute life of reason, yet that to which we thus surrender ourselves is in reality our truer self. The life of absolute reason is not a life that is foreign to us."

Nevertheless, Principal Caird goes on to say, so far as we are able outwardly to realize this doctrine, the balm it offers remains incomplete. Whatever we may be *in posse,* the very best of us *in actu* falls very short of being absolutely divine. Social morality, love, and self-sacrifice even, merge our Self only in some other finite self or selves. They do not quite identify it with the Infinite. Man's ideal destiny, infinite in abstract logic, might thus seem in practice forever unrealizable.

"Is there, then," our author continues, "no solution of the contradiction between the ideal and the actual? We answer, There is such a solution, but in order to reach it we are carried beyond the sphere of morality into that of religion. It may be said to be the essential characteristic of religion as contrasted with morality, that it changes aspiration into fruition, anticipation into realization; that instead of leaving man in the interminable pursuit of a vanishing ideal, it makes him the actual partaker of a divine or infinite life. Whether we view religion from the human side or the divine—as the surrender of the soul to God, or as the life of God in the soul—in either aspect it is of its very essence that the Infinite has ceased to be a far-off vision, and has become a present reality. The very first pulsation of the spiritual life, when we rightly apprehend its significance, is the indication that the division between the Spirit and its object has vanished, that the ideal has become real, that the finite has reached its goal and become suffused with the presence and life of the Infinite.

"Oneness of mind and will with the divine mind and will is not the future hope and aim of religion, but its very beginning and birth in the soul. To enter on the religious life is to terminate the struggle. In that act which constitutes the beginning of the religious life—call it faith, or trust, or self-surrender, or by whatever name you will—there is involved the identification of the finite with a life which is eternally realized. It is true indeed that the religious life is progressive; but understood in the light of the foregoing idea, religious progress is not progress *towards,* but *within* the sphere of the Infinite. It is not the vain attempt by endless finite additions or increments to become possessed of infinite wealth, but it is the endeavor, by the constant exercise of spiritual activity to appropriate that infinite inheritance of which we are already in possession. The whole future of the religious life is given in its beginning, but it is given implicitly. The position of the man who has entered on the religious life is that evil, error, imperfection, do not really belong to him: they are excrescences which have no organic relation to his true nature: they are already virtually, as they will be actually, suppressed and annulled, and in the very process of being annulled they become the means of spiritual progress. Though he is not exempt from temptation and conflict, [yet] in that inner sphere in which his true life lies, the struggle is over, the victory already achieved. It is not a finite but an infinite life which the spirit lives. Every pulse-beat of its [existence] is the expression and realization of the life of God."

You will readily admit that no description of the phenomena of the religious consciousness could be better than these words of your lamented preacher and philosopher. They reproduce the very rapture of those crises of conversion of which we have been hearing; they utter what the mystic felt but was unable to communicate; and the saint, in hearing them, recognizes his own experience. It is indeed gratifying to find the content of religion reported so unanimously. But when all is said and done, has Principal Caird—and I only use him as an example of that whole mode of thinking—transcended the sphere of feeling and of the direct experience of the individual, and laid the foundations of religion in impartial reason? Has he made religion universal by coercive reasoning, transformed it from a private faith into a public certainty? Has he rescued its affirmations from obscurity and mystery?

I believe that he has done nothing of the kind, but that he has simply reaffirmed the individual's experiences in a more generalized vocabulary. And again, I can be excused from proving technically that the transcendentalist reasonings fail to make religion universal, for I can point to the plain fact that a majority of scholars, even religiously disposed ones, stubbornly refuse to treat them as convincing. The whole of Germany, one may say, has positively rejected the Hegelian argumentation. As for Scotland, I need only mention Professor Fraser's and Professor Pringle-Pattison's memorable criticisms, with which so many of you are familiar. Once more, I ask, if transcendental idealism were as objectively and absolutely rational as it pretends to be, could it possibly fail so egregiously to be persuasive?

What religion reports, you must remember, always purports to be a fact of experience: the divine is actually present, religion says, and between it and ourselves relations of give and take are actual. If definite perceptions of fact like this cannot stand upon their own feet, surely abstract reasoning cannot give them the support they are in need of. Conceptual processes can class facts, define them, interpret them; but they do not produce them, nor can they reproduce their individuality. There is always a *plus*, a *thisness*, which feeling alone can answer for. Philosophy in this sphere is thus a secondary function, unable to warrant faith's veracity, and so I revert to the thesis which I announced at the beginning of this lecture.

In all sad sincerity I think we must conclude that the attempt to demonstrate by purely intellectual processes the truth of the deliverances of direct religious experience is absolutely hopeless.

It would be unfair to philosophy, however, to leave her under this negative sentence. Let me close, then, by briefly enumerating what she can do for religion. If she will abandon metaphysics and deduction for criticism and induction, and frankly transform herself from theology into science of religions, she can make herself enormously useful.

The spontaneous intellect of man always defines the divine which it feels in ways that harmonize with its temporary intellectual prepossessions. Philosophy can by comparison eliminate the local and the accidental from these definitions. Both from dogma and from worship she can remove historic incrustations. By confronting the spontaneous religious constructions with the results of natural science, philosophy can also eliminate doctrines that are now known to be scientifically absurd or incongruous.

Sifting out in this way unworthy formulations, she can leave a residuum of conceptions that at least are possible. With these she can deal as *hypotheses,* testing them in all the manners, whether negative or positive, by which hypotheses are ever tested. She can reduce their number, as some are found more open to objection. She can perhaps become the champion of one which she picks out as being the most closely verified or verifiable. She can refine upon the definition of this hypothesis, distinguishing between what is innocent over-belief and symbolism in the expression of it, and what is to be literally taken. As a result, she can offer mediation between different believers, and help to bring about consensus of opinion. She can do this the more successfully, the better she discriminates the common and essential from the individual and local elements of the religious beliefs which she compares.

I do not see why a critical Science of Religions of this sort might not eventually command as general a public adhesion as is commanded by a physical science. Even the personally non-religious might accept its conclusions on trust, much as blind persons now accept the facts of optics—it might appear as foolish to refuse them. Yet as the science of optics has to be fed in the first instance, and continually verified later, by facts experienced by seeing persons; so the science of religions would depend for its original material on facts of personal experience, and would have to square itself with personal experience through all its critical reconstructions. It could never get away from concrete life, or work in a conceptual vacuum. It would forever have to confess, as every science confesses, that the subtlety of nature flies beyond it, and that its formulas are but approximations. Philosophy lives in words, but truth and fact well up into our lives in ways that exceed verbal formulation. There is in the living act of perception always something that glimmers and twinkles and will not be caught, and for which reflection comes too late. No one knows this as well as the philosopher. He must fire his volley of new vocables out of his conceptual shotgun, for his profession condemns him to this industry, but he secretly knows the hollowness and irrelevancy. His formulas are like stereoscopic or kinetoscopic photographs seen outside the instrument; they lack the depth, the motion, the vitality. In the religious sphere, in particular, belief that formulas are true can never wholly take the place of personal experience.

Friedrich Wilhelm Nietzsche

(1844–1900)

From

BEYOND GOOD AND EVIL

The Religious Mood

The human soul and its limits, the range of man's inner experiences hitherto attained, the heights, depths and distances of these experiences, the entire history of the soul *up to the present time,* and its still unexhausted possibilities: this is the preordained hunting-domain for a born psychologist and lover of a "big hunt." But how often must he say despairingly to himself: "A single individual! alas, only a single individual! and this great forest, this virgin forest!" So he would like to have some hundreds of hunting assistants, and fine trained hounds, that he could send into the history of the human soul, to drive *his* game together. In vain: again and again he experiences, profoundly and bitterly, how difficult it is to find assistants and dogs for all the things that directly excite his curiosity. The evil of sending scholars into new and dangerous hunting-domains, where courage, sagacity, and subtlety in every sense are required, is that they are no longer serviceable just when the *"big hunt,"* and also the great danger commences—it is precisely then that they lose their keen eye and nose. In order, for instance, to divine and determine what sort of history the problem of *knowledge and conscience* has hitherto had in the souls of *homines religiosi,* a person would perhaps himself have to possess as profound, as bruised, as immense an experience as the intellectual conscience of Pascal; and then he would still require that wide-spread heaven of clear, wicked spirituality, which, from above, would be able to oversee, arrange, and effectively formulize this mass of dangerous and painful experiences.— But who could do me this service! And who would have time to wait for such servants!—they evidently appear too rarely, they are so improbable at all times! Eventually one must do every-

thing *oneself* in order to know something; which means that one
has *much* to do!—But a curiosity like mine is once for all the
most agreeable of vices—pardon me! I mean to say that the
love of truth has its reward in heaven, and already upon earth.

Faith, such as early Christianity desired, and not infrequently
achieved in the midst of a skeptical and southernly free-spirit-
ed world, which had centuries of struggle between philosophical schools behind it and in it, counting besides the education
in tolerance which the *imperium Romanum* gave—this faith is
not that sincere, austere slave-faith by which perhaps a Luther
or a Cromwell, or some other northern barbarian of the spirit
remained attached to his God and Christianity; it is much
rather the faith of Pascal, which resembles in a terrible manner
a continuous suicide of reason—a tough, long-lived, wormlike
reason, which is not to be slain at once and with a single blow.
The Christian faith from the beginning, is sacrifice: the sacrifice of all freedom, all pride, all self-confidence of spirit; it is
at the same time subjection, self-derision, and self-mutilation.
There is cruelty and religious Phoenicianism in this faith,
which is adapted to a tender, many-sided, and very fastidious
conscience; it takes for granted that the subjection of the spirit is indescribably *painful*, that all the past and all the habits
of such a spirit resist the *absurdissimum*, in the form of which
"faith" comes to it. Modern men, with their obtuseness as
regards all Christian nomenclature, have no longer the sense
for the terribly superlative conception which was implied to an
antique taste by the paradox of the formula, "God on the
Cross." Hitherto there had never and nowhere been such bold-
ness in inversion, nor anything at once so dreadful, questioning, and questionable as this formula: it promised a transvalu-
ation of all ancient values.—It was the Orient, the *profound*
Orient, it was the Oriental slave who thus took revenge on
Rome and its noble, light-minded toleration, on the Roman
"Catholicism" of nonfaith; and it was always, not the faith, but
the freedom from the faith, the half-stoical and smiling indifference to the seriousness of the faith, which made the slaves
indignant at their masters and revolt against them.
"Enlightenment" causes revolt: for the slave desires the unconditioned, he understands nothing but the tyrannous, even in

morals; he loves as he hates, without *nuance,* to the very depths, to the point of pain, to the point of sickness—his many *hidden* sufferings make him revolt against the noble taste which seems to *deny* suffering. The skepticism with regard to suffering, fundamentally only an attitude of aristocratic morality, was not the least of the causes, also, of the last great slave-insurrection which began with the French Revolution.

Wherever the religious neurosis has appeared on the earth so far, we find it connected with three dangerous prescriptions as to regimen: solitude, fasting, and sexual abstinence—but without its being possible to determine with certainty which is cause and which is effect, or *if* any relation at all of cause and effect exists there. This latter doubt is justified by the fact that one of the most regular symptoms among savage as well as among civilized peoples is the most sudden and excessive sensuality; which then with equal suddenness transforms into penitential paroxysms, world-renunciation, and will-renunciation: both symptoms perhaps explainable as disguised epilepsy? But nowhere is it *more* obligatory to put aside explanations: around no other type has there grown such a mass of absurdity and superstition, no other type seems to have been more interesting to men and even to philosophers—perhaps it is time to become just a little indifferent here, to learn caution, or, better still, to look away, *to go away.*—Yet in the background of the most recent philosophy, that of Schopenhauer, we find almost as the problem in itself, this terrible note of interrogation of the religious crisis and awakening. How is the negation of will *possible?* how is the saint possible?—that seems to have been the very question with which Schopenhauer made a start and became a philosopher. And thus it was a genuine Schopenhauerian consequence, that his most convinced adherent (perhaps also his last, as far as Germany is concerned), namely, Richard Wagner, should bring his own life-work to an end just here, and should finally put that terrible and eternal type upon the stage as Kundry, *type vécu,* and as it loved and lived, at the very time that the mad-doctors in almost all European countries had an opportunity to study the type close at hand, wherever the religious neurosis—or as I call it, "the religious mood"—made its latest epidemical outbreak and display as the "Salvation Army."—If it be a question, however, as to what has been so extremely interesting to men of all sorts in all ages, and even to philosophers, in the whole phenomenon of the saint, it is undoubtedly the appearance of the miraculous therein—namely, the immediate *succession of opposites*, of states of the soul regarded as morally antithetical: it was believed here to be self-evident that a "bad man" was all at once turned into a "saint," a good man. The hitherto existing psychology was wrecked at this point; it is not possible it may have happened principally because psychology had placed itself under the dominion of morals, because it *believed* in oppositions of moral values, and saw, read, and *interpreted* these oppositions into the text and facts of the case? What? "Miracle" only an error of interpretation? A lack of philology?

It seems that the Latin races are far more deeply attached to their Catholicism than we Northerners are to Christianity generally, and that consequently unbelief in Catholic countries means something quite different from what it does among Protestants—namely, a sort of revolt against the spirit of the race, while with us it is rather a return to the spirit (or non-spirit) of the race. We Northerners undoubtedly derive our origin from barbarous races, even as regards our talents for religion—we have *poor* talents for it. One may make an exception in the case of the Celts, who have theretofore furnished also the best soil for Christian infection in the north: the Christian ideal blossomed forth in France as much as ever the pale sun of the north would allow it. How strangely pious for our taste are still these later French skeptics, whenever there is any Celtic blood in their origin! How Catholic, how un-German does Auguste Comte's Sociology seem to us, with the Roman logic of its instincts! How Jesuitical, that amiable and shrewd cicerone of Port-Royal, Sainte-Beuve, in spite of all his hostility to Jesuits! And even Ernest Renan: how inaccessible to us Northerners does the language of such a Renan appear, in whom every instant the merest touch of religious thrill throws his refined voluptuous and comfortably couching soul off its balance! Let us repeat after him these fine sentences—and what wickedness and haughtiness is immediately aroused by way of answer in our probably less beautiful but harder souls, that is to say, in

our more German souls!—"*Disons donc hardiment que la religion est un produit de l'homme normal, que l'homme est le plus
dans le vrai quand il est le plus religieux et le plus assuré d'une
destinée infinie. . . . C'est quand il est bon qu'il veut que la virtu
corresponde à un order éternal, c'est quand il contemple les
choses d'une manière désintéressée qu'il trouve la mort
révoltante et absurde. Comment ne pas supposer que c'est dans
ces moments là, que l'homme voit le mieux?*" . . . These sentences are so extremely *antipodal* to my ears and habits of
thought, that in my first impulse of rage on finding them, I wrote
on the margin, "*la niaiserie religieuse par excellence!*"—until
in my later rage I even took a fancy to them, these sentences
with their truth absolutely inverted! It is so nice and such a distinction to have one's own antipodes!

That which is so astonishing in the religious life of the ancient
Greeks is the irrestrainable stream of *gratitude* which it pours
forth—it is a very superior kind of man who takes *such* an attitude towards nature and life.—Later on, when the populace got
the upper hand in Greece, *fear* became rampant also in religion; and Christianity was preparing itself.

The passion for God: there are churlish, honest-hearted, and
importunate kinds of it, like that of Luther—the whole of
Protestantism lacks the southern *delicatezza*. There is an
Oriental exaltation of the mind in it, like that of an unde-
servedly favored or elevated slave, as in the case of St.
Augustine, for instance, who lacks in an offensive manner, all
nobility in bearing and desires. There is a feminine tenderness
and sensuality in it, which modestly and unconsciously longs
for a *unio mystica et physica*, as in the case of Madame de
Guyon. In many cases it appears, curiously enough, as the disguise of a girl's or youth's puberty; here and there even as the
hysteria of an old maid, also as her last ambition. The Church
has frequently canonized the woman in such a case.

The mightiest men have hitherto always bowed reverently
before the saint, as the enigma of self-subjugation and utter
voluntary privation—why did they thus bow? They divined in
him—and as it were behind the questionableness of his frail

and wretched appearance—the superior force which wished to test itself by such a subjugation; the strength of will, in which they recognized their own strength and love of power, and knew how to honor it: they honored something in themselves when they honored the saint. In addition to this, the contemplation of the saint suggested to them a suspicion: such an enormity of self-negation and anti-naturalness will not have been coveted for nothing—they have said, inquiringly. There is perhaps a reason for it, some very great danger, about which the ascetic might wish to be more accurately informed through his secret interlocutors and visitors? In a word, the mighty ones of the world learned to have a new fear before him, they divined a new power, a strange, still unconquered enemy:—it was the "Will to Power" which obliged them to halt before the saint. They had to question him.

In the Jewish "Old Testament," the book of divine justice, there are men, things, and sayings on such an immense scale, that Greek and Indian literature has nothing to compare with it. One stands with fear and reverence before those stupendous remains of what man was formerly, and one has sad thoughts about old Asia and its little out-pushed peninsula Europe, which would like, by all means, to figure before Asia as the "Progress of Mankind." To be sure, he who is himself only a slender, tame house-animal, and knows only the wants of a house-animal (like our cultured people of today, including the Christians of "cultured" Christianity), need neither be amazed nor even sad amid those ruins—the taste for the Old Testament is a touchstone with respect to "great" and "small": perhaps he will find that the New Testament, the book of grace, still appeals more to his heart (there is much of the odor of the genuine, tender, stupid beadsman and petty soul in it). To have bound up this New Testament (a kind of *rococo* of taste in every respect) along with the Old Testament into one book, as the "Bible," as "The Book in Itself," is perhaps the greatest audacity and "sin against the Spirit" which literary Europe has upon its conscience.

Why Atheism nowadays? "The father" in God is thoroughly refuted; equally so "the judge," "the rewarder." Also his "free will": he does not hear—and even if he did, he would not know how to

274 🐌 Friedrich Wilhelm Nietzsche

help. The worst is that he seems incapable of communicating himself clearly; is he uncertain?—This is what I have made out (by questioning and listening at a variety of conversations) to be the cause of the decline of European theism; it appears to me that though the religious instinct is in vigorous growth—it rejects the theistic satisfaction with profound distrust.

What does all modern philosophy mainly do? Since Descartes—and indeed more in defiance of him than on the basis of his procedure—an *attentat* has been made on the part of all philosophers on the old conception of the soul, under the guise of a criticism of the subject and predicate conception— that is to say, an *attentat* on the fundamental presupposition of Christian doctrine. Modern philosophy, as epistemological skepticism, is secretly or openly *anti-Christian*, although (for keener ears, be it said) by no means anti-religious. Formerly, in effect, one believed in "the soul" as one believed in grammar and the grammatical subject: one said, "I" is the condition, "think" is the predicate and is conditioned—to think is an activity for which one *must* suppose a subject as cause. The attempt was then made, with marvelous tenacity and subtlety, to see if one could not get out of this net—to see if the opposite was not perhaps true: "think" the condition, and "I" the condi- tioned; "I," therefore, only a synthesis which has been *made* by thinking itself. *Kant* really wished to prove that, starting from the subject, the subject could not be proved—nor the object either: the possibility of an *apparent existence* of the subject, and therefore of "the soul," may not always have been strange to him—the thought which once had an immense power on earth as the Vedanta philosophy.

There is a great ladder of religious cruelty, with many rounds; but three of these are the most important. Once upon a time men sacrificed human beings to their God, and perhaps just those they loved the best—to this category belong the firstling sacrifices of all primitive religions, and also the sacrifice of the Emperor Tiberius in the Mithra-Grotto on the Island of Capri, that most terrible of all Roman anachronisms. Then, during the moral epoch of mankind, they sacrificed to their God the strongest instincts they possessed, their "nature"; *this* festal joy shines in the cruel glances of ascetics and "anti-natural" fanatics. Finally, what still remained to be sacrificed? Was it not necessary in the end for men to sacrifice everything comforting, holy, healing, all hope, all faith in hidden harmonies, in future blessedness and justice? Was it not necessary to sacrifice God himself, and out of cruelty to themselves to worship stone, stupidity, gravity, fate, nothingness? To sacrifice God for nothingness—this paradoxical mystery of the ultimate cruelty has been reserved for the rising generation; we all know something thereof already.

Whoever, like myself, prompted by some enigmatical desire, has long endeavored to go to the bottom of the question of pessimism and free it from the half-Christian, half-German narrowness and stupidity in which it has finally presented itself to this century, namely, in the form of Schopenhauer's philosophy; whoever, with an Asiatic and super-Asiatic eye, has actually looked inside, and into the most world-renouncing of all possible modes of thought—beyond good and evil and no longer like Buddha and Schopenhauer, under the dominion and delusion of morality—whoever has done this, has perhaps just thereby, without really desiring it, opened his eyes to behold the opposite ideal: the ideal of the most world-approving, exuberant and vivacious man, who has not only learned to compromise and arrange with that which was and is, but wishes to have it again *as it was and is,* for all eternity, insatiably calling out *de capo,* not only to himself, but to the whole piece and play; and not only the play, but actually to him who requires the play—and makes it necessary; because he always requires himself anew—and makes himself necessary.—What? And this would not be—*circulus vitiosus deus?*

The distance, and as it were the space around man, grows with the strength of his intellectual vision and insight: his world becomes profounder; new stars, new enigmas, and notions are ever coming into view. Perhaps everything on which the intellectual eye has exercised its acuteness and profundity has just been an occasion for its exercise, something of a game, something for children and childish minds. Perhaps the most solemn conceptions that have caused the most fighting and suffering, the conceptions "God" and "sin," will one day seem to us of no more importance than a child's plaything or a child's pain seems to an old man—and perhaps another plaything and another pain will then be necessary once more for "the old man"—always childish enough, an eternal child!

Has it been observed to what extent outward idleness, or semi-idleness, is necessary to a real religious life (alike for its favorite microscopic labor of self-examination, and for its soft placidity called "prayer," the state of perpetual readiness for the "coming of God"), I mean the idleness with a good conscience, the idleness of olden times and of blood, to which the aristocratic sentiment that work is *dishonoring*—that it vulgarizes body and soul—is not quite unfamiliar? And that consequently the modern, noisy, time-engrossing, conceited, foolishly proud laboriousness educates and prepares for "unbelief" more than anything else? Amongst these, for instance, who are at present living apart from religion in Germany, I find "freethinkers" of diversified species and origin, but above all a majority of those in whom laboriousness from generation to generation has dissolved the religious instincts; so that they no longer know what purpose religions serve, and only note their existence in the world with a kind of dull astonishment. They feel themselves already fully occupied, these good people, be it by their business or by their pleasures, not to mention the "Fatherland," and the newspapers, and their "family duties"; it seems that they have no time whatever left for religion; and above all, it is not obvious to them whether it is a question of a new business or a new pleasure—for it is impossible, they say to themselves, that people should go to church merely to spoil their tempers. They are by no means enemies of religious customs; should certain circumstances, state affairs perhaps, require their participation in such customs, they do what is required, as so many things are done—with a patient and unassuming seriousness, and without much curiosity or discomfort—they live too much apart and outside to feel even the necessity for a *for* or *against* in such matters. Among those indifferent persons may be reckoned nowadays the majority of German Protestants of the middle classes, especially in the great laborious centers of trade and also the majority of laborious scholars, and the entire University personnel (with the exception of the theologians, whose existence and possibility there always give psychologists new and more subtle puzzles to solve). On the part of pious, or merely church-going people, there is seldom any idea of *how much* good will, one might say arbitrary will, is now necessary for a German scholar to take the problem of religion seriously; his whole profession (and as I have said, his whole workmanlike laboriousness, to which he is compelled by his modern conscience) inclines him to a lofty and almost charitable serenity as regards religion, with which is occasionally mingled a slight disdain for the "uncleanliness" of spirit which he takes for granted wherever anyone still professes to belong to the Church. It is only with the help of history (*not* through his own personal experience, therefore) that the scholar succeeds in bringing himself to a respectful seriousness, and to a certain timid deference in presence of religions; but even when his sentiments have reached the stage of gratitude towards them, he has not personally advanced one step nearer to that which still maintains itself as Church or as piety; perhaps even the contrary. The practical indifference to religious matters in the midst of which he has been born and brought up, usually sublimates itself in his case into circumspection and cleanliness, which shuns contact with religious men and things; and it may be just the depth of his tolerance and humanity which prompts him to avoid the delicate trouble which tolerance itself brings with it.—Every age has its own divine type of naiveté, for the discovery of which other ages may envy it: and how much naiveté—adorable, childlike, and boundlessly foolish naiveté is involved in this belief of the scholar in his superiority, in the good conscience of his tolerance, in the unsuspecting, simple certainty with which his instinct treats the religious man as a lower and less valuable type, beyond, before, and *above* which he himself has developed—he, the little arrogant dwarf and mob-man, the sedulously alert, head-and-hand drudge of "ideas," of "modern ideas"!

Whoever has seen deeply into the world has doubtless divined what wisdom there is in the fact that men are superficial. It is their preservative instinct which teaches them to be flighty, lightsome, and false. Here and there one finds a passionate and exaggerated adoration of "pure forms" in philosophers as well as in artists: it is not to be doubted that whoever has *need* of the cult of the superficial to that extent, has at one time or another made an unlucky dive *beneath* it. Perhaps there is even an order of rank with respect to those burnt children, the born artists who find the enjoyment of life only in trying to *falsify* its image (as if taking wearisome revenge on it); one might guess to what degree life has disgusted them, by the extent to which they wish to see its image falsified, attenuated, ultrafied, and deified—one might reckon the *homines religiosi* amongst the artists, as their *highest* rank. It is the profound, suspicious fear of an incurable pessimism which compels whole centuries to fasten their teeth into a religious interpretation of existence: the fear of the instinct which divines that truth might be attained *too soon*, before man has become strong enough, hard enough, artist enough. . . . Piety, the "Life in God," regarded in this light, would appear as the most elaborate and ultimate product of the *fear* of truth, as artist-adoration and artist-intoxication in presence of the most logical of all falsifications, as the will to the inversion of truth, to untruth at any price. Perhaps there has hitherto been no more effective means of beautifying man than piety; by means of it man can become so artful, so superficial, so iridescent, and so good, that his appearance no longer offends.

To love mankind *for God's sake*—this has so far been the noblest and remotest sentiment to which mankind has attained. That love to mankind, without any redeeming intention in the background, is only an *additional* folly and brutishness, that the inclination to this love has first to get its proportion, its delicacy, its grain of salt and sprinkling of ambergris from a higher inclination—whoever first perceived and "experienced" this, however his tongue may have stammered as it attempted to express such a delicate matter, let him for all time be holy and respected, as the man who has so far flown highest and gone astray in the finest fashion!

The philosopher, as *we* free spirits understand him—as the man of the greatest responsibility, who has the conscience for the general development of mankind—will use religion for his disciplining and educating work, just as he will use the contemporary political and economic conditions. The selecting and disciplining influence—destructive, as well as creative and fashioning—which can be exercised by means of religion is manifold and varied, according to the sort of people placed under its spell and protection. For those who are strong and independent, destined and trained to command, in whom the judgment and skill of a ruling race is incorporated, religion is an additional means for overcoming resistance in the exercise of authority—as a bond which binds rulers and subjects in common, betraying and surrendering to the former the conscience of the latter, their inmost heart, which would fain escape obedience. And in the case of the unique natures of noble origin, if by virtue of superior spirituality they should incline to a more retired and contemplative life, reserving to themselves only the more refined forms of government (over chosen disciples or members of an order), religion itself may be used as a means for obtaining peace from the noise and trouble of managing *grosser* affairs, and for securing immunity from the *unavoidable* filth of all political agitation. The Brahmins, for instance, understood this fact. With the help of a religious organization, they secured to themselves the power of nominating kings for the people, while their sentiments prompted them to keep apart and outside, as men with a higher and super-regal mission. At the same time religion gives inducement and opportunity to some of the subjects to qualify themselves for future ruling and commanding: the slowly ascending ranks and classes, in which, through fortunate marriage customs, volitional power and delight in self-control are on the increase. To them religion offers sufficient incentives and temptations to aspire to higher intellectuality, and to experience the sentiments of authoritative self-control, of silence, and of solitude. Asceticism and Puritanism are almost indispensable means of educating and ennobling a race which seeks to rise above its hereditary baseness and work itself upward to future supremacy. And finally, to ordinary men, to the majority of the people, who exist for service and general utility, and are only so far entitled to exist, religion gives invaluable contentedness with their lot and condition, peace of heart, ennoblement of obedience, additional social happiness and sympathy, with something of transfiguration and embellishment, something of justification of all the commonplaceness, all the meanness, all the semi-animal poverty of their souls. Religion, together with the religious significance of life, sheds sunshine over such perpetually harassed men, and makes even their own aspect endurable to them; it operates upon them as the Epicurean philosophy usually operates upon sufferers of a higher order, in a refreshing and refining manner, almost *turning* suffering *to account,* and in the end even hallowing and vindicating it. There is perhaps nothing so admirable in Christianity and Buddhism as their art of teaching even the lowest to elevate themselves by piety to a seemingly higher order of things, and thereby to retain their satisfaction with the actual world in which they find it difficult enough to live—this very difficulty being necessary.

To be sure—to make also the bad counter-reckoning against such religions, and to bring to light their secret dangers—the cost is always excessive and terrible when religions do *not* operate as an educational and disciplinary medium in the hands of the philosopher, but rule voluntarily and *paramountly,* when they wish to be the final end, and not a means along with other means. Among men, as among all other animals, there is a surplus of defective, diseased, degenerating, infirm, and necessarily suffering individuals; the successful cases, among men also, are always the exception; and in view of the fact that man is *the animal not yet properly adapted to his environment,* the rare exception. But worse still. The higher the type a man represents, the greater is the improbability that he will *succeed;* the accidental, the law of irrationality in the general constitution of mankind, manifests itself most terribly in its destructive effect on the higher orders of men, the conditions of whose lives are delicate, diverse, and difficult to determine. What, then, is the attitude of the two greatest religions above-mentioned to the *surplus* of failures in life? They endeavor to preserve and keep alive whatever can be preserved; in fact, as the religions *for sufferers,* they take the part of these upon principle; they are always in favor of those who suffer from life as from a disease, and they would fain treat every other experience of life as false and impossible. However highly we may esteem this indulgent and preservative care (inasmuch as in applying to others, it has applied, and applies also to the highest and usually the most suffering type of man), the hitherto *paramount religions*—to give a general appreciation of them—are among the principal causes which have kept the type of "man" upon a lower level— they have preserved too much *that which should have perished.* One has to thank them for invaluable services; and who is sufficiently rich in gratitude not to feel poor at the contemplation of all that the "spiritual men" of Christianity have done for Europe hitherto! But when they had given comfort to the sufferers, courage to the oppressed and despairing, a staff and support to the helpless, and when they had allured from society into convents and spiritual penitentiaries the brokenhearted and distracted: what else had they to do in order to work systematically in that fashion, and with a good conscience, for the preservation of all the sick and suffering, which means, in deed and in truth, to work for *the deterioration of the European race?* To *reverse* all estimates of value—*that* is what they had to do! And to shatter the strong, to spoil great hopes, to cast suspicion on the delight in beauty, to break down everything autonomous, manly, conquering, and imperious—all instincts which are natural to the highest and most successful type of "man"—into uncertainty, distress of conscience, and self-destruction; forsooth, to invert all love of the earthly and of supremacy over the earth, into hatred of the earth and earthly things—*that* is the task the Church imposed on itself, and was obliged to impose, until, according, to its standard of value, "unworldliness," "unsensuousness," and "higher man" fused into one sentiment. If one could observe the strangely painful equally coarse and refined comedy of European Christianity with the derisive and impartial eye of an Epicurean god, I should think one would never cease marveling and laughing; does it not actually seem that some single will has ruled over Europe for eighteen centuries in order to make a *sublime abortion* of man? He, however, who, with opposite requirements (no longer Epicurean) and with some divine hammer in his hand, could approach this almost voluntary degeneration and stunting of mankind, as exemplified in the European Christian (Pascal, for instance), would he not have to cry aloud with rage, pity, and horror: "Oh, you bunglers, presumptuous pitiful bunglers, what have you done! Was that a work for your hands? How you have hacked and botched my finest stone! What have *you* presumed to do!"—I should say that Christianity has hitherto been the most portentous of presumptions. Men, not great enough, nor hard enough to be entitled as artists to take part in fashioning *man*; men, not sufficiently strong and far-sighted to *allow*, with sublime self-constraint, the obvious law of the thousandfold failures and perishings to prevail; men, not sufficiently noble to see the radically different grades of rank and intervals of rank that separate man from man—*such* men, with their "equality before God," have hitherto swayed the destiny of Europe; until at last a dwarfed, almost ludicrous species has been produced, a gregarious animal, something obliging, sickly, mediocre, the European of the present day.

Sigmund Freud

(1856–1939)

From

THE INTERPRETATION OF DREAMS

The Analysis of a Specimen Dream

The epigraph on the title-page of this volume indicates the tradition to which I prefer to ally myself in my conception of the dream. I am proposing to show that dreams are capable of interpretation; and any contributions to the solution of the problem which have already been discussed will emerge only as possible byproducts in the accomplishment of my special task. On the hypothesis that dreams are susceptible of interpretation, I at once find myself in disagreement with the prevailing doctrine of dreams—in fact, with all the theories of dreams, excepting only that of Scherner, for "to interpret a dream" is to specify its "meaning," to replace it by something which takes its position in the concatenation of our psychic activities as a link of definite importance and value. But, as we have seen, the scientific theories of the dream leave no room for a problem of dream-interpretation; since, in the first place, according to these theories, dreaming is not a psychic activity at all, but a somatic process which makes itself known to the psychic apparatus by means of symbols. Lay opinion has always been opposed to these theories. It asserts its privilege of proceeding illogically, and although it admits that dreams are incomprehensible and absurd, it cannot summon up the courage to deny that dreams have any significance. Led by a dim intuition, it seems rather to assume that dreams have a meaning, albeit a hidden one; that they are intended as a substitute for some other thought process, and that we have only to disclose this substitute correctly in order to discover the hidden meaning of the dream.

The unscientific world, therefore, has always endeavored to "interpret" dreams, and by applying one or the other of two essentially different methods. The first of these methods envisages the dream-content as a whole, and seeks to replace it by another content, which is intelligible and in certain respects analogous. This is symbolic dream-interpretation; and of course it goes to pieces at the very outset in the case of those dreams which are not only unintelligible but confused. The construction which the biblical Joseph placed upon the dream of Pharaoh furnishes an example of this method. The seven fat kine, after which came seven lean ones that devoured the former, were a symbolic substitute for seven years of famine in the land of Egypt, which according to the prediction were to consume all the surplus that seven fruitful years had produced. Most of the artificial dreams contrived by the poets are intended for some such symbolic interpretation, for they reproduce the thought conceived by the poet in a guise not unlike the disguise which we are wont to find in our dreams.

The idea that the dream concerns itself chiefly with the future, whose form it surmises in advance—a relic of the prophetic significance with which dreams were once invested—now becomes the motive for translating into the future the meaning of the dream which has been found by means of symbolic interpretation.

A demonstration of the manner in which one arrives at such a symbolic interpretation cannot, of course, be given. Success remains a matter of ingenious conjecture, of direct intuition, and for this reason dream-interpretation has naturally been elevated into an art which seems to depend upon extraordinary gifts. The second of the two popular methods of dream-interpretation entirely abandons such claims. It might be described as the "cipher method," since it treats the dream as a kind of secret code in which every sign is translated into another sign of known meaning, according to an established key. For example, I have dreamt of a letter, and also of a funeral or the like; I consult a "dream-book," and I find that "letter" is to be translated by "vexation" and "funeral" by "engagement." It now remains to establish a connection, which I am again to assume as pertaining to the future, by means of the rigmarole which I have deciphered. An interesting variant of this cipher procedure, a variant in which its character of purely mechanical transference is to a certain extent corrected, is presented in the work on dream-interpretation by Artemidoros of Daldis. Here not only the dream-content, but also the personality and social position of the dreamer are taken into consideration, so that the same dream-content has a significance for the rich man, the married man, or the orator, which is different from that which applies to the poor man, the bachelor, or, let us say, the merchant. The essential point, then, in this procedure is that the work of interpretation is not applied to the entirety of the dream, but to each portion of the dream-content severally, as though the dream were a conglomerate in which each fragment calls for special treatment. Incoherent and confused dreams are certainly those that have been responsible for the invention of the cipher method.

The worthlessness of both these popular methods of interpretation does not admit of discussion. As regards the scientific treatment of the subject, the symbolic method is limited in its application, and is not susceptible of a general exposition. In the cipher method everything depends upon whether the "key," the dream-book, is reliable, and for that all guarantees are lacking. So that one might be tempted to grant the contention of the philosophers and psychiatrists, and to dismiss the problem of dream-interpretation as altogether fanciful.

I have, however, come to think differently. I have been forced to perceive that here, once more, we have one of those not infrequent cases where an ancient and stubbornly retained popular belief seems to have come nearer to the truth of the matter than the opinion of modern science. I must insist that the dream actually does possess a meaning, and that a scientific method of dream-interpretation is possible. I arrived at my knowledge of this method in the following manner:

For years I have been occupied with the resolution of certain psychopathological structures—hysterical phobias, obsessional ideas, and the like—with therapeutic intentions. I have been so occupied, in fact, ever since I heard the significant statement of Joseph Breuer, to the effect that in these structures, regarded as morbid symptoms, solution and treatment go hand in hand. Where it has been possible to trace a pathological idea back to those elements in the psychic life of the patient to which it owed its origin, this idea has crumbled away, and the patient has been relieved of it. In view of the failure of our other therapeutic efforts, and in the face of the mysterious character of these pathological conditions, it seemed to me tempting, in spite of all the difficulties, to follow the method initiated by Breuer until a complete elucidation of the subject had been achieved. I shall have occasion elsewhere to give a detailed account of the form which the technique of this procedure has finally assumed, and of the results of my efforts. In the course of these psychoanalytic studies, I happened upon the question of dream-interpretation. My patients, after I had pledged them to inform me of all the ideas and thoughts which occurred to them in connection with a given theme, related their dreams, and thus taught me that a dream may be interpolated in the psychic concatenation, which may be followed backwards from a pathological idea into the patient's memory. The next step was to treat the dream itself as a symptom, and to apply to it the method of interpretation which had been worked out for such symptoms.

For this a certain psychic preparation on the part of the patient is necessary. A twofold effort is made, to stimulate his attentiveness in respect of his psychic perceptions, and to eliminate the critical spirit in which he is ordinarily in the habit of viewing such thoughts as come to the surface. For the purpose of self-observation with concentrated attention it is advantageous that the patient should take up a restful position and close his eyes; he must be explicitly instructed to renounce all criticism of the thought-formations which he may perceive. He must also be told that the success of the psychoanalysis depends upon his noting and communicating everything that passes through his mind, and that he must not allow himself to suppress one idea because it seems to him unimportant or irrelevant to the subject, or another because it seems nonsensical. He must preserve an absolute impartiality in respect to his ideas; for if he is unsuccessful in finding the desired solution of the dream, the obsessional idea, or the like, it will be because he permits himself to be critical of them.

I have noticed in the course of my psychoanalytical work that the psychological state of a man in an attitude of reflection is entirely different from that of a man who is observing his psychic processes. In reflection there is a greater play of psychic activity than in the most attentive self-observation; this is shown even by the tense attitude and the wrinkled brow of the man in a state of reflection, as opposed to the mimic tranquillity of the man observing himself. In both cases there must be concentrated attention, but the reflective man makes use of his critical faculties, with the result that he rejects some of the thoughts which rise into consciousness after he has become aware of them, and abruptly interrupts others, so that he does not follow the lines of thought which they would otherwise open up for him; while in respect of yet other thoughts he is able to behave in such a manner that they do not become conscious at all—that is to say, they are suppressed before they are perceived. In self-observation, on the other hand, he has but one task—that of suppressing criticism; if he succeeds in doing this, an unlimited number of thoughts enter his consciousness which would otherwise have eluded his grasp. With the aid of the material thus obtained—material which is new to the self-observer—it is possible to achieve the interpretation of pathological ideas, and also that of dream-formations. As will be seen, the point is to induce a psychic state which is in some degree analogous, as regards the distribution of psychic energy (mobile attention), to the state of the mind before falling asleep—and also, of course, to the hypnotic state. On falling asleep the "undesired ideas" emerge, owing to the slackening of a certain arbitrary (and, of course, also critical) action, which is allowed to influence the trend of our ideas; we are accustomed to speak of fatigue as the reason of this slackening; the emerging undesired ideas are changed into visual and auditory images. In the condition which it utilized for the analysis of dreams and pathological ideas, this activity is purposely and deliberately renounced, and the psychic energy thus saved (or some part of it) is employed in attentively tracking the undesired thoughts which now come to the surface—thoughts which retain their identity as ideas (in which the condition differs from the state of falling asleep). *"Undesired ideas" are thus changed into "desired" ones.*

There are many people who do not seem to find it easy to adopt the required attitude toward the apparently "freely rising" ideas, and to renounce the criticism which is otherwise applied to them. The "undesired ideas" habitually evoke the most violent resistance, which seeks to prevent them from com-

ing to the surface. But if we may credit our great poet-philoso-
pher Friedrich Schiller, the essential condition of poetical creation includes a very similar attitude. In a certain passage in
his correspondence with Körner (for the tracing of which we are
indebted to Otto Rank), Schiller replies in the following words
to a friend who complains of his lack of creative power: "The
reason for your complaint lies, it seems to me, in the constraint
which your intellect imposes upon your imagination. Here I
will make an observation, and illustrate it by an allegory.
Apparently it is not good—and indeed it hinders the creative
work of the mind—if the intellect examines too closely the
ideas already pouring in, as it were, at the gates. Regarded in
isolation, an idea may be quite insignificant, and venturesome
in the extreme, but it may acquire importance from an idea
which follows it; perhaps, in a certain collocation with other
ideas, which may seem equally absurd, it may be capable of
furnishing a very serviceable link. The intellect cannot judge
all these ideas unless it can retain them until it has considered
them in connection with these other ideas. In the case of a creative mind, it seems to me, the intellect has withdrawn its
watchers from the gates, and the ideas rush in pell-mell, and
only then does it review and inspect the multitude. You worthy
critics, or whatever you may call yourselves, are ashamed or
afraid of the momentary and passing madness which is found in
all real creators, the longer or shorter duration of which distinguishes the thinking artist from the dreamer. Hence your complaints of unfruitfulness, for you reject too soon and discriminate too severely" (letter of December 1, 1788).

And yet, such a withdrawal of the watchers from the gates of
the intellect, as Schiller puts it, such a translation into the condition of uncritical self-observation, is by no means difficult.

Most of my patients accomplish it after my first instructions.
I myself can do so very completely, if I assist the process by
writing down the ideas that flash through my mind. The quan-
tum of psychic energy by which the critical activity is thus
reduced, and by which the intensity of self-observation may be
increased, varies considerably according to the subject-matter
upon which the attention is to be fixed.

The first step in the application of this procedure teaches us
that one cannot make the dream as a whole the object of one's

attention, but only the individual components of its content. If I ask a patient who is as yet unpracticed: "What occurs to you in connection with this dream?" he is unable, as a rule, to fix upon anything in his psychic field of vision. I must first dissect the dream for him; then, in connection with each fragment, he gives me a number of ideas which may be described as the "thoughts behind" this part of the dream. In this first and important condition, then, the method of dream-interpretation which I employ diverges from the popular, historical and legendary method of interpretation by symbolism and approaches more nearly to the second or "cipher method." Like this, it is an interpretation in detail, not *en masse*; like this, it conceives the dream, from the outset, as something built up, as a conglomerate of psychic formations.

In the course of my psychoanalysis of neurotics I have already subjected perhaps more than a thousand dreams to interpretation, but I do not wish to use this material now as an introduction to the theory and technique of dream-interpretation. For quite apart from the fact that I should lay myself open to the objection that these are the dreams of neuropaths, so that the conclusions drawn from them would not apply to the dreams of healthy persons, there is another reason that impels me to reject them. The theme to which these dreams point is, of course, always the history of the malady that is responsible for the neurosis. Hence every dream would require a very long introduction, and an investigation of the nature and etiological conditions of the psychoneuroses, matters which are in themselves novel and exceedingly strange, and which would therefore distract attention from the dream-problem proper. My purpose is rather to prepare the way, by the solution of the dream-problem, for the solution of the more difficult problems of the psychology of the neuroses. But if I eliminate the dreams of neurotics, which constitute my principal material, I cannot be too fastidious in my treatment of the rest. Only those dreams are left which have been incidentally related to me by healthy persons of my acquaintance, or which I find given as examples in the literature of dream-life. Unfortunately, in all these dreams I am deprived of the analysis without which I cannot find the meaning of the dream. My mode of procedure is, of course, less easy than that of the popular cipher method, which

translates the given dream-content by reference to an established key; I, on the contrary, hold that the same dream-content
may conceal a different meaning in the case of different persons, or in different connections. I must, therefore, resort to my
own dreams as a source of abundant and convenient material,
furnished by a person who is more or less normal, and containing references to many incidents of everyday life. I shall certainly be confronted with doubts as to the trustworthiness of
these "self-analyses," and it will be said that arbitrariness is
by no means excluded in such analyses. In my own judgment,
conditions are more likely to be favorable in self-observation
than in the observation of others; in any case, it is permissible
to investigate how much can be accomplished in the matter of
dream-interpretation by means of self-analysis. There are other
difficulties which must be overcome in my own inner self. One
has a comprehensible aversion to exposing so many intimate
details of one's own psychic life, and one does not feel secure
against the misinterpretations of strangers. But one must be
able to transcend such considerations. *"Tout psychologiste,"*
writes Delboeuf, *"est obligé de faire l'aveu même de ses faib-
lesses s'il croît par là jeter du jour sur quelque problème obscur."*
And I may assume for the reader that his initial interest in the
indiscretions which I must commit will very soon give way to an
exclusive engrossment in the psychological problems elucidat-
ed by them.

I shall therefore select one of my own dreams for the purpose
of elucidating my method of interpretation. Every such dream
necessitates a preliminary statement; so that I must now beg
the reader to make my interests his own for a time, and to
become absorbed, with me, in the most trifling details of my
life; for an interest in the hidden significance of dreams imper-
atively demands just such a transference.

Preliminary Statement

In the summer of 1895 I had treated psycho-analytically a
young lady who was an intimate friend of mine and of my family.
It will be understood that such complicated relations may
excite manifold feelings in the physician, and especially the
psychotherapist. The personal interest of the physician is

greater, but his authority less. If he fails, his friendship with the patient's relatives is in danger of being undermined. In this case, however, the treatment ended in partial success; the patient was cured of her hysterical anxiety, but not of all her somatic symptoms. At that time I was not yet quite sure of the criteria which denote the final cure of an hysterical case, and I expected her to accept a solution which did not seem acceptable to her. In the midst of this disagreement we discontinued the treatment for the summer holidays. One day a younger colleague, one of my most intimate friends, who had visited the patient—Irma—and her family in their country residence, called upon me. I asked him how Irma was, and received the reply: "She is better, but not quite well." I realize that these words of my friend Otto's, or the tone of voice in which they were spoken, annoyed me. I thought I heard a reproach in the words, perhaps to the effect that I had promised the patient too much, and—rightly or wrongly—I attributed Otto's apparent "taking sides" against me to the influence of the patient's relatives, who, I assumed, had never approved of my treatment. This disagreeable impression, however, did not become clear to me, nor did I speak of it. That same evening I wrote the clinical history of Irma's case, in order to give it, as though to justify myself, to Dr. M., a mutual friend, who was at that time the leading personality in our circle. During the night (or rather in the early morning) I had the following dream, which I recorded immediately after waking:

DREAM OF JULY 23-24, 1895

A great hall—a number of guests, whom we are receiving— among them Irma, whom I immediately take aside, as though to answer her letter, and to reproach her for not yet accepting the "solution." I say to her: "If you still have pains, it is really only your own fault."—She answers: "If you only knew what pains I have now in the throat, stomach, and abdomen—I am choked by them." I am startled, and look at her. She looks pale and puffy. I think that after all I must be overlooking some organic affection. I take her to the window and look into her throat. She offers some resistance to this, like a woman who has a set of false teeth. I think, surely, she doesn't need them.—The mouth then opens wide, and I find a large white spot on the right, and elsewhere I see extensive grayish-white scabs adhering to curiously curled formations, which are evidently shaped like the turbinal bones of the nose.—I quickly call Dr. M., who repeats the examination and confirms it. . . . Dr. M. looks quite unlike his usual self; he is very pale, he limps, and his chin is clean-shaven. . . . Now my friend Otto, too, is standing beside her, and my friend Leopold percusses her covered chest, and says: "She has a dullness below, on the left," and also calls attention to an infiltrated portion of skin on the left shoulder (which I can feel, in spite of the dress) . . . . M. says: "There's no doubt that it's an infection, but it doesn't matter; dysentery will follow and the poison will be eliminated." . . . We know, too, precisely how the infection originated. My friend Otto, not long ago, gave her, when she was feeling unwell, an injection of a preparation of propyl . . . propyls . . . propionic acid . . . trimethylamin (the formula of which I see before me, printed in heavy type). . . . One doesn't give such injections so rashly. . . . Probably, too, the syringe was not clean.

This dream has an advantage over many others. It is at once obvious to what events of the preceding day it is related, and of what subject it treats. The preliminary statement explains these matters. The news of Irma's health which I had received from Otto, and the clinical history, which I was writing late into the night, had occupied my psychic activities even during sleep. Nevertheless, no one who had read the preliminary report, and had knowledge of the content of the dream, could guess what the dream signified. Nor do I myself know. I am puzzled by the morbid symptoms of which Irma complains in the dream, for they are not the symptoms for which I treated her. I smile at the nonsensical idea of an injection of propionic acid, and at Dr. M.'s attempt at consolation. Towards the end the dream seems more obscure and quicker in tempo than at the beginning. In order to learn the significance of all these details I resolve to undertake an exhaustive analysis.

Analysis

The hall—a number of guests, whom we are receiving. We were living that summer at *Bellevue,* an isolated house on one of the hills adjoining the Kahlenberg. This house was originally built as a place of entertainment, and therefore has unusually lofty, hall-like rooms. The dream was dreamed in *Bellevue,* a few days before my wife's birthday. During the day my wife had mentioned that she expected several friends, and among them Irma, to come to us as guests for her birthday. My dream, then, anticipates this situation: It is my wife's birthday, and we are receiving a number of people, among them Irma, as guests in the large hall of *Bellevue.*

I reproach Irma for not having accepted the "solution," I say, "If you still have pains, it is really your own fault." I might even have said this while awake; I may have actually said it. At that time I was of the opinion (recognized later to be incorrect) that my task was limited to informing patients of the hidden meaning of their symptoms. Whether they then accepted or did not accept the solution upon which success depended—for that I was not responsible. I am grateful to this error, which, fortunately, has now been overcome, since it made life easier for me at a time when, with all my unavoidable ignorance, I was expected to effect successful cures. But I note that in the speech which I make to Irma in the dream I am above all anxious that I shall not be blamed for the pains which she still suffers. If it is Irma's own fault, it cannot be mine. Should the purpose of the dream be looked for in this quarter?

Irma's complaints—pains in the neck, abdomen, and stomach; she is choked by them. Pains in the stomach belonged to the symptom-complex of my patient, but they were not very prominent; she complained rather of qualms and a feeling of nausea. Pains in the neck and abdomen and constriction of the throat played hardly any part in her case. I wonder why I have decided upon this choice of symptoms in the dream; for the moment I cannot discover the reason.

She looks pale and puffy. My patient had always a rosy complexion. I suspect that here another person is being substituted for her.

I am startled at the idea that I may have overlooked some organic affection. This, as the reader will readily believe, is a constant fear with the specialist who sees neurotics almost exclusively, and who is accustomed to ascribe to hysteria so many manifestations which other physicians treat as organic. On the other hand, I am haunted by a faint doubt—I do not know whence it comes—whether my alarm is altogether honest. If Irma's pains are indeed of organic origin, it is not my duty to cure them. My treatment, of course, removes only hysterical pains. It seems to me, in fact, that I wish to find an error in the diagnosis; for then I could not be reproached with failure to effect a cure.

I take her to the window in order to look into her throat. She resists a little, like a woman who has false teeth. I think to myself, she does not need them. I had never had occasion to inspect Irma's oral cavity. The incident in the dream reminds me of an examination, made some time before, of a governess who at first produced an impression of youthful beauty, but who, upon opening her mouth, took certain measures to conceal her denture. Other memories of medical examinations, and of petty secrets revealed by them, to the embarrassment of both physician and patient, associate themselves with this case.— "She surely does not need them," is perhaps in the first place a compliment to Irma; but I suspect yet another meaning. In a careful analysis one is able to feel whether or not the *arrière-pensées* which are to be expected have all been exhausted. The way in which Irma stands at the window suddenly reminds me of another experience. Irma has an intimate woman friend of whom I think very highly. One evening, on paying her a visit, I found her at the window in the position reproduced in the dream, and her physician, the same Dr. M., declared that she had a diphtheritic membrane. The person of Dr. M. and the membrane return, indeed, in the course of the dream. Now it occurs to me that during the past few months I have had every reason to suppose that this lady too is hysterical. Yes, Irma herself betrayed the fact to me. But what do I know of her condition? Only the one thing, that like Irma in the dream she suffers from hysterical choking. Thus, in the dream I have replaced my patient by her friend. Now I remember that I have often played with the supposition that this lady, too, might ask me to relieve her of her symptoms. But even at the time I thought it improbable, since she is extremely reserved. She *resists,* as the dream shows. Another explanation might be that *she does not need it*; in fact, until now she has shown herself strong enough to master her condition without outside help. Now only a few features remain, which I can assign neither to

Irma nor to her friend; pale, puffy, false teeth. The false teeth
led me to the governess; I now feel inclined to be satisfied with
bad teeth. Here another person, to whom these features may
allude, occurs to me. She is not my patient, and I do not wish
her to be my patient, for I have noticed that she is not at her
ease with me, and I do not consider her a docile patient. She is
generally pale, and once, when she had not felt particularly
well, she was puffy. I have thus compared my patient Irma with
two others, who would likewise resist treatment. What is the
meaning of the fact that I have exchanged her for her friend in
the dream? Perhaps that I wish to exchange her; either her
friend arouses in me stronger sympathies, or I have a higher
regard for her intelligence. For I consider Irma foolish because
she does not accept my solution. The other woman would be
more sensible, and would thus be more likely to yield. *The
mouth then opens readily;* she would tell more than Irma.

*What I see in the throat: a white spot and scabby turbinal
bones.* The white spot recalls diphtheria, and thus Irma's friend,
but it also recalls the grave illness of my eldest daughter two
years earlier, and all the anxiety of that unhappy time. The
scab on the turbinal bones reminds me of my anxiety concerning my own health. At that time I frequently used cocaine in
order to suppress distressing swellings in the nose, and I had
heard a few days previously that a lady patient who did likewise had contracted an extensive necrosis of the nasal mucous
membrane. In 1885 it was I who had recommended the use of
cocaine, and I had been gravely reproached in consequence. A
dear friend, who had died before the date of this dream, had
hastened his end by the misuse of this remedy.

I quickly call Dr. M., who repeats the examination. This would
simply correspond to the position which M. occupied among us.
But the word "quickly" is striking enough to demand a special
examination. It reminds me of a sad medical experience. By
continually prescribing a drug (sulphonal), which at that time
was still considered harmless, I was once responsible for a condition of acute poisoning in the case of a woman patient, and
hastily turned for assistance to my older and more experienced
colleague. The fact that I really had this case in mind is confirmed by a subsidiary circumstance. The patient who suc-
cumbed to the toxic effects of the drug, bore the same name as

my eldest daughter. I had never thought of this until now; but now it seems to me almost like a retribution of fate as though the substitution of persons had to be continued in another sense: this Matilda for that Matilda; an eye for an eye, a tooth for a tooth. It is as though I were seeking every opportunity to reproach myself for a lack of medical conscientiousness.

Dr. M. is pale; his chin is shaven, and he limps. Of this so much is correct, that his unhealthy appearance often arouses the concern of his friends. The other two characteristics must belong to another person. An elder brother living abroad occurs to me, for he, too, shaves his chin, and if I remember him rightly, the M. of the dream bears on the whole a certain resemblance to him. And some days previously the news arrived that he was limping on account of an arthritic affection of the hip. There must be some reason why I fuse the two persons into one in my dream. I remember that, in fact, I was on bad terms with both of them for similar reasons. Both had rejected a certain proposal which I had recently made them.

My friend Otto is now standing next to the patient, and my friend Leopold examines her and calls attention to a dullness low down on the left side. My friend Leopold also is a physician, and a relative of Otto's. Since the two practice the same specialty, fate has made them competitors, so that they are constantly being compared with one another. Both of them assisted me for years, while I was still directing a public clinic for neurotic children. There, scenes like that reproduced in my dream had often taken place. While I would be discussing the diagnosis of a case with Otto, Leopold would examine the child anew and make an unexpected contribution towards our decision. There was a difference of character between the two men like that between Inspector Brasig and his friend Karl. Otto was remarkably prompt and alert; Leopold was slow and thoughtful, but thorough. If I contrast Otto and the cautious Leopold in the dream I do so, apparently, in order to extol Leopold. The comparison is like that made above between the disobedient patient Irma and her friend, who was believed to be more sensible. I now become aware of one of the tracks along which the association of ideas in the dream proceeds: from the sick child to the children's clinic. Concerning the dullness low on the left side, I have the impression that it corresponds with a certain case of which all the details were similar, a case in which Leopold impressed me by his thoroughness. I thought vaguely, too, of something like a metastatic affection, but it might also be a reference to the patient whom I should have liked to have in Irma's place. For this lady, as far as I can gather, exhibited symptoms which imitated tuberculosis.

An infiltrated portion of skin on the left shoulder. I know at once that this is my own rheumatism of the shoulder, which I always feel if I lie awake long at night. The very phrasing of the dream sounds ambiguous: "Something which I can feel, as he does, in spite of the dress." "Feel on my own body" is intended. Further, it occurs to me how unusual the phrase "infiltrated portion of skin" sounds. We are accustomed to the phrase: "an infiltration of the upper posterior left"; this would refer to the lungs, and thus, once more, to tuberculosis.

In spite of the dress. This, to be sure, is only an interpolation. At the clinic the children were, of course, examined undressed; here we have some contrast to the manner in which adult female patients have to be examined. The story used to be told of an eminent physician that he always examined his patients through their clothes. The rest is obscure to me; I have, frankly, no inclination to follow the matter further.

Dr. M. says: "It's an infection, but it doesn't matter; dysentery will follow and the poison will be eliminated." This, at first, seems to me ridiculous; nevertheless, like everything else, it must be carefully analyzed; more closely observed it seems after all to have a sort of meaning. What I had found in the patient was a local diphtheritis. I remember the discussion about diphtheritis and diphtheria at the time of my daughter's illness. Diphtheria is the general infection which proceeds from local diphtheritis. Leopold demonstrates the existence of such a general infection by the dullness, which also suggests a metastatic focus. I believe, however, that just this kind of metastasis does not occur in the case of diphtheria. It reminds me rather of pyaemia.

It doesn't matter is a consolation. I believe it fits in as follows: The last part of the dream has yielded a content to the effect that the patient's sufferings are the result of a serious organic affection. I begin to suspect that by this I am only trying to shift the blame from myself. Psychic treatment cannot be held responsible for the continued presence of a diphtheritic affection. Now, indeed, I am distressed by the thought of having invented such a serious illness for Irma, for the sole purpose of exculpating myself. It seems so cruel. Accordingly, I need the assurance that the outcome will be benign, and it seems to me that I made a good choice when I put the words that consoled me into the mouth of Dr. M. But here I am placing myself in a position of superiority to the dream; a fact which needs explanation.

But why is this consolation so nonsensical?

Dysentery. Some sort of far-fetched theoretical notion that the toxins of disease might be eliminated through the intestines. Am I thereby trying to make fun of Dr. M.'s remarkable store of far-fetched explanations, his habit of conceiving curious pathological relations? Dysentery suggests something else. A few months ago I had in my care a young man who was suffering from remarkable intestinal troubles; a case which had been treated by other colleagues as one of "anemia with malnutrition." I realized that it was a case of hysteria; I was unwilling to use my psychotherapy on him, and sent him off on a seavoyage. Now a few days previously I had received a despairing letter from him; he wrote from Egypt, saying that he had had a fresh attack, which the doctor had declared to be dysentery. I suspect that the diagnosis is merely an error on the part of an ignorant colleague, who is allowing himself to be fooled by the hysteria; yet I cannot help reproaching myself for putting the invalid in a position where he might contract some organic affection of the bowels in addition to his hysteria. Furthermore, dysentery sounds not unlike diphtheria, a word which does not occur in the dream.

Yes, it must be the case that with the consoling prognosis, "Dysentery will develop, etc.," I am making fun of Dr. M., for I recollect that years ago he once jestingly told a very similar story of a colleague. He had been called in to consult with him in the case of a woman who was very seriously ill, and he felt obliged to confront his colleague, who seemed very hopeful, with the fact that he found albumen in the patient's urine. His colleague, however, did not allow this to worry him, but answered calmly: "*That does not matter,* my dear sir; the albumen will soon be excreted!" Thus I can no longer doubt that this part of the dream expresses derision for those of my colleagues who are ignorant of hysteria. And, as though in confirmation, the thought enters my mind: "Does Dr. M. know that the appearances in Irma's friend, his patient, which gave him reason to fear tuberculosis, are likewise due to hysteria? Has he recognized this hysteria, or has he allowed himself to be fooled?"

But what can be my motive in treating this friend so badly? That is simple enough: Dr. M. agrees with my solution as little as does Irma herself. Thus, in this dream I have already revenged myself on two persons: on Irma in the words, "If you still have pains, it is your own fault," and on Dr. M. in the wording of the nonsensical consolation which has been put into his mouth.

We know precisely how the infection originated. This precise knowledge in the dream is remarkable. Only a moment before this we did not yet know of the infection, since it was first demonstrated by Leopold.

My friend Otto gave her an injection not long ago, when she was feeling unwell. Otto had actually related during his short visit to Irma's family that he had been called in to a neighboring hotel in order to give an injection to someone who had been suddenly taken ill. Injections remind me once more of the unfortunate friend who poisoned himself with cocaine. I had recommended the remedy for internal use only during the withdrawal of morphia; but he immediately gave himself injections of cocaine.

With a preparation of propyl . . . propyls . . . propionic acid. How on earth did this occur to me? On the evening of the day after I had written the clinical history and dreamed about the case, my wife opened a bottle of liqueur labeled "Ananas," which was a present from our friend Otto. He had, as a matter of fact, a habit of making presents on every possible occasion; I hope he will some day be cured of this by a wife. This liqueur smelt so strongly of fusel oil that I refused to drink it. My wife suggested: "We will give the bottle to the servants," and I, more prudent, objected, with the philanthropic remark: "They shan't be poisoned either." The smell of fusel oil (amyl . . .) has now apparently awakened my memory of the whole series: propyl, methyl, etc., which furnished the preparation of propyl mentioned in the dream. Here, indeed, I have effected a substitution: I dreamt of propyl after smelling amyl; but substitutions of this kind are perhaps permissible, especially in organic chemistry.

Trimethylamin. In the dream I see the chemical formula of this substance—which at all events is evidence of a great effort on the part of my memory—and the formula is even printed in heavy type, as though to distinguish it from the context as something of particular importance. And where does trimethylamin, thus forced on my attention, lead me? To a conversation with another friend, who for years has been familiar with all my germinating ideas, and I with his. At that time he had just informed me of certain ideas concerning a sexual chemistry, and had mentioned, among others, that he thought he had found in trimethylamin one of the products of sexual metabolism. This substance thus leads me to sexuality, the factor to which I attribute the greatest significance in respect of the origin of these nervous affections which I am trying to cure. My patient Irma is a young widow; if I am required to excuse my failure to cure her, I shall perhaps do best to refer to this condition, which her admirers would be glad to terminate. But in what a singular fashion such a dream is fitted together! The friend who in my dream becomes my patient in Irma's place is likewise a young widow.

I surmise why it is that the formula of trimethylamin is so insistent in the dream. So many important things are centered about this one word: trimethylamin is an allusion, not merely to the all-important factor of sexuality, but also to a friend whose sympathy I remember with satisfaction whenever I feel isolated in my opinions. And this friend, who plays such a large part in my life, will he not appear yet again in the concatenation of ideas peculiar to this dream? Of course; he has a special knowledge of the results of affections of the nose and the sinuses, and has revealed to science several highly remarkable relations between the turbinal bones and the female sexual organs. (The three curly formations in Irma's throat.) I got him to examine Irma, in order to determine whether her gastric pains were of nasal origin. But he himself suffers from suppurative rhinitis, which gives me concern, and to this perhaps there is an allusion in pyaemia, which hovers before me in the metastasis of the dream.

One doesn't give such injections so rashly. Here the reproach of rashness is hurled directly at my friend Otto. I believe I had some such thought in the afternoon, when he seemed to indicate, by word and look, that he had taken sides against me. It was, perhaps: "How easily he is influenced; how irresponsibly he pronounces judgment." Further, the above sentence points once more to my deceased friend, who so irresponsibly resorted to cocaine injections. As I have said, I had not intended that injections of the drug should be taken. I note that in reproaching Otto I once more touch upon the story of the unfortunate Matilda, which was the pretext for the same reproach against me. Here, obviously, I am collecting examples of my conscientiousness, and also of the reverse.

Probably too the syringe was not clean. Another reproach directed at Otto, but originating elsewhere. On the previous day I happened to meet the son of an old lady of eighty-two, to whom I am obliged to give two injections of morphia daily. At present she is in the country, and I have heard that she is suffering from phlebitis. I immediately thought that this might be a case of infiltration caused by a dirty syringe. It is my pride that in two years I have not given her a single infiltration; I am always careful, of course, to see that the syringe is perfectly clean. For I am conscientious. From the phlebitis I return to my wife, who once suffered from thrombosis during a period of pregnancy, and now three related situations come to the surface in my memory, involving my wife, Irma, and the dead Matilda, whose identity has apparently justified my putting these three persons in one another's places.

I have now completed the interpretation of the dream. In the course of this interpretation I have taken great pains to avoid all those notions which must have been suggested by a comparison of the dream-content with the dream-thoughts hidden behind this content. Meanwhile the "meaning" of the dream has dawned upon me. I have noted an intention which is realized through the dream, and which must have been my motive in dreaming. The dream fulfills several wishes, which were awakened within me by the events of the previous evening (Otto's news, and the writing of the clinical history). For the result of the dream is, that it is not I who am to blame for the pain which Irma is still suffering, but that Otto is to blame for it. Now Otto has annoyed me by his remark about Irma's imperfect cure; the dream avenges me upon him, in that it turns the reproach upon himself. The dream acquits me of responsibility for Irma's condition, as it refers this condition to other causes (which do, indeed, furnish quite a number of explanations). The dream represents a certain state of affairs, such as I might wish to exist; *the content of the dream is thus the fulfillment of a wish; its motive is a wish.*

This much is apparent at first sight. But many other details of the dream become intelligible when regarded from the standpoint of wish-fulfillment. I take my revenge on Otto, not merely for too readily taking sides against me, in that I accuse him of careless medical treatment (the injection), but revenge myself also for the bad liqueur which smells of fusel oil, and I find an expression in the dream which unites both these reproaches: the injection of a preparation of propyl. Still I am not satisfied, but continue to avenge myself by comparing him with his more reliable colleague. Thereby I seem to say: "I like him better than you." But Otto is not the only person who must be made to feel the weight of my anger. I take my revenge on the disobedient patient, by exchanging her for a more sensible and more docile one. Nor do I pass over Dr. M.'s contradiction; for I express, in an obvious allusion, my opinion of him: namely, that his attitude in this case is that of an ignoramus ("Dysentery will develop, etc."). Indeed, it seems as though I were appealing from him to someone better informed (my friend, who told me about trimethylamin), just as I have turned from Irma to her friend, and from Otto to Leopold. It is as though I were to say: Rid me of these three persons, replace them by three others of my own choice, and I shall be rid of the reproaches which I am not willing to admit that I deserve! In my dream the unreasonableness of these reproaches is demonstrated for me in the most elaborate manner. Irma's pains are not attributable to me, since she herself is to blame for them, in that she refuses to accept my solution. They do not concern me, for being as they are of an organic nature, they cannot possibly be cured by psychic treatment.—Irma's sufferings are satisfactorily explained by her widowhood (trimethylamin!); a state which I cannot alter.—Irma's illness has been caused by an incautious injection administered by Otto, an injection of an unsuitable drug, such as I should never have administered.— Irma's complaint is the result of an injection made with an unclean syringe, like the phlebitis of my old lady patient, whereas my injections have never caused any ill effects. I am aware that these explanations of Irma's illness, which unite in acquitting me, do not agree with one another; that they even exclude one another. The whole plea—for this dream is nothing else—recalls vividly the defense offered by a man who was accused by his neighbor of having returned a kettle in a damaged condition. In the first place, he said, he had returned the kettle undamaged; in the second place it already had holes in it when he borrowed it; and in the third place, he had never borrowed it at all. A complicated defense, but so much the better; if only one of these three lines of defense is recognized as valid, the man must be acquitted.

Still other themes play a part in the dream, and their relation to my non-responsibility for Irma's illness is not so apparent: my daughter's illness, and that of a patient with the same name; the harmfulness of cocaine; the affection of my patient, who was traveling in Egypt; concern about the health of my wife; my brother, and Dr. M.; my own physical troubles, and anxiety concerning my absent friend, who is suffering from suppurative rhinitis. But if I keep all these things in view, they combine into a single train of thought, which might be labeled: concern for the health of myself and others; professional conscientiousness. I recall a vaguely disagreeable feeling when Otto gave me the news of Irma's condition. Lastly, I am inclined, after the event, to find an expression of this fleeting sensation in the train of thoughts which forms part of the dream. It is as though Otto had said to me: "You do not take your medical duties seriously enough; you are not conscientious; you do not perform what you promise." Thereupon this train of thought placed itself at my service, in order that I might give proof of my extreme conscientiousness, of my intimate concern about the health of my relatives, friends and patients. Curiously enough, there are also some painful memories in this material, which confirm the blame attached to Otto rather than my own exculpation. The material is apparently impartial, but the connection between this broader material, on which the dream is based, and the more limited theme from which emerges the wish to be innocent of Irma's illness, is, nevertheless, unmistakable.

I do not wish to assert that I have entirely revealed the meaning of the dream, or that my interpretation is flawless.

I could still spend much time upon it; I could draw further explanations from it, and discuss further problems which it seems to propound. I can even perceive the points from which further mental associations might be traced; but such considerations as are always involved in every dream of one's own prevent me from interpreting it farther. Those who are overready to condemn such reserve should make the experiment of trying to be more straightforward. For the present I am content with the one fresh discovery which has just been made: If the method of dream-interpretation here indicated is followed, it will be found that dreams do really possess a meaning, and are by no means the expression of a disintegrated cerebral activity, as the writers on the subject would have us believe. *When the work of interpretation has been completed the dream can be recognized as a wish-fulfillment.*